THE
ESCAPE

THE
ESCAPE

PIPPA YORK & DAVID WALSH

THE TOUR,
THE CYCLIST
AND ME

MUDLARK

Mudlark
HarperCollins*Publishers*
1 London Bridge Street
London SE1 9GF

www.harpercollins.co.uk

HarperCollins*Publishers*
Macken House, 39/40 Mayor Street Upper
Dublin 1, D01 C9W8, Ireland

First published by Mudlark 2025
This edition published 2026

10 9 8 7 6 5 4 3 2 1

The opening of Duncan Macmillan's essay 'The Caledonian Antisyzygy'
from *Barbara Rae: The Lammermuirs,* published by the Royal Academy
of Arts, London, in 2022, quoted with permission.

A catalogue record of this book is
available from the British Library

ISBN 978-0-00-851063-3

Printed and bound in the UK using 100%
renewable electricity at CPI Group (UK) Ltd

MIX
Paper | Supporting
responsible forestry
FSC® C013604
FSC
www.fsc.org

The Caledonian antisyzygy is a term invented to describe the supposed harnessing of conflicting opposites under the common yoke of the Scottish character ...

Perhaps it goes even deeper than that, however, and this anti-syzygy is actually rooted in the Scottish landscape itself. There is hardly a piece of fertile land in Scotland where, as you look at it, you are not aware at the same time of the wild hills beyond or around it. Nor are they just a backdrop; like the antisyzygy, they are an integral but starkly contrasting aspect of the same landscape. Away from the wilder mountains where there is no cultivation, in both the Highlands and the Lowlands it is this relationship of green fields and wild hills that forms the distinctive Scottish landscape. Although very different, they belong together, for it is the shelter given by the high ground that makes possible the fertility of the fields of the low ground.

Duncan Macmillan

Prologue

I meet up with Pippa York again. We're about to board an Air France flight to Paris, and in no time at all we've picked up where we left off at the last Tour de France, just ten months ago.

That 2020 edition of the Tour was one of the stranger instalments of cycling's epic story. Covid moved the Tour from its usual July home into an August/September rental. The crowds couldn't gather by the roadsides in their usual numbers, but when I look back, the 2020 Tour stands as tall as the others – a beautiful race, held together by defiance and enriched by an ending no one foresaw. That had been our first Tour together, Pippa and me, and it had gone well. So we decided to do it all again.

The odds on a happy outcome hadn't been good. I am David Walsh, a white Irish sportswriter, winding down the last descent as the summit of my 60th birthday recedes into the distance. Pippa is a little younger. I know her now as Pippa, although formally she's Philippa York and formerly she was Robert Millar.

We first met in the early 1980s. I was in love with cycling and it was a good time to be an Irishman covering the Tour. Sean

1

Kelly was then a godfather of the peloton, a taciturn spokesman for the English speakers. We referred to Kelly as the 'Irish Flamand', so tough he could have been Flemish. His compatriot Stephen Roche was then fresh-faced and a few years off his historic Tour de France win in 1987.

Roche had turned up in France after his name had been suggested to the ACBB (Athletic Club de Boulogne-Billancourt) amateur team in Paris by a young Scottish rider who'd arrived 12 months earlier. That was the tradition. Each 'Anglo' nominated another recruit at the end of their first year. So Paul Sherwen begat Graham Jones who begat Robert Millar who begat Stephen Roche.

I was keen to write cycling stories, and Kelly and Roche were my go-to men. Millar, however, was a different kettle of smoked cod. Around him, any question could be the wrong question, so just like the house with the visible alarm system, us criminals of the press centre moved on to the house round the corner. The truth was, I didn't much like Millar, not that he'd have noticed.

When his career ended, Millar's life began all over again, if that's the right way of putting it. After a long and painstaking transition, Robert metamorphosed into Pippa York, the wry, sharp woman with whom I'm looking forward to spending the next month. I'm still a sportswriter, I still enjoy telling stories, and I'm grateful that Pippa York is less reticent than Robert Millar. She seems more at ease with the world than he was.

We both did our first Tours in 1983, Millar on a road bike, me on a motorbike. That was the first of Laurent Fignon's two Tour wins. Without the controlling presence of Bernard Hinault, '83 was a wild race. Millar was just a kid, but on the first mountain stage – a 125-mile trek from Pau to Bagnères-de-

Luchon in the Pyrenees – he attacked on the final climb, the Col de Peyresourde, to claim a sensational victory.

I remember that day. For four hours on an intensely hot afternoon, I waited high up on the Col d'Aspin. It was the only time Sean Kelly ever wore the yellow jersey in the Tour, while Roche had the white jersey, marking him out as the leading young rider. Both were crushed that afternoon. Millar and his breakaway companion José Patrocinio Jiménez were first to fly past on the Aspin. Eight long minutes elapsed before Kelly appeared, his yellow jersey soaked in sweat, the man himself wasted. Three minutes later, Roche struggled past. Millar's performance made things worse. If a Scot could cope with the heat, why not the two Irishmen? I never got to know Millar, but in the Pyrenees that afternoon he proved himself a gifted climber. In any era he'd have won mountain races.

But this is more the story of Pippa York and how she became who she is – and why her life and the Tour are so intertwined. For three Tours – 2020, 2021 and 2022 – we spoke as we drove, laughed and argued together. Twelve weeks of togetherness. We got to find out about each other, learned to live with each other and even ended up liking each other.

It's also a love letter to the Tour, a collection of vignettes of our time on the road together and reflections from Pippa herself, looking back on her life in cycling. We tell of times on the Tour, random days chosen as much for the conversation we had that day as for any particular details of the stage we'd watched. We're not trying to recount the story of one Tour, nor are we following any of these three editions chronologically. Instead we give you slices from our Tours, in no particular order, so that by the end you might have a finer understanding of what it is to 'follow' the Tour de France.

It's also a tale of a friendship that grew over this time, something I never had with Robert when he was riding all those years ago.

*   *   *

Hi. My name is Pippa York.

It's quite a nice name. You've a better chance when you choose your own name. And my name choice is all the better for not being a consequence of marriage or being part of a witness protection programme, although you might end up thinking that the latter would have been appropriate for me.

I rode the Tour de France 11 times, and it wasn't the female edition. As Robert Millar I was the first person from Britain to win a major Tour de France classification, the polka dot jersey in 1984. I set standards that weren't equalled for two decades.

I was Robert Millar then.

I am Pippa York now.

Parts of Robert Millar remain, and there are other parts that – looking back – I barely recognise. Being trans is complicated; sometimes it's awful. But I understand that people find it interesting. Even I find it fascinating.

When David Walsh first asked me to join him on the Tour de France I had serious concerns. This is the guy who brought down Lance Armstrong. I consider him to be a serious journalist, which I am definitely not. I write. I just tell stories. Sometimes I make stories out of other people's words. And sometimes I just say what's in my head. David was bound to find me out.

And then there was the other thing as well. He talks a lot. A. LOT. Never stops. He's Irish and charming in a way that you might even find suspicious. Three weeks in a car? He'd probably drive me nuts.

Then I heard somebody whose voice sounded a bit like mine say yes. So we did it. Drove the Tour de France. And then we did it again, and again. Strangely our friendship works.

I'm not sure what my Wee Gran, who was actually my great-gran, would make of it all. In the Glasgow of my youth she was a dyed-in-the-wool Orange woman, all five feet nothing of her. There was no form of integration that wouldn't have been a problem for Wee Gran. We weren't allowed to mix with those of a Catholic persuasion. The Irish, that is. The Tims. The Taigs. They had horns and cloven feet. No doubt they all talked a lot too.

And now I'm sharing a car for three weeks with a southern Irishman. Forgive me, Wee Gran, though I know she won't.

Gran, I'd have explained, our friendship is built on a shared love for the Tour de France. It's one of the most beautiful pieces of madness, an epic in an age that doesn't do epics anymore. A race that's flawed and fascinating, human and inhuman. A race that lasts too long and ends too soon.

David is one of those people who, if asked to identify himself, would say 'Journalist' and leave it at that. He's interested, of course, in my gender change, but when we first talk he asks if my attitude to journalists has softened since my days as a Tour rider.

'Your face used to be like a sign that said "Beware of the Dog",' he told me. 'You were a bit scary.'

This notion is hilarious to me. The guy who took on Lance Armstrong being wary of me? Really?

'I'm not that difficult a person, definitely not now. Was I that difficult back then?'

'Well, you had no trouble telling a journalist to fuck off? Do you not remember that?'

He has a point. I did that to protect myself. I could only give so much. If I allowed people to take all of my recovery time it would have affected my performance, and racing was more important to me than time spent speaking to a journalist.

So I made a choice. I felt I was being selective, not difficult. Journalists might say I was unhelpful. And there were times when I was rude. The way I saw it, I was being judged on my performance, and why couldn't I judge people who came from the media? If they didn't like my manner, fuck them.

By the way, as Robert Millar I did like to swear. There's not a lot of point in being from Glasgow, a son/daughter of the Gorbals, if you're always going to be obliging and never swearing. That's your edge gone straight away.

But Pippa York, I'm pleased to say, is nice to journalists. David isn't buying this. He calls it revisionism, and says that at some point on our road trip, the inner Robert will resurface. He thinks the wasp still carries a sting.

Almost everywhere I go, the place names remind me of races I've ridden in another life. Yet the stories I remember aren't always about the races. This story is like that. It's more about David and me travelling through France, following the Tour, the race that David has been covering since 1983. Like all of my cycling stories, this one's mostly about something else.

Chapter 1

Late June 2021
Somewhere in Brittany

By the time we come through arrivals at Charles de Gaulle Airport the heavens have opened and unleashed a deluge of torrential rain. We find the Hertz desk and make our way to the car that will be our home for the daylight hours of the next 26 days. It has taken us approximately seven hours to get from our homes in England, and now there's the small matter of 640 kilometres to our destination in Brittany.

Pippa drives the first 200 kilometres. She likes driving. Being chivalrous, I graciously allow her to do more than her share. I take the next 200, and by the time my shift is finished, night has fallen.

'My eyes hurt when I drive in the dark,' Pippa says.

'My eyes actually close,' I say, before taking a left turn into the minutiae of narcolepsy.

I win by virtue of the need for both of us to stay alive. Pippa drives the last 240 kilometres. Having left the airport in Paris at five o'clock in the afternoon, we reach our hotel 20 minutes after midnight.

We're billeted in the tiny hamlet of La Pointe Saint-Mathieu on France's north-west coast, just a 20-minute drive from Brest, where the Tour starts in two days. On our way back from a short walk to the ruins of the 6th-century abbey at Saint-Mathieu we stumble across La Crêpe Dantel', an attractive little restaurant inside an old granite cottage.

'How about a coffee and a crêpe?' I say, partly from the need to make up for Pippa having to do most of the driving the night before.

'Nah,' Pippa says, 'I had a bad experience in a crêperie a long time ago and I haven't been able to touch one since. It all happened here in Brittany about 40 years ago, a place called Concarneau.'

'I know Concarneau. In 1984 I went there to see a criterium.'

'That'll have been the same criterium! The place where I had my bad experience.'

'Such a small flipping world,' I say, and we trade our Concarneau stories.

Pippa first. She was then Robert Millar, an up-and-coming second-year professional, living in Paris, riding with the Peugeot team and earning £300 a week. Criteriums offered extra cash. Millar travelled to Concarneau with a Peugeot teammate, the English rider Graham Jones. Also in the company was the late Paul Sherwen, who rode with the La Redoute team. They got there three hours before the race, time enough for something to eat.

'Paul Sherwen said he knew of a place from having ridden the Concarneau criterium before. He took us to a crêperie. "This is good," he said.'

In the parts of Glasgow that Millar spent his childhood, crêpes weren't much of a thing. Even now in the UK we expect them to come with sugar, cream, ice cream or Nutella. In Brittany, this understanding of the crêpe announces you as a philistine. Here they can be sweet or savoury. Your choice.

In Concarneau, Paul Sherwen showed Millar a world where they put virtually anything on their crêpes. 'As a rider,' says Pippa, 'I was really picky and conservative about food. I worried about it a lot. So in this place that served everything on crêpes, I opted for eggs.'

'A safe choice, I'd have thought,' I say.

'Well, half an hour later I knew I'd made a mistake. My stomach was rumbling and groaning. I had cramps. I needed to get to a toilet and I needed to get there fast. When I got there, things got worse. I had the works.'

Pippa explained 'the works'. Diarrhoea. Vomiting. A cold sweat. Weak as a kitten. The feeling of being profoundly sick. Profoundly and very inconveniently sick.

'I found the agent who'd got me into the race and told him just how sick I felt. Agents don't become agents because they're lovely people, but he wasn't too bad about it.

'He said, "Look, it's good you've told me all this, but you've got to ride at least half of the race to get your fee." Fortunately Paul Sherwen had brought a supply of medicines. He gave me something to settle my stomach.

'I felt terrible but still started. There were so many laps. You could take one lap out, pretending you had a puncture. I did that, and then I hung on until precisely one lap after halfway. Then I stopped. I waited to see if I'd get the money and was relieved when I did.'

The race fee was 1,500 francs, which translated into £150. It wasn't a common-or-garden case of gastroenteritis. After returning to Paris, Millar still felt pretty unwell.

'I needed a lot of medication. There was a prescription for this and a prescription for that. I had a French social security number, but the total cost of the treatment was still 1,800 francs. So, all in all the criterium and the crêpe in Concarneau cost me 300 francs, not to mention all the time in the bathroom.'

That was 1981. Forty years later, Pippa York still won't look at a crêpe.

My own Concarneau story took place three years later. I'd travelled with Sean Kelly to experience a few days on the criterium circuit. There was Kelly, his then-fiancée Linda and me. It was August, but it rained non-stop in Concarneau. Back then, Kelly was much higher up the food chain than Millar and due to get 20,000 francs (£2,000) for his appearance.

After racing and showering he went to the race headquarters, a small house near the finish, to collect his fee. He was gone for a while, and on his return he explained the delay by the need for one of the organisers to count out 20,000 francs from the evening's takings. Alhough Kelly wasn't the sort a pickpocket would choose to rob, he still took precautions. So as his tracksuit bottoms didn't have pockets, he stuffed the twenty grand into his underpants.

Sitting in the front seat of his Citroën car, he pulled the cash from his jocks, handed it to Linda and said, 'Count that for 20,000.'

The money was counted. It tallied, and only then did Kelly start the car and point it east. The next day's criterium was in the Netherlands, and we'd drive through the night to get there.

'How do you do this?' I asked when we stopped to refuel at 3.30 a.m., somewhere in the middle of nowhere.

'I'll do it for a couple of weeks. If I was a long-haul lorry driver, this would be my life.'

Kelly was like that. 'Chary of words when not downright hostile,' the American author Robin Magowan wrote of him.

We used to joke that Sean once nodded in answer to a question on radio. Pippa says she liked Kelly, which doesn't surprise me.

Recalling our Concarneau experiences, it strikes me how deep the roots of our relationship with France and the Tour went. What was it that made Robert Millar want to ride the race and me want to report on it? Who can say? We love lots of things at different points in our lives. Loves bloom and wither, passions come and go. Not much that you loved 40 years ago endures.

Pippa and I are still here, four decades after first falling in love with the race, coming back with more or less the same enthusiasm we had at the beginning, still crazy after all these years.

Gorbals

Robert Millar?

He's that watchful sparrow of a kid over there. He's a child of the famous Gorbals slum, a place where it really is better to be a big man than it is to be a wiry wee lad.

Like any kid he plays in the cracked streets. Once upon a time, so they say, lepers stood here in this endless Scottish rain and cadged for alms. Immigrants of every mark have trudged here in their heavy work boots, trudged along these melting-pot pavements.

Robert is in the chasing pack before he even has a bicycle. In the evenings when the coal lorries come belching into Wellcroft Place, having done their rounds across the grey city, the kids give chase. They leap and then hang from the swaying back boards of the flat bed while the drivers jostle into the parking spaces underneath the old railway arches, just opposite the Millar home, at Number 4.

The arches are a forbidden playground, but their darkness is as black as a coalmine and it draws kids like an ice cream van on a sunny day. The black dust hangs in the air and it speckles your snot. It gets in your hair and later the dust tells tales on you. There's no lying about where you've been when your ma bawls that it's time to be home. Every squeaky-clean boy that goes out their front door comes back home as a grimy urchin and he best be braced for a skelpin'.

The streets and the tenements in this poxed part of Glasgow are famous for the hard men and the criminals that they produce, but the Gorbals of reality is different. The myth is threadbare, worn thin by outsiders. The Gorbals is more sinned against than sinning. Nobody here shits on their own doorstep. Nobody has much worth stealing. Life is something to be going on with. If you're curious about your future, just look at the faces of your ma and da. It's written there for you, in those lines and crow's feet.

Life? You'll be old before your time, most probably. Life will beat you early and then they'll bury you in the Southern Necropolis with the rest.

schoolyard

Abbotsford Primary School has been staring down Devon Street since the Victorian days. For most of that time it has been raining. The mizzling, drizzling, occasionally down-pouring rain of Glasgow. You know that line about Scots having to scrape the moss off each other first thing every morning? Well, yes.

The school is an austere stone building with grey slate roofs laid out under a slate-grey sky. After years of cobwebs Abbotsford is an all-Muslim school now, but the building into which five-year-old Robert Millar walked many years ago for his first day of education just teemed with kids who scrubbed up pale and scrawny.

The school still has a palazzo-style facade and is built around a central hallway and staircase. If you've just come from the downstairs tenement of Number 4 it might be quite intimidating. Robert is the youngest of three bairns, however, and his siblings have been the pathfinders. Anyway, this is the

Gorbals. Show your tough face or else you go home crying for yer maw and you'll never be let forget about it.

When the bell goes for class, the boys are corralled to one side, the girls to the other. Never the twain. Odd, thinks wee Robert. He never expected this. For half a morning of minutes he sits, fidgety in his scarred little wood desk with its hole where a long missing ceramic inkwell once sat. His energy goes unburned until the bell sets everybody free to play in the yard.

The boys run around, all noise and no design. They bruise each other and kick out. They thump and roar, their voices still soprano but Gorbals harsh. Curses are an ornament to speech. The boys make their pecking order out of each other's toughness.

Robert Millar is not a very biddable boy. He's small and solitary and he wonders where all the girls have gone. He finds them in an adjacent reservation on the other side of the railings. His small, gloveless hands are cold but he grasps a railing in each and he peers through.

The scuffling boy bedlam behind him fades away. They're fascinating to him, these girls. Their games are imaginative and varied. Hopscotch! Skipping! Their laughter is free, their bonds are quiet. No dog-eat-dog stuff here.

Every day from then on he likes to stand and look into this other world. One lunchtime, slanty rain as usual, the noise behind him causes him to turn. A gang of the older boys are pounding on easy prey. They're punching and kicking a wee bony fellow. Calling him a sissy and a weirdo. Yeah!

Robert Millar gets it. The kid had showed his hand. Any weakness, you get eaten. That's just the way of the jungle. He turns back to the railing. As a boy he has to be big and strong.

He has to take his lumps and eat his red meat. He has to support Rangers and he has to hide his weaknesses.

And the girls? They can do whatever they like. He doesn't want to play with the girls over there. He wants to be one of them.

Already he knows that in his gut. But that's his own business. Robert Millar's wee secret. He pulls the hood of his anorak up and turns his tough, cagey face back towards the stunted world that he's stuck in.

bloodlines

Later, his permed, curly hair cascaded down over his shoulders. Later, he'd wear an earring and carry a scalded look on a face that you could never impress, no matter how hard you tried. Later, whenever he spoke of home, he was unsentimental. Later, the tree grew no broader than the sapling, his legs muscular but his torso remaining pencil-thin. Later, he had pipe-cleaner arms. Later, he descended mountains as if living a long life didn't concern him very much. Later, he looked as if he'd been especially bred for cycling up and down those large mountains.

That was all later. The bloodlines weren't a promising start.

*   *   *

Bill Millar worked in the ironmongery business. When the family moved from the Gorbals to Pollokshaws as part of a slum clearance, the tenement houses were all demolished and the Millars lived in a high rise.

If you were old enough and Glaswegian enough, you knew that jeely was jam and you knew the Matt McGinn song about the council-flat cuisine.

Oh yae cannae fling pieces oot a twenty-storey flat,
Seven hundred hungry wains will testify to that.
If it's butter, cheese or jeely, if the breid is plain or pan,
The odds against it reaching earth are ninety-nine tae wan.

The Millar family was complete by the time of the move. Ian, Elizabeth and Robert. There was a child after Robert who had died at birth and never got talked about.

Bill Millar changed job around the time the family moved and thereafter worked for a company called Hills, an Australian outfit that made rotary dryers. Bill drove around the new-build housing estates selling or delivering the rotary dryers. He was away a lot, three days a week at least, away off on the road.

Bill had polio as a child. One of his legs was withered or underdeveloped. His wife Mary suffered from arthritis. Any genetic dividend of athletic ability wasn't immediately visible to young Robert. Bill and Mary did as everybody else did. They drank and they smoked. Bill played some snooker. Mary went to bingo as an occasional treat. Nobody in the Millar family or the small world surrounding them indulged in any type of sport at all.

Everybody was as poor as sin. Nobody felt poorer than anybody else and there was nothing for anyone to covet or envy. Nobody went too hungry but nobody threw food away either. It was a standard working-class life for the time. In due time it would be sentimentalised.

When the Millars left the Gorbals behind they no longer had to travel to Queen's Park just to see some grass. They lived now in the 11th floor of a Pollokshaws high-rise and there was a park down below. Robert was nine, ten maybe, and he was growing up in this family without a sporting gene between them.

If life were like the fairytales a kindly uncle would have arrived with a second-hand Raleigh bicycle that he'd gleamed up. The skinny wee boy would be wide-eyed. He'd master riding that Raleigh after just a few wobbles and then we'd see his family chasing him down the roadway, beseeching him to come back, begging him to be careful, shouting advice till he became just a dot on the horizon, a boy cycling his way all the way to Ayr, the place where the road ran out and the sea began. That lad, they'd say, shaking their heads, he's a natural.

But he had a three-wheeler bike, an old clunker of a thing, not toddler stuff. There was nothing cute about being ten years old in Glasgow and riding a three-wheeler. Nothing cool.

In Pollok Park he found himself a slight downhill run. No alpine descent thrill ride but just enough gradient for a wee man to get a little head of steam going. He'd rattle the three-wheeler down the path and squeeze the last bit of speed out of the thing. He liked the sensation straight away. The bike responded grudgingly to his pedalling and as he clanged down the slope he pedalled harder again. And then, just to see what might happen, he shut his eyes.

What happened first was a swooshing tingle of exhilaration. Yessssssssss.

What happened next was that he opened his eyes.

Nooooooo.

What happened immediately after that was a lamppost.

The three-wheeler wrapped itself around the lamppost like it was a long-lost lover back from a war. Robert Millar's head hit the lamppost so hard that he and the lamppost exchanged valuable molecules.

He left the three-wheeler there. Screw that for a game of soldiers.

clothes horse

Picture this, the so-called nuclear family of olden times. On any given evening the grown-ups are having a beverage, maybe just milky tea with too much sugar, and they're also smoking because it's the 1970s and everybody just has to get through the hell of it all. Two kids are squashed between the adults. Everybody is settled in to watch one of the three channels that make up the whole galaxy of television.

Behind the row of his seated family, the youngest member of the household, Robert, scuttles across the hallway from the foot of the stairs to the bathroom. He's nine or ten, and he's a little bit withdrawn. He lives in his head in his own wee world, but he's a good kid.

He's wearing his sister's clothes.

His sister, Elizabeth, is a year older, and she's plonked there on the sofa. She's roughly the same size as Robert. He tries on her clothes occasionally and to him they feel good. Elizabeth is oblivious to all this.

The voice nags his head, though. *You get found doing this and you're in real trouble. You could get a good beating from your parents, maybe not at first but if they keep finding you in girls' clothes …*

He's not big but he's not scared either. At school if you want to fight him for any reason – and at school you don't need reasons – he'll fight you back. No question. He'll lose most times because height is reach, and he has neither. He'll give you plenty, though, because everybody knows that wee Robert Millar doesn't take shit.

He knows that fights are brief and chaotic things, and that the winner is decided quickly. It's better to be a scrappy loser in a 12-second scuffle than always to be branded the kid who ran away. He fights back, because needs must. He plays football too and he isn't bad at it, but being honest he isn't too bothered with football.

He's not unhappy with being a boy. It's not that. Not yet anyway. But if he'd bought his gender in a local shop, he'd just bring his boyness back and ask for a swap, please. He knows that he'd be much happier as a girl. Nothing sexual about it. Never. Girlworld just feels like a preferable place to be. A better world.

He has no idea about what might happen later, it's just that now 11 floors up in a Glasgow high-rise this dress of his sister's feels more normal than anything about being a boy. In girl clothes he feels settled. The world just feels better.

If there's a problem, it's only that the mirror's in the bathroom and the bathroom's downstairs. He must wait in his sister's girl clothes till the family settles on the sofa. He hangs back till the theme tune plays, waits till he hears them laughing. He tiptoes down the stairs, darts across the hallway and locks the bathroom door after himself

Minutes later he returns his sister's clothes to exactly where he found them. He's careful. What he felt on the inside, that happy – happier – state, melts away quickly.

sunshine getaway

The listlessness of the days gets broken on Saturdays. It's not long past midday. Robert Millar has planted himself on the sofa. He has a cup of tea in one hand and a plate with a bacon sandwich in the other. Dickie Davies, this Tango-tanned guy with his big moustache, oozes onto the screen with *World of Sport*. This is what Robert is here for.

The Tour de France reaches Glasgow in grainy highlight snippets, dispatches on how the British boys are faring in this strange race that brings new instalments every Saturday. So it seems. This Saturday? Last Saturday. All the Saturdays, is it? The boy is hooked on this Tour de France thing.

Today there's an English guy, it's a Barry Hoban from Wakefield. And this Barry Hoban wins a mad sprint to take a stage. Everybody is very excited. It always looks boiling hot and exotic over there on the 'continent'. And they're all going, balls out, really fast, trying to catch this Barry Hoban of Wakefield, and there's dust and paper and everything flying up in the air.

And Robert Millar leans forward and thinks, *I wouldn't mind trying a bit of that*.

Wakefield? Surely Wakefield can't have any more olive groves or vineyards than Glasgow has? If Barry Hoban can do it … surely Pollokshaws can have its own *paysan* who pedals.

Robert has a paper round. He walks the streets of Pollokshaws heaving his massive paperboy bag, brimful of newspapers. His bag weighs as much as he does. At weekends it's the *Sunday Post* mainly, and the *Sunday Times* for the really posh people. Weekdays it's generally the *Daily Record* and the

Sun for the flats, because posh people are rare as hen's teeth in the flats of Pollokshaws.

He does his rounds on foot. A bike would be no easier. You leave it at the foot of a high-rise and it will be gone, nicked, vanished by the time you get back. So he yomps up the stair-wells and shoves newspapers through letterboxes or under doors.

It pays not a lot, this paperboy racket, but Barry Hoban and Dickie Davies have given him a new interest in life. He'll have to divide his paper money into three now.

Money for his parents.

Money for a bike.

Money for the other thing.

platforms

He has saved sufficient of his paper-round money, stashing a little every week until he has enough. He has walked the mile or so down to Shawlands on a Saturday morning. It's early now, tennish. Glasgow is still waking up after its Friday night. He dawdles outside the shop window for an age. He has a lot to think about.

Inside, two women are serving the early customers. The shop women are both around the same age as his mum. For some time he peers through the glass. He needs to reassure himself that there's nobody from school working a Saturday job in the shop. He doesn't want a fuss, not even from the two mum types. He wants none of that 'How can we help you this morning, wee man?' patter. No smarmy, charmy stuff, thanks.

He lingers outside on the pavement until a father enters the shop with his young son. The women begin fussing over the boy. It's time.

He walks into the shop and tells one of the women that he's got to buy a present for his sister. His sister has indicated to him that she might like some shoes. Helpfully, she has shown him some pictures of what sort of shoes, by way of style. He reckons that the brown platforms in the window would be just the ticket. Thank you. He points out the very pair. The heels aren't too high. His sister will like them, he's pretty sure.

So that's it. Nothing to see here. Just a diffident 11-year-old boy buying a present for his sister.

The shop assistant asks if he knows which size his sister takes. He does indeed. She vanishes into the store room and returns with a box into which they both peer when she lifts the lid.

'Yes,' the boy says. 'I think they'll be OK for her.'

'Don't worry,' the woman says. 'If they don't fit, ye could always bring them back to be swapped to the right size.'

That's true, he could return them. But – probably – he wouldn't.

He hands over his money and scuttles away off home. It has taken six weeks of saving his paper-round money to buy the shoes.

They fit him just fine. He doesn't have to go back for a swap.

components

Cycling just wouldn't let go of him. He was still doing his paper round, he was buying girls' clothes and he was buying bike bits. What he spent his money on depended on what the priority was in his head on a given Saturday. It all made no sense.

Then he discovered that top cyclists shaved their legs. *You didn't have to wear two pairs of tights to hide your hairy legs? You could shave your legs and no busybody could say boo to you? This was acceptable? You were a cyclist and you just got a shaved-leg pass?* Ye have to shave yer bloody legs because when ye fell off yer bike ye could get infections and ye need your sticky plasters to stick to yer smooth calves and all the rest of it, so there, ye bampot.

OK, he thought, *that's an advantage. A young man could fit riding a bike into the whole business of wanting to be a girl.*

Somehow he came into possession of an old Flying Scot bicycle frame. It dated from the late 1950s or early 60s, a hefty rake on forks with weedy little tubing. It was something you might have seen in a *Carry On* comedy film, but it was his bike. Anyway, it wasn't about the frame. It was about the bits that you could put on the frame.

There was a little bike shop over by Hampden Park, where the football stadium is. The place sells cars now, but back in the day there used to be three little shops in a row. The bike shop. And then the newsagents. And then a chip shop at the end.

He was a cyclist and from the start he limited his visits to chip shops. He knew in his waters that the Glasgow diet was his unnatural enemy. Eating spam or a bag of chips? Even the thought felt unhealthy.

What drew him to the little row was that the bike shop stocked Campagnolo components. They were there in the window, catching the light like treasure, their perfection and workmanship calling out to him. Flange hubs, cassettes, chains, derailleurs, chainsets, pedals, brakes, brake levers, gear shifters, bottom brackets, steering heads ... any single component as appealing as a pretty summer dress.

Anything Campagnolo might manufacture would demand three months of his wages. But what were three months for something so gorgeous? Campagnolo Brevetti Internazionali. These were words to dream about. Brevetti Internazionali! Whatever it meant, it danced on the tongue! It was a battle cry. From Vicenza, Italia to Pollokshaws, Glasgow.

Beauty and function. Each piece he bought added magic and elegance to his clunky old frame. It took a mean commitment to put aside that money. The commitment meant less money to spare for the other thing. *Maybe*, he thought, *that's no harm either*.

He felt misaligned with the world. He thought that maybe the solution would be cycling. Make your choice and stick to it. One thing or the other, sonny boy. He could devote his money and his energy to his bike and not to girls' clothes. He'd be a cyclist, which he loved being. He'd be a bike rider, a racer – nothing else. Unless he felt the need to have access to kind of feminine stuff again. Could he suffocate that need?

He'd ride over that bridge when he came to it.

Chapter 2

3 July 2022
Stage 3, Vejle to Sønderborg – 182 km

In my early years, it was common for journalists to be honoured by Tour organisers for their length of service. A low-key ceremony in the press centre – handshakes, smiles and a memento to mark 25 years at the race. I tended to look away. We were journalists, they were organisers. We weren't on the same side. So you can already tell, I'm not going to be everyone's cup of tea.

This year the race begins in Copenhagen, so far from France that after three stages the riders will take a flight from Sønderborg to Lille. To compensate for this inconvenience, the fourth day is declared a rest day. In explaining the rationale, Tour boss Christian Prudhomme speaks of the need to take the race to new places.

For Denmark, it's a big deal. Never before has the Tour pitched its tent on Danish soil and the Danes do have a particular love for the bicycle. In Copenhagen, Pippa and I agree that the chances of being run over by a car are nowhere near as likely as being run over by a bike. They travel at speed and the city teems with them.

Walk through the revolving door to the race headquarters at the Bella Centre in the city, then follow the yellow-painted path and it's on the ground beneath your feet: '7 out of 10 Danes own a bike – in Copenhagen it is 9 out of 10'; 'Copenhagen was ranked the world's best cycling city in 2019, and this wasn't the first time'. The next message confirms what your eyes have already seen: 'Bicycles outnumber cars by five to one in Copenhagen.' And still more: 'Forty-four per cent of all trips to the workplace and places of education in Copenhagen are done by bicycle.' Then a message sure to alarm the sedentary. 'Adults who bike to work have 30 per cent lower morbidity rates than those who do not.'

What isn't printed on the yellow-painted paths inside the Bella Centre is the fee that Copenhagen has paid to have the Tour start in the city. Now more than ever, the race begins outside France – and this happens because non-French cities are prepared to pay more. There are many sides to the Tour de France, the least of which is not the commercial side. Meanwhile, Pippa and I are discussing an age-old problem: parking.

PIPPA: Remember what you were saying earlier about that
  field in Nyborg yesterday?
DAVID: The field where I said you've got to park here, you
  disagreed and you were right? That one?
PIPPA: Well, there's a really interesting dynamic in that.
  When you join the female world, you realise that men think
  they run the world but women know they do. We just let
  the men go on thinking that they do. Men tend to adopt a
  quite protective role, in the sense of: 'Oh, you don't know
  what you're doing, so we'll lead you.' A smart woman
  exploits that.
DAVID: Well, at least in our relationship, I'm aware that I've
  ceded all power to you. You like driving. So you drive. It
  scares me that I surrender so much power to you.

PIPPA: See? I don't believe that. Because you're in charge of the hotels and the timings, when we get to the press centre, when we leave, and I tend to agree with you because it's easier than arguing. And what have I got to argue about?

DAVID: Well, you could easily complain about how long it takes me to write my stuff. Tolstoy got *War and Peace* done in less time. We're usually the last to leave the Centre de Presse and you never complain. I appreciate that.

PIPPA: Well, it's your job.

DAVID: I've got a job for you. Further on, we're going to some places where we don't yet have a hotel. As a modern man, committed to inclusivity, I'm going to share some of the responsibility with you to find places.

PIPPA: But because of my female side, I won't be able to take decisions without first consulting with you.

DAVID: Ah no. Absolutely no need to consult me, Pippa. You just go ahead and book them. I'll just imagine that I have the power.

*   *   *

Further along the road to Sønderborg, Margaret, the third person in our car, continually interrupts Pippa and me.

MARGARET: Please follow the road for 900 metres.

DAVID: Aw, Margaret, go fuck yourself and stop interrupting.

PIPPA: Yeah, go and join Boris Johnson and all that House of Commons fuckery.

DAVID: She does sound a bit Tory. Pippa, I've been thinking about your transition and how oestrogen might be the solution to my problem?

MARGARET: Follow the road for 800 metres, then turn left.

PIPPA: There's always a solution. All testosterone does is mess with your prostate. Turns it to toast.

DAVID: My eldest brother Eamonn died from prostate cancer. You women are so lucky not to have a prostate.

PIPPA: Yep. Fun fact, David. Women have all the luck! That's why I changed sides. Look at the trouble caused by testosterone when young men are on a night out. Not that women are that much better, because they have a level of testosterone as well. Especially when they're younger – teenage years and early 20s.

DAVID: Teenage rebellion.

PIPPA: Among other things.

DAVID: What would be the benefits of oestrogen for me, from your experience?

MARGARET: In 200 metres at the traffic lights, turn left.

PIPPA: You'd be able to grow your hair. Well, some hair. You wouldn't have to shave so often.

MARGARET: In 200 metres at the traffic lights, turn left.

DAVID: That would be an advantage. 'Why does it take you so long in the bathroom,' my wife says most mornings. Women don't have to shave, I say.

PIPPA: Maybe you're both lucky she doesn't have to shave every day. Is shaving compulsory for men? Just grow a beard.

MARGARET: Please follow the road for two kilometres.

PIPPA: Aw, Margaret, give it a bloody rest.

* * *

PIPPA: Can we just revisit the football field incident in that place again?

DAVID: Yesterday? In Nyborg. Yes. I merely suggested that we park near where we entered, and you very politely ignored my advice and drove all the way in and out around the back.

PIPPA: I think there might be another lesson here.

DAVID: We were really early, but I had a radio interview and needed to get to the press centre. I said, 'OK, just park here.' All the 'official' cars were there, so I said it again, 'Let's park here,' close to where I thought the entrance was.

PIPPA: And?

DAVID: And? And you completely ignored me! You kept on driving and you went right round the back into some cow field or pasture, and you drove to the far end of the field, and I'm thinking, I hope there's some kind of shuttle bus back to take us back to where we should have been in the first place.

PIPPA: Yes, and what happened next?

DAVID: Well, this Danish guy comes over to us out of nowhere and he says, 'You can just walk in through there.'

PIPPA: Into where?

DAVID: Into where the press centre actually was.

PIPPA: The lesson?

DAVID: Basically, you guessed and got it right.

PIPPA: Or did I just figure it all out? You know, the way women do. Looking at signs and all that other witchcraft?

MARGARET: Reconfiguring route.

PIPPA: Poor Margaret's really bad with her direction today. She has me confused.

DAVID: OK, Ms Pathfinder Superior. I wanted to know this. Do you think that you're calmer now?

PIPPA: Calmer than Margaret? You do know that Margaret's not a real person, David?

DAVID: Calmer than you were before.

PIPPA: Before? Ah yeah. Yeah.

DAVID: Significantly?

PIPPA: Massively. There's no conflict in my head anymore. There's no anger, there's no angst about feeling weird. Before I transitioned, people felt I was normal and I felt I was weird. Now people think I'm weird and I feel that I'm normal. They're judging me on the outside.

DAVID: You're confusing me.

PIPPA: Basically, I'm not living to please other people anymore. And once you get to that point, things just calm down.

DAVID: So, all the changes have left you pretty serene?

PIPPA: If you haven't been dysphoric about your gender and your identity, then I can't imagine you'd be too happy about the changes, you know? It's fairly stark how a tiny amount of female hormone changes the way you react to things, and how you feel more vulnerable. You try not to put yourself in confrontational situations.

DAVID: So, you feel more vulnerable and sensitive, apart from the more obvious changes?

MARGARET: In 500 metres, turn left.

PIPPA: Oh, just fuck the hell off, Margaret. Yes.

DAVID: Margaret, have you been introduced to Pippa? Why not join Pippa on her path to deep serenity?

PIPPA: Same to you as to Margaret!

DAVID: I only asked about the changes because occasionally, at the end of a very long drive, you do revert to something more like your previous self.

PIPPA: Yeah? I do have the odd wobbly, and I do have a crazy turn every now and then, but I like to think that's just my competitive nature. I'm used to driving slightly aggressively, and if something happens then I can revert back to the male model. 'Right, I'm going through that gap, you suckers.' And I don't really care if it upsets people. It's quite rare, but it happens.

DAVID: It's rare. Sort of.

MARGARET: In 300 metres, turn left.

PIPPA: Maybe once a week I'll get ratty.

DAVID: Sometimes it seems like more. In those moments, you remind me of Robert Millar, this cyclist I once knew. Bit cranky.

MARGARET: In 100 metres, turn left.

PIPPA: Oh, for fuck's sake, I heard you, Margaret. I may not be able to park anymore because I'm now a woman, David, but if I see a gap in traffic, I'm going for it. No apologies.

DAVID: None expected.

PIPPA: Some people would take all that as a slight on their femininity. I recognise that I live with both identities attached to me. It doesn't offend me. Lucky for you. I see myself doing it and I think, this isn't good for my female persona. But then, unlucky for you, I do it anyway.

DAVID: You can't resist.

PIPPA: I can't resist. Some people don't expect a woman to drive like that. And I'm thinking, 'Well, that'll teach you.'

DAVID: Don't stereotype women drivers, Pippa. You're not too weird to be cancelled.

MARGARET: Now go straight for 300 metres.

DAVID: Does that sound right?

PIPPA: I don't know, the signs have disappeared. Margaret's really struggling to get us out onto the motorway. We'll just go back. The signs are really poor. I don't know if we're meant to be going this way … There are signs here, but to a different autoroute.

MARGARET: Now exit the roundabout at the second exit.

DAVID: Fuck. I think we need to stop listening to Margaret. She's wearing your empathy out.

PIPPA: Reversing years of progress.

DAVID: Did I ever tell you about the time on tour when I shared a car with an Australian friend, Rupert Guinness, and an American, Gregor Brown?

PIPPA: No.

DAVID: 2015. We started in Utrecht – I got there a day after the two lads. They've got the car, and the Margaret that was doling out the satnav instructions had a really strange accent. Couldn't make it out, but English wasn't her first language and for whatever reason her accent grated on me.

PIPPA: Are you hinting for me or Margaret to shut the hell up? Just come out and say it.

DAVID. On the second day, I could take no more. So I said, 'If we have to listen to that fucking woman for the next three weeks I'm going to lose the will to live.' And Gregor says, 'Actually, that's my wife you're talking about.' Holy fuck! I didn't even know you could input your own voice or your wife's into the satnav. Did you know that?

PIPPA: No.

DAVID. I think I recovered well though.

PIPPA: Oh God. What did you say?
DAVID: I said, 'Well, Gregor, she does sound sexy.'

*   *   *

A curious thing happened over those three days of racing in Denmark. A certain rider finished second all three days: runner-up in the opening 13.2-kilometre time trial, and then just beaten in mass sprints on the second and third days. It might have simply remained a curiosity – tinged no doubt with a little sadness – if it had been any old rider, but Wout van Aert isn't any old rider. In a conversation about the best all-round rider in the peloton, Van Aert's name is going to be mentioned, probably second only to Tadej Pogačar.

Van Aert is from Herentals in Belgium, a rider in the great tradition of Flemish bike racers. There's a natural hauteur about him – no need to tell me how good I am, the results are there for all to see. But three second places isn't what he's accustomed to.

Before he was chauffeured to the airport in Sønderborg for the riders' chartered flight to Lille, poor Van Aert had to do a video conference with journalists in the press centre. Who wants to explain a third consecutive second-place finish? Don't feel too sorry for him, because he did have the yellow jersey going into this early first rest day. Someone asked if he'd sleep happily knowing he had the leader's jersey or restlessly because he had been second three days running.

'I'd better force myself to be happy with this position,' he said. 'Everything is going well, but when you get this close three times, you've got to have mixed feelings.'

I smiled to myself when he said that and thought, *That's a first, the yellow jersey going to bed with mixed feelings.*

After its return to France and a rest day, the Tour recommenced with a stage from Dunkirk to Calais. Van Aert won after a solo breakaway, which was one way of banishing mixed feelings.

Chapter 3

August 2022

Transfer day, Hamburg to Dunkirk – countless miles

We had a plan for the transfer day: drop the car off at Hamburg Airport and fly to France from there. This involved a very early morning Eurowings flight from Hamburg to Paris at 6.40, which meant getting up at 3.30, well before the local roosters, and arriving in Paris at ten past eight. In the morning! Pick up a new rental car at Charles de Gaulle and hit Dunkirk by midday, giving us ample time to be ready for the resumption of the race the following morning. We were actually looking forward to some relaxing down time in Dunkirk. The best-laid plans …

Fate throws us a spanner. Eurowings cancelled the 6.40 from Hamburg, the email dropping around 10.30 the previous evening. I immediately break the news to Pippa that we've been denied the chance of rising at 3.30 a.m., but she takes it well.

'We were only going to feel shit all day anyway,' she says calmly.

This is a positive. I didn't know Robert Millar very well, but I wouldn't have liked to have broken the news of a cancelled flight to him. Instead, Pippa and I huddle to come up with a Plan B.

We study the train route first. It's nine hours from Hamburg to Paris. We could possibly get some work done on the train, but we'd then have to find our way to the airport to pick up a car – another hour – followed by a three-hour drive to Dunkirk. Estimated time of arrival at Dunkirk, 3.30 a.m., all going well.

DAVID: You're taking this much better than I expected.

PIPPA: That's experience.

DAVID: Not oestrogen?

PIPPA: No, experience. When you've been on cycling teams, it's part of the deal. If you're at a race and you fall off and you have to quit and you feel like crap, usually your return ticket hasn't been booked and you're in the middle of nowhere. You're feeling shit, and with the best will in the world you just can't get out of that place until the next day. So you kind of get used to it and go with it.

DAVID: Another thing. In these post-pandemic times, airports are so congested.

PIPPA: If there's 400 people crammed into a small area, at least ten of them have Covid. And nine of them would be standing next to me.

DAVID: Put it that way it really has worked out well. Thanks Eurowings.

Finally, we decide to just get a hotel at Hamburg Airport and relax. In the morning we can look at the options afresh.

PIPPA: You see people who go on their annual summer holiday and the flight gets delayed and it's a complete disaster. Panic. They spend £3,000 to get home from somewhere. We're not doing that. And if it means that we have to miss Wednesday's stage, we could watch it on TV and do our work from that. You were saying no one would notice the difference?

DAVID: That was off the record.

*   *   *

It's an ongoing joke between us that I'm relieved to be travelling with Pippa York instead of Robert Millar. She's good humoured and flexible, and she treats my tendency to compare her to Millar as a bit of a joke, but deep down I *am* really relieved. I thought I'd be sharing a car with Robert Millar, and that worried me.

In the 1980s I spent a lot of time around Millar's world, but I never got to know him. This now feels like my loss: if I'd got to know him, I'd have seen the good sides, the qualities that others saw.

No longer having an early morning flight, we chat late into the night in our hotel close to Hamburg Airport.

DAVID: Journalists were afraid of him, or wary at least, but Robert Millar seemed to get on well with quite a few of the other riders. LeMond, Kelly, Roche, Allan Peiper, they all had a high opinion of you. Different, they said, but a really good person.

PIPPA: I did get on with them. They didn't see the surliness and if they did, they wouldn't let me get away with it. This cancelled flight stuff reminds me of an incident years ago going through Heathrow with Allan. I abused one of the immigration officers. I didn't really abuse her, but I did disrespect her. I was then whisked away into a nearby room.

DAVID: What exactly did you say?

PIPPA: Well, we got to immigration and we had 20 minutes to get on the plane. We'd done a one-day race in England, and it was a time when you travelled with bike bags. So we're in a rush to get to the gate. We're going through security and get stopped. The woman says, 'What's in the bag?' We're as stressed as we could be. I'm stressed and I'm about to lose my rag. I say, 'What do you think it is?' Now I suppose I'm a little pee'd off because it has the words 'Peugeot Cycles Racing Team' written on the bag. In big letters. She says, 'I don't know what you have in the bag, sir.' I say, 'It's a parachute.'

DAVID: Really?

PIPPA: I might have said, 'It's a fucking parachute.'

DAVID: More believable.

PIPPA: Then I say, 'I'm going to jump out of the plane somewhere between here and Brussels.' At that she calls over her colleague and he says, 'Come this way.'

DAVID: Seriously? And you have 20 minutes to get on the plane?

PIPPA: Yes. In we go to the interrogation room, and I realise this is going really badly.

DAVID: Really? What gave you that idea?

PIPPA: Anyway, Allan was like my parent. He was younger than me but wiser, and he's heard me make an idiot of myself. After five minutes I eventually get out. They've gone through my paperwork, they've looked in the bike bag to make sure there isn't a parachute. Then they let me off.

DAVID: You were lucky. I'd have made you miss your flight.

PIPPA: Now, I've got ten minutes to get to the gate. I run there and I hand over my bike so it goes in the hold. We're still waiting for the last people to get on, and Allan says to me, 'If you ever do that again, I'm going to punch you. You're an effing idiot.' I felt six inches tall.

DAVID: Allan would have meant it.

PIPPA: Oh yeah, he meant it.

DAVID: What did you say?

PIPPA: I just said to him, 'Yeah, I know. I'm really sorry. That was bad.' I never ever did that again. It's one of those moments where you just mess up completely, because you're an idiot, you're not an adult yet. You might be a pro and famous and all the rest of it, but you're still an idiot. Twenty-five or 26 and still a twat.

DAVID: I'll handle the stuff at the desk tomorrow.

*   *   *

My experiences with airport car-hire desks haven't always been smooth. 'What do you mean you've got no record of my booking?' etc. People say, always read the small print. One day I will. So with this chequered history, Pippa and I present ourselves at the Europcar desk in Hamburg Airport.

I explain our predicament to a very tall, very thin, very young German man. He's more understanding than anyone I've ever encountered at a car-hire desk.

DAVID: You see, we're covering this race and we'd thought that a flight from Hamburg to Paris would spare us a very long drive and also allow us to drop off the rental car we'd picked up in Copenhagen five days ago. The plan was to fly from here to Paris, pick up a new car there and carry on. But our flight was cancelled last night and, as you can see, we're still here ... So I don't even want to ask you how much it's going to cost to keep our Europcar car for a further three weeks.

PIPPA: Don't tell us. Maybe it's best if we don't know.

The man's fingers dance over his keyboard. He looks up.

VERY TALL, VERY THIN, VERY YOUNG GERMAN: It will be €50 extra

DAVID: €50 extra for the extra three weeks?

VERY TALL, VERY THIN, VERY YOUNG GERMAN: Yes.

DAVID: Fifty extra in total?

VERY TALL, VERY THIN, VERY YOUNG GERMAN: Yes. If you can just sign here?

PIPPA (whispering): Don't snatch it out of the man's hand, David.

DAVID (whispering back): I didn't.

PIPPA. You did. I've never seen you move so quick.

DAVID: Thank you very much. You've been very helpful.

VERY TALL, VERY THIN, VERY YOUNG GERMAN: Have a good trip!

We walk away. I'm trying not to skip or run, but I tell Pippa to move quickly because this young German has just made a big mistake.

We're about to drive away in our Mercedes C Class estate. We'd been expecting to be stuffing ourselves and our bags into a Nissan Micra every morning for the next three weeks. This is joy. Also, I've saved Rupert Murdoch somewhere between two and three grand. I honestly don't understand why I'm so pleased.

PIPPA: If it was my name on the contract, you'd have accused me of sleeping with that young German guy.
DAVID: Accuse you? I'd have lauded you. Fifty euros! The ultimate in taking one for the team. Now let's get out of here before he realises his mistake.

Pippa has undergone another transition. From mere driver to getaway driver. Soon I'm feeling G forces pinning me to the lovely leather.

DAVID: It feels like we're Bonnie and Clyde.
PIPPA: Which of us is which? Or are you suggesting that I'm both?

* * *

It's early morning when we get out of Hamburg Airport. Ten kilometres later I stop looking in the rearview mirror. Bonnie and Clyde are headed for the Hotel Ibis Dunkerque Centre, a 730-kilometre drive. Well, at least there's plenty of time to talk.

This is our third Tour together, and days that bring the unexpected don't upset us anymore. Pippa is imperturbable. Though I'm thoroughly used to her company and at ease with it, I sometimes glance across at my friend in the driver's seat and think of the man she used to be.

The thing is, these times of sharing so much with her on the Tour have helped me to better appreciate who Robert Millar was. Back in the day he was the best climber in the peloton, and though I was wary of the man, I had huge admiration for the bike rider. Now I realise Robert was much more than that.

I want Pippa to feel the same way about Robert but am not sure she can. And, of course, I'm not one for leaving things unsaid.

DAVID: I've asked this before, but surely you must have enjoyed being Robert Millar, the highly successful bike rider? He gave you a life that was good and he helped you to cope with your gender dysphoria. You were so good as Robert Millar, it had to have been compensation for who you couldn't be? If you were back in your teens, and attitudes were as liberal then as they are now, I'm guessing you wouldn't want to give up on Robert Millar's cycling career?

PIPPA: No, you're not right. If Robert Millar had been born in 1998 not 1958, I'd never have been a pro bike rider.

DAVID: Seriously?

PIPPA: You're asking if being Robert Millar, the great cyclist, was some kind of compensation. It wasn't. Some people who'll eventually transition go to the heights of masculinity. They think if I join the army, the paras, or whatever, it will knock the femininity out of me. These guys in the army will reprogram me and I'll be OK. That's not what happens in professional sport. You step into a world of masculinity and ego, but no one's trying to force you into manhood.

DAVID: But surely if you're Robert Millar and you're so talented, sport gives you fame, recognition, excitement and a decent salary. A lot of people looked up to Millar.

PIPPA: But that couldn't compensate you for something you're not dealing with. Something you know deep down you should be dealing with.

DAVID: But at the time it helped you to deal with the fallout of not dealing with it?

PIPPA: Yes, it helped me to bury it. Because I was so invested in that career, I wasn't thinking about gender dysphoria every day, every moment. If I throw myself into this cycling thing 100 per cent, I'm not thinking about it.

DAVID: So it worked? Being Robert Millar.

PIPPA: Then it hits you, unexpectedly. You see a woman somewhere, and you think, *Shit, that could be me. Why isn't that me?* Then I'd have to go back to being Robert Millar, the guy in the bike race.

DAVID: But when you were flying down the Col de Peyresourde in 1983 on your way to winning your first Tour de France stage win, with Pedro Delgado trying to chase you down, that must have been some adrenaline surge?

PIPPA: You're the bike rider at that moment. You're not thinking about the other thing.

DAVID: But you're achieving something that very, very few people get to achieve, something you've worked incredibly hard for. When you cross the finish line, it must have felt like all the dreams have been realised.

PIPPA: I'm aware of that.

DAVID: Are you saying the euphoria of your greatest victories was diminished by internal strife?

PIPPA: No, in that moment, it's not going to arise.

DAVID: When you look back, do you think that while it might not have been an ideal situation, it was a pretty good situation?

PIPPA: I do look back and say, 'Yes, wow, that was a good thing.'

DAVID: Does that allow you to look back with affection on Robert Millar?

PIPPA: I look at my career and who I was. I was missing 1 or 2 per cent to be as good a rider as I could be. As a person, much more was missing. Because of gender dysphoria, the whole social side was really stunted. I was emotionally closed to most people. Because I was so demanding and harsh with the bike rider, I was also harsh with people around cycling. In my private life I was closed. I didn't share things.

DAVID: Maybe it's the fan in me, but I want to think Robert Millar was a happy person.

* * *

From Hamburg we drive south west on the A1, travelling for more than 500 kilometres before crossing the German border into Belgium. There are stops at motorway services: petrol for the car, coffee for the humans. Conversation ebbs and flows.

DAVID: Do you think this is the most content you've been in your life? The point of total contentment?

PIPPA: Well, David, I do enjoy these trips – and these epic drives are a bonus – and don't take this the wrong way, but being with you in a car all day every day falls just short of total contentment …

DAVID: All I know is that you're so much easier to get along with than Robert Millar was.

PIPPA: I'll concede that much, yes.

DAVID: I can tell you have learned to enjoy life.

PIPPA: But I wouldn't want every trans person to think the ultimate reward was driving through France every summer with an over-talkative Irishman and an annoying GPS system. I'm resilient enough to cope with these things, but is everyone?

DAVID: Probably not. But you've not answered the question. Has transition made you happier than you ever were before?

PIPPA: I feel 95 per cent content. Before, when I was the cyclist, I was about 5 per cent content. I'm speaking about me as a person, not as a cyclist. I've got wrinkles now. I wish I was taller, slimmer, whatever. All that stuff. But not having that stuff only takes away a small part of my contentment, like 5 per cent.

DAVID: Ninety-five per cent contentment is about as good as it gets?

PIPPA: I'm a totally different person to who I was as a rider. Very, very different.

DAVID: Do you put that down to transition?

PIPPA: No, it relates to who you are.

DAVID: Did you ever consider coming back to the Tour as, say, a team directeur sportif?

PIPPA: I remember people asking me late in my career if I wanted to do that. I said no, I didn't. I can remember the specific time I realised I didn't want to do that. I was in the TVM team, late in my career. At a race in Spain I felt ill. I stopped just before the feed zone, handed my race number to a commissaire and got into the team car. We were behind the race and soon came to a long hill. I could see guys getting dropped, one after the other. I looked at their faces and saw how much suffering they were enduring. The pain in their faces. That's something you don't realise when you're in the thick of a race. Seeing that, I knew I couldn't do this as a job. I couldn't drive past those guys and not feel some kind of compassion and not want to help them. These guys looked ten or fifteen years older. I couldn't drive past them every day. There are other things I could have done in a cycling team, but I didn't want to be in the car. I just didn't.

DAVID: When you were suffering in the peloton, and you were very good at suffering, it didn't bother you that everybody else was suffering. You step back from the sport, start seeing it from the outside and you end up with a completely different perspective.

PIPPA: I had conversations with directors that I had ridden with. Talked about the admin side, interacting with sponsors, visiting the bike factory, sorting out equipment. All that I could have learned. The race-day stuff, I didn't want any of that.

DAVID: I'm pleased that you're free to be who you always wanted to be, not having to deal with the guilt you once felt when dressing as a girl. That must have made your early life so difficult?

PIPPA: Not really, because I buried it that deeply so the wrongness of it didn't affect me. Since then, I've done all kinds of psychological assessments. Now, you can even go on a course to learn self-improvement. Back then it was just the odd book, and what I found is that no matter how hard I pushed the dysphoria to the bottom of the pile, it would still rumble away.

DAVID: Still, 95 per cent content now, that is some climb. You could be the poster person for transitioning!

PIPPA: Did you have to stop yourself saying 'poster boy' just there, David?

DAVID: You don't miss much, do you?

Chapter 4

4 September 2020
Stage 7, Millau to Lavaur – 168 km

I remember Lavaur in 2020. It marked the last time we thought of Tadej Pogačar as a normal bike rider. In his first Tour de France, the 21-year-old from Slovenia had ridden well through the first six days and, remarkably, was third overall when they set off from Millau, just seven seconds down on race leader Adam Yates.

It was almost as if we were patting him on the head. You're not bad for a kid. In hindsight, we should have paid more attention to what he'd done in the Vuelta a España the previous year. How could a 20-year-old win three mountain stages and fight for overall victory without being truly exceptional?

That late afternoon in 2020, Pogačar was the 43rd rider over the finish line at Lavaur, 1 minute and 21 seconds behind the day's winner. He lost time to his principal rivals and plummeted from third to 16th on general classification. His fall didn't merit much of a mention in that day's reports.

He was a kid who'd got caught out in the crosswinds towards the end. It happens. He's still learning his trade. Not many went to the trouble of enquiring. Who was Pogačar at that moment? Some talented young guy who'd done well in last year's Vuelta. Let's not get carried away.

*   *   *

The sun is setting as we skirt round Toulouse on our south-westerly journey from Lavaur to Cugnaux. This Covid-affected Tour de France should feel different, but it doesn't. Sure, we don masks and remember not to shake the hand of anyone inside the Tour bubble, but the inconveniences are minor.

After seven days the racing feels no different, nor has the late-August start changed much. The September weather is as warm as July. And it's here, on the A68 autoroute, that a familiar thought resurfaces: France is particularly beautiful at this time in the evening. On our drive to the two-star Le Patio Occitan in Cugnaux, the light slowly wanes.

What we don't want in Cugnaux is another Auberge Les Cardabelles. That had been our resting place the previous night. A nightmare. 'What's wrong with your mobile phone?' *la patronne* growled as we walked through the door. She was an older woman who didn't seem, let's say, much in love with life. 'Do you not have a mobile phone?' she snarled. It was only 9.30. Perhaps we should have called ahead, but we're not talking crime of the century. Where was the hospitality? '*Désolé*,' we said, but to no avail. From the moment we arrived, she crucified us.

Pippa and I needed to talk about it.

PIPPA: We probably shouldn't have stopped at the pizzeria in that village before Les Cardabelles. But had we not stopped, it would have been another night without food.
DAVID: We had to eat.
PIPPA: The McDonald's the night before hadn't been good and the pizza joint wasn't bad.

DAVID: Pretty basic, but an upgrade. Things aren't great when a late-night €10 pizza feels like an upgrade on the previous evening. *La belle vie!* Anyway, I tried calling the hotel from the pizzeria but there was no signal.

PIPPA: Straightaway she started on at us! 'You were supposed to be here hours ago, you should have called, yap, yap, yap.'

DAVID: She was like an angry mother saying, 'You treat this place like a hotel.' Except …

PIPPA: You said we didn't have a phone signal, but she wasn't having it. She started rabbiting on about having to get up in the morning and this being very unsatisfactory.

DAVID: She was so aggressive. If she'd had a gun and had seen a way of getting away with it, we were both dead.

PIPPA: It wasn't even a nice place. Old and rundown. Halfway up the rickety stairs there was a stuffed bear on the landing, a bear's body with what looked like a goat's head. Like something from the film *Jeepers Creepers*. Everything was decrepit. She'd had it all painted in an attempt to hide the dinginess. Everything creaked and the communal bathroom was down the corridor.

DAVID: Plus, we were the only people staying there, which was a giveaway. Then this morning she serves us fresh orange juice at breakfast.

PIPPA: It was a decent breakfast, but she spoiled it with the side dish of whingeing. Check-out is ten o'clock! 'Where's your friend?'

DAVID: Where was I? Did she think I'd done a runner?

PIPPA: You were still in the room, I was sitting in the shade outside waiting for you, and she was going berserk. 'I've got other people coming, he should be out of his room by now.' Then you come strolling down and you're in good form because you've filed an extra piece to *The Times*. She nabs you and starts on again.

DAVID: Water off a duck's back.

PIPPA: People shoot ducks.

*   *   *

Sallanches, long ago …

The most brutal bike race I've ever witnessed took place on the last Sunday in August 1980. Nobody who saw that race has forgotten it. I was a young reporter and trading on the possibility that Sean Kelly might win a title without an Irish journalist being present, I sold the idea to my sports editor in Dublin. The *Irish Press* newspaper sent their rookie reporter off to France to cover the World Road Race Championships.

The race was held in Sallanches in Haute-Savoie, at the foot of Mont Blanc. Twenty laps of a 13.4-kilometre circuit. That's a marathon 268.4 km in total. But there was a sadistic twist. The Côte de Domancy, on the outskirts of the town, was the cruellest of climbs, 2.7 km of sheer torture, with some gradients of up to 16 per cent. To win the Worlds, a rider would have to do the Category 2 climb 20 times and still have enough in the tank to finish ahead of his rivals.

Of course, this was France and the route had been chosen to provide a coronation for the national hero, Bernard Hinault. They called Hinault 'Le Blaireau' (the Badger) because of his super-aggressive riding style. That climb would be to his liking.

That summer the Badger's teeth were bared into a snarl. Having won the 1978 and 1979 Tours de France, he was leading the 1980 Tour after almost two weeks of the race, but a knee injury meant he couldn't start stage 13. The forced with-drawal hurt. He vanished in the night without a word.

In Sallanches before the race, Jacques Anquetil, the legendary rider who was managing the French team that year, predicted that only 15 starters would finish. To make matters even worse, it was raining as the 106 riders set off to claim the rainbow jersey.

Seven and a half hours later, the winner crossed the line. Twenty minutes passed while the other 14 survivors wearily crossed the finish line. Anquetil had called it. Fifteen finishers. Hinault had dominated. Kelly, the would-be winner according to the *Irish Press* correspondent, dropped out soon after half-way. I had sold my sports editor a pup.

Apart from Hinault crushing every rival, what I remember from that brutal race is the skinny 21-year-old Glaswegian in the GB team shirt. Robert Millar was one of two riders to still be with Hinault near the end. The brilliant Italian climber Gianbattista Baronchelli was the other.

On the last lap Millar ran out of energy and faded to 11th, but that was of minor relevance. He'd shown he had the talent and the fearlessness to compete on the toughest terrain with the greatest rider of that era. Millar was then a first-year pro.

* * *

The drive from Millau to Cugnaux in the lovely evening light took us about an hour. Through the departments of Aveyron, Tarn and Haute-Garonne we weaved, making a long half-circle to get round Toulouse. The views should have been enough, but I wanted to relive that Sallanches ride with Pippa.

'Tell me,' I ask, 'how did the still-wet-behind-the-ears Millar produce a ride like that?'

You may think I'm harking back too much because these were difficult years in Pippa's life, but I know that even though she wasn't happy being Robert Millar, she's proud of what he did on the bike.

PIPPA: Well, I was a first-year pro in survival mode in every race. Most races I don't see the front. Maybe a couple of small ones, but I certainly didn't see Hinault and Baronchelli in any race I'd ridden. When I found myself with them in the lead group, basically I didn't want to get in their way. The most shocking part for me came when it was down to just four, Hinault, Baronchelli, [Michel] Pollentier and me, it was Pollentier who got dropped. *Bloody hell*. I thought, *Oh shit, there's just the three of us now. I'll get a medal if I keep this up.* That was easier said than done. Hinault was riding like ten men, Baronchelli was glued to his wheel and I was just hanging on.

DAVID: I remember it. It was only on the last lap you wilted?

PIPPA: When I cracked, I was seeing stars.

A postscript to that long day in Sallanches. Spain's Juan Fernández got the bronze medal that could so easily have been Robert's. Fernández later said he was so wasted at the end, his fingers locked when signing an autograph and for a few moments he couldn't put the pen down.

Doping control was on the second floor of a sports hall with no elevator. Robert looked at the stairs and the thought of another climb, however short, was too much. He gripped the rail by the side of the stairs and slowly hauled himself upwards.

Soon Hinault was there, pounding on the steps behind him, bounding past him, throwing out a cheery '*Ça va?*' that wasn't seeking a reply. Then he was gone.

*   *   *

As we near Cugnaux, the evening has dimmed to twilight. We're bound for Le Patio Occitan, a two-star hotel whose rating makes me a little giddy. Pippa, however, is tired. Not of driving, nor of the Tour, but of the interrogations.

PIPPA: OK, David, a question for you. Mary is your wife, right. Say we go back in time. You're five or ten years into your marriage. You have two kids. Work is going well. One day Mary says, 'David, I've got something to tell you.'

DAVID: I'm not liking where this is going.

PIPPA: She announces she's going to change sides, transition. The clumsy way of putting it was, 'I'm going to have a sex change.' What would you do, David?

DAVID: Well, my first thought would be, *What are the ladies at the golf club going to think?* Only joking.

PIPPA: Let me put it another way. You love this person and if she was in a car accident, lost an arm or was disfigured, you wouldn't leave her. You'd want to do the right thing. How we appear to others matters to people.

DAVID: OK. I don't disagree with that.

PIPPA: So, how would you process what she's just said to you because it's not the same as an accident or someone you love being laid low by long Covid? Knowing this is the change that will make her happy, would you be able to go with Mary becoming a man?

DAVID: Being honest, I wouldn't be. In the car with you now, I'm uneasy admitting this.

PIPPA: Exactly. You see, I understand that. You wouldn't be comfortable. Yet inside Mary would still be the person you love. I admit if it happened to me, I wouldn't be OK with it at first. I'd have to get my head round it. It's a lot to ask, and you wonder what people will think of me if my partner transitions.

DAVID: I'm relieved to hear you say this.

PIPPA: People ask me, why did you change? How did your partner deal with it? Your kids? Honestly, I don't really know how they've dealt with it because I've got enough crap going on in my head. I can't imagine what it's done to them. And I'm aware of that. I'm aware of that every day. So I say to people, you know, how would you deal with this?

DAVID: What's the answer that you usually get?

PIPPA: Well, some people just say, no. It's not happening. No, because it takes them outside of what they're comfortable with. Or it's about others judging them on what they are and who they are with. Or they can't, you know, they can't relate to the mechanics of it.

DAVID: So are you saying that in the eyes of the public or just people who know me, I'd be a hero for sticking by my wife who had a horrible medical condition, but if she decides she wants to be a man, and I stick with her, I'd be seen as a weirdo?

PIPPA: Exactly. And people care deeply about what other people think. What I'm getting to is this: there's a perception that the person who's changing sides hasn't thought about all this. As if the person who's transitioning is completely insensitive. But the opposite is the case, from the moment you start dealing with the problem. If you've got any kind of emotional intelligence about you, you're very aware of how it's going to affect everybody. You're maybe not understanding exactly how it's hitting them, but you do know that it's going to impact them. How can it not? They love you, but you're asking a lot.

DAVID: From what you're saying, I'm guessing you got accused of being selfish?

PIPPA: I did, but I'd been dealing with it in my head for 25 years. So I knew it wasn't selfish. It wasn't an impulse. It would have been more selfish to keep hiding that part of me and making everybody unhappy. I was a difficult person.

DAVID: When you eventually spoke to your partner Linda about it, was it a gradual thing?

PIPPA: Acceptance? Yeah, really gradual.

DAVID: Are you consciously beginning the conversation, feeling the temperature of the water before you immerse?

PIPPA: It's, you know, it's hard to say how people are going to react. With Linda, it first came out that I'd dress in girls' clothes and I suppose it seemed to Linda that, maybe, there's some kind of transvestite, cross-dresser thing going on with me. Something for a kind of mental relief. For my well-being, some days I'd have to dress as a woman. But that became more frequent and a bit more difficult. So then finally we got to it. 'Are you going to have a sex change? You don't know? I mean, you must know.' And you do know. In the back of your head, you know. Inside you're screaming, yeah, I want to have a sex change. I want to live full-time as a woman. But you can't communicate that to the person with you. You can't just throw that grenade into the room. At least I couldn't.

*   *   *

Until Pippa, I'd never known a trans person. Spending time with her has been revelatory, and I find myself caring about her in ways I'd never have imagined. During the early part of the Tour she'd been in touch with Sandra Forgues, a French woman with whom she has much in common. In previous lives they were both elite athletes. Sandra had been an Olympic gold medallist in canoe-slalom at a time when she was Wilfrid Forgues. In Millau, where Pogačar had once come in so far back, Sandra and Pippa made time for a coffee.

'How did it go?' I ask, when she returns to the press centre.

'Really well,' Pippa says. 'It was good for me to speak with her. We're similar in how we want transition to work. Ideally, I want to be totally comfortable in the company of my women friends, and I hope they can be comfortable with me. Sandra talked about not wanting to die as an old man and that resonated with me. I too never wanted to die as an old man.'

away the Crow Road

He loved riding. He liked speed. He couldn't bear to plod along. He enjoyed the pulse-quickening danger.

He discovered that he was decent at 15. His first race came when he was 16. He lacked the skill to ride on the wheels of others or the knowledge of how to pace himself. He just threw himself out there. If he blew up, well, that was it. But he didn't. He finished sixth. Last of the finishers. Thirty boys dropped out.

The excitement was a drug. Chasing buses out the length of the Ayr Road gave him a hit. His family took annual holidays at Butlin's, and how epic that journey had seemed to him as a kid. Now he could cycle well past Butlin's and spin home again in the space of an afternoon. The bike took him out of ordinary life, away from the city. Trees, hills, animals, the coast, and the vast, grey Firth of Clyde.

On empty days he'd cycle the seven miles or so out to the airport and put down a few hours just looking at the planes and wondering about the places they flew to and came from. And then his mind fell back to earth and his bike. All the places a bike might take him had yet to be fully considered.

For now, though, he could generally head northwards. He did a lot of his training riding between Lennoxtown and Fintry, where the Crow Road rises northwards out from Lennoxtown and through Crosshill Street, leaving the stone houses behind. The way sent him toiling across the face of the Campsie Fells to the Kilsyth Hills, just bloody climbing and climbing for over five kilometres up the old drovers' road. Heaven was freedom.

When one of their number passed, kicked the bucket or shuffled off the mortal coil, the old timers used to say that he was *away the Crow Road*. No more struggle for him. Heaven, freedom or whatever you wanted to call it.

The Crow Road was often used, others said, by Rob Roy and the MacGregors. Any mention of quarrelsome outlaws who passed this way drew just a scolding eye-roll from young Robert Millar. He did? Aye? And what gear ratio did he use?

He needed no myths or havering for his imagination.

summer wedges

As Robert got used to going out into the world as a girl, he ventured further afield. At weekends, if he'd saved enough money, he'd catch the train up to Glasgow Central and mooch around the city centre, browsing the stores. On Saturdays the city was busy and nobody threw a second glance at a small girl with long hair flicking through the rails for affordable new fashion.

His confidence grew quickly. Instead of just looking at what girls of his age were wearing, he thought about what he might buy. He carefully trawled shops like Dorothy Perkins or Frasers department store trying on girls' clothes. He bought what he liked and could afford.

It was scary in the beginning. What if a cashier asked a question? He had only his cracked boy's voice to reply with. He never spoke to the assistants on the tills when it came time to pay. That was OK. On Saturday afternoons he looked like just another grumpy teenager with a long queue behind her.

He rarely had to guess sizes as there were usually changing rooms to slip into. His shopping trips gradually became less daunting. He looked like a girl for most of his adolescence, and he got used to the image he saw reflected back at himself when he was in girl mode. At first it was perplexing – not strange and not troubling. There was a slight taint of wrongness to it, but he forgot about that once he was out in the world and immersed in girlness.

Once he bought a pair of Ravel shoes, beige summer wedges that he'd coveted. In the shop he'd been hurrying and hadn't tried them on. Shoes had become tricky since he'd stopped saying he was buying them for his sister. Assistants asked awkward questions. How are they on ye? Bit tight? Little bit narrow? Walk up and down there.

So he took a chance and bought his size in wedges. When he got them home one shoe was smaller than the other. He kicked himself with the shoe that fitted. Somebody had messed with the display pair.

A boy had to deliver a lot of papers to be able to afford new shoes, and Robert just couldn't afford to take the hit financially. He yearned to walk around in those new shoes. He went back to the shop the next weekend.

He proffered the shoes to an assistant and, using as few words as possible, he explained the size problem. His girl voice wasn't girlish enough and he got a funny look in return. It was more the second glance given to a girl with a boyish voice than the gaze directed at a boy dressed as a girl. He settled for that. The swap was done. He nodded his thanks and left.

sunny day

Overall, he thought he looked OK as a girl. He had really long hair. His skin was smooth, and when he applied a little of the make-up he'd purchased from Boots the look was almost complete. He wore inappropriate shoes, just as some teenage girls did. The trickiest part of a shopping trip was always leaving his parents' flat and returning. So easy to get spotted by a neighbour or any of the kids hanging about.

He was resourceful. He fashioned a crawl-in wardrobe for himself in the cupboard under the stairs. The space wasn't in the flat where they lived but outside in the corridor and, as such, it was seldom used. Robert stored his bike there, but it was also where he hid his girls' clothes. It was a place where he could get changed before shopping.

Mostly Robert had been dressing up at home and staying there. The first time he went outside in girls' clothes was a summer's day when he was 12 years old. He needed to know what it felt like having the warm wind on his legs. He wanted freedom to not have to wear denim jeans. He bided his time and got ready when everyone else had gone out. He slipped into his space under the stairs. He put on a skirt, tights, a short-sleeve top that he'd 'borrowed' from his sister. Transformed, he stepped out again and made for the back stairwell. The Millars lived on the 11th floor of 22, but the lift was too risky.

Outside the sun shone and the afternoon was his. He went to the park, staying well away from the football pitches. He avoided the crowds lolling on the grass and enjoyed the sense of naturalness he felt when dressed as a girl. Part of him knew this wasn't what boys were supposed to do on a Saturday afternoon. It was confusing because he felt good, not in any kind of sexual way but just at peace with himself and the world.

Having walked for a long time feeling like he was wrapped in the cloak of femininity, the experience was just as he hoped it would be.

bus stop

One Saturday he walked down the back stairs. Dressed as a girl, he was heading for the bus. The walk down from the 11th floor to fresh air and freedom was always stressful, but it got a little less so every time he did it. Robert had long since figured out that people paid less attention to long-haired teenagers than he paid to people.

This Saturday, though, he got just past the second level and it happened. He met a kid that he knew from school. The kid was running up the stairs to his second-floor flat. Robert was descending. It was a younger kid. Two pairs of eyes locked.

'Howzitgoin?'

'Nae bad.'

There was a moment of recognition on the other kid's face, followed by a moment of confusion. Then it was over.

So it seemed. By the time Robert got out the door of the building, the kid had absorbed the sight he'd seen and was already at his bedroom window shouting down, 'Aye, you're goin' out dressed as a wee girl?'

Oh fuck, said Robert to himself.

By the time Robert got to the bus stop he'd forgotten about it. That's the kid he was, onto the next thing. It was like fighting in the school yard – bad moments only lasted so long. A few punches, the moments stop and then you get consumed by something else. Well, doncha?

So in his dress he calmly waited for the bus and he didn't think about it anymore until he was coming home again. Then the whole guilt started to beat him up. What if the little fucker tells somebody? What if he tells everybody? What if I go to school tomorrow and they all say, 'Hey, wee fella, you were dressed as a girl goin' to town.'

What then?

He decided that he'd just say that the girl heading down the stairs was his sister. He looked like his sister. What was more likely? Really? That wee kid was mistaken?

Ye must have seen it was my sister? What's wrong with ye see, you've got one eye or something? Ye know that? Bin drinkin', have ye? Was nae me, ya bampot.

He changed back into his boy clothes in the understairs space and had tea with the family.

caught

The mirror was always the draw and always the problem. He'd save money to have one in his bedroom if it didn't draw questions. Instead, he'd tiptoe the stairs through the hallway and into the bathroom. It was never comfortable.

He was in the downstairs toilet, checking his outfit in the mirror. Make-up was a work in progress. He shot over-the-shoulder glances, turned this way and that. He looked good and felt that way too. Then his dad came home early. Men in 1970s Glasgow never came home early from work.

The bathroom door was unlocked and ajar when his dad opened the front door. *Early! Sweet Jesus! Was somebody dead? Was it war? Early?*

There was Robert Millar, dressed as a girl. Tights, skirt, top, make-up, the whole she-bang. And there was Bill Millar in the hallway. For God's sake.

Neither Dad nor Robert said a word. The bathroom door closed quickly. Bill Millar went upstairs. Robert pressed his back to the door.

He hasn't seen me. He hasn't said anything. I've got away with it.

He began removing everything. De-girling. Clothes gone. Face scrubbed.

And then from upstairs, the shout. 'Are you finished in there yet?'

Robert went upstairs in silence. Waited. Bill Millar didn't come to his son's room. Robert sat on his bed, not knowing. It was worse than knowing. *Had he been seen? Maybe his father had just noticed a blur. A blur in girls' clothes? Maybe not? He'd have said something. Of course he would. There was nothing to go on.* He upgraded the 'maybe not' to a 'probably not'.

Then the worst outcome.

Robert had gone to bed when his father came to the bedroom. A man wrestling with words and losing.

He could have said: 'You know, I saw you dressed as a girl today, Robert.'

He could have said: 'What the fuck are you playing at, kid?'

He could have said: 'No son of mine, etc., etc.'

Instead, Bill Millar tried to understand. Tried his best to express something soft through all the vagueness a working-class Glaswegian man in the 1970s could muster.

'You're going through puberty, adolescence. We all went through it. It's a natural time. It's confusing too.'

And his son, the boy who wants to be a girl, isn't relieved to hear the pastoral tone. He's crawling under his bedsheets. It's excruciating.

Oh Jesus. Don't, Dad. Anything but this. Be angry even, but not this.

Bill confirms that he and Mum have had a talk.

Oh, no, he's told my mum. Oh Jesus. What's she gonna say? Why the fuck would you tell her?

'This puberty, son, it's really confusing … You know we all go through these really confusing phases in our teenage years … it happens to everybody … It happened to me … I went through it.'

Please stop … Is it really just a phase? … If you want a gas-mask bag as your school bag, that's a phase, isn't it? … Playing tennis on the street when Wimbledon's on the telly? That's a phase?

'So, your mum and I, we don't want you to worry … you're a good wee lad … and this is just a thing that you're going through … As I said, lots of people go through it … puberty and all that … I went through it … Yes, when I was growing up, I was a bit confused as well …'

The boy who wants to be a girl is now listening more than he's squirming.

You've dressed as a girl as well? … It's not just me, then … Why didn't you say that at the start? … Maybe it really is just a phase … Maybe I'm not a freak show like they say in the magazines or papers … My dad was confused as well … and it passed for him … Look at him, he doesn't wear dresses anymore … Just look at him … He's fine now.

His dad gets up to leave. Bill Millar walks out of his child's bedroom in Glasgow in the 1970s. Touchy-feely is years away. Man to man is all there is, even if one man is a boy whose sole contribution has been a mortified grunt. Bill Millar has that face on. The face says, it's OK, I've talked about that. Whatever it was, I've talked about it. I've dealt with that. I've done my bit. I've asked you. You've listened. I can report back downstairs. Job done.

'So that's it, son. Yeah. Now go to sleep.'

Bill Millar's footsteps faded down the stairs. Robert lay there, a curled-up comma of a boy, fretting in his bed. Questions he wanted to ask now raised their hands, too late.

I have a dream where I'd rather just wake up as a girl? … Did you have those dreams, Dad? … They don't seem like a phase … I dream that dream a lot, the 'I'd rather be a girl' kind of dream … Is there some kind of magic that I can perform on myself? Did you do that?

And his mum never, ever mentions the subject. Nobody ever mentions it again.

Chapter 5

7 September 2020

Rest day at Hôtel La Jetée Sud, La Rochelle

Three days after Tadej Pogačar suffered his first bad moment at the 2020 Tour de France and three minutes after we checked into our rest-day hotel, Pippa and I knew two things. One, Pogačar, the Tour debutant, already knows he's wrapped in the warm cloak of destiny. Two, La Jetée Sud is perhaps the worst hotel in all of France.

Let's talk about Pogačar.

After unluckily losing 1 minute 21 seconds, he said he'd try another day. On his way to signing on the following morning, he had an update. 'I intend to attack today,' he said matter-of-factly. With three tough Pyrenean climbs, it wasn't a bad day to pick a fight, but why forewarn the others?

If you'd put that to Pogačar, he'd have laughed. 'Why not? It's what I'm going to do.' Allan Peiper, his director sportif at the time, who'd been unusually upset at the loss of time the previous day, told him that reactive attacks rarely work and advised him to keep his powder dry.

After Jumbo-Visma's Tom Dumoulin had stretched out the GC group on the final climb, the Col de Peyresourde, Pogačar just took off. His Slovenian compatriot Primož Roglič countered, then Nairo Quintana. Behind, every other rider toiled. It had the potential to be an important moment, but Roglič wasn't sure, nor was Quintana, and with Egan Bernal working at the front of the pursuers, the gap closed.

In reactive mode, Pogačar attacked again. Roglič had neither the energy, nor perhaps the stomach, for another pursuit. And that was the last they saw of young Tadej. Early breakaways, allowed to build a big lead, dominated the finish. Pogačar finished ninth but, importantly, clawed back 40 of the 81 seconds he'd lost to the Tour favourites.

For him, that wasn't enough. On the second day in the Pyrenees he attacked on the Col de Marie-Blanque, but now the others were ready, Roglič especially. He chased down his compatriot, making him see there was no point. After getting over the Marie-Blanque, they descended to the finish, a select group of favourites eyeing each other like hawks. Unable to break clear, Pogačar switched to Plan B. Approaching the end, he was one of five with a chance of winning.

Laruns is a small Pyrenean town of 1,200 inhabitants. On the outskirts, Pogačar knew Roglič was dangerous, so too the Swiss rider Marc Hirschi. He latched on to Hirschi's wheel, then accelerated past him. Roglič surged down the left side of the road. Though well apart, there was nothing between them. In a fiercely contested sprint, Pogačar shaded it. That's him. He makes good things happen.

That afternoon, Laruns became the place Tadej Pogačar enjoyed his first victory at the Tour de France. It will be remembered for that.

Hôtel La Jetée Sud will also be remembered. After two days in the Pyrenees, we overnighted at the Aliotel in Cazères-sur-l'Adour and left early the next morning. It was a 335-kilometre drive to the Jetée Sud, and because the hotel was in La Rochelle and close to the sea, we assumed it would be fine. From the outside, it certainly looked OK.

'You've got the last two rooms,' the patron said. 'One has an en-suite, the other a communal bathroom across the corridor.'

At this moment the gentleman doesn't have a choice. 'The lady,' I say, 'will have the room with the en-suite.' Pippa doesn't demur. Settled. My double room is very basic, the bathroom is across the corridor. It, too, is pretty basic. Feeling a little like a victim and looking for comfort, I go to Pippa's room.

DAVID: What's that toilet doing in the middle of your bedroom?

PIPPA: It's a macerator, David.

DAVID: A macerator? No, I mean the toilet bowl.

PIPPA: Yeah, at the end of the bed.

DAVID: Yes.

PIPPA: Macerator. It's got a rotational blade inside that turns what you deposit into slurry. Just so you know, it's a Saniflo system.

DAVID: Why in the middle of the room?

PIPPA: I don't know. Maybe the pipes aren't big enough to get rid of the waste and it must be chopped up first. It works the same as your food processor except this is for food you have already processed. And then it gets pumped out through the small pipe.

DAVID: But it's at the end of your bed.

PIPPA: I know. Believe me, I know where it is.

DAVID: On booking.com they called it an en-suite.

PIPPA: A non-suite. Technically, it has what you'd expect in an en-suite. But with a twist. There's a shower and a toilet, but they're both in the actual room, by the actual bed.

Between the bed and the toilet there's about four feet. More a non-suite than an en-suite.

DAVID: Does it smell?

PIPPA: Yes. Non-sweet.

DAVID: I thought I was the one taking the hit here, but I've actually drawn the long straw. I'd rather walk across the corridor, if it's all the same to you!

PIPPA: Chivalry has paid off for you. I have a smelly room, and the other thing about having a macerator at the foot of the bed is that it makes a horrendous noise.

DAVID: Do you press a button?

PIPPA: Yeah, very high-tech. Just press a button and it mushes the waste. It's this loud, whizzing noise. Like the grinder you have in some kitchen sinks. It's not just the macerator.

DAVID: Don't tell me.

PIPPA: The electricity is also unsafe, the television is high up on the wall so people can't knock it off and a wire runs down to the socket, but it's just a wire. No plug, so you just have a wire stuck into the socket. You wouldn't dare touch it. As for the shower? It's one of the dirtiest I've ever seen.

DAVID: I can see this is pretty upsetting for you. Well, there's some good news.

PIPPA: Yeah?

DAVID: Yeah. We're here for two nights.

*   *   *

We survived.

Even a dreadful hotel is going to have one upside. We left on a Wednesday morning with a very short drive to the start at

Châtelaillon-Plage. Short drives at the Tour are about as frequent as snow. The sky was blue, the day was warm and as we travelled, it felt good to be alive.

DAVID: That place in La Rochelle really wasn't so bad.

PIPPA: It wasn't so great either.

DAVID: At least the owner wasn't rushing us out the door this morning.

PIPPA: I've had a look on Tripadvisor.

DAVID: What, to check the reviews?

PIPPA: Just the latest one. The headline says, 'Only If You Must!' Then it reads, 'Couldn't find anywhere else and this was the last resort!! More a truckers' stop over, the showers were in the room, no separate shower room!! Breakfast was coffee and one stingy croissant!! Guy was nice enough. If you're one guy on his own or with a couple of mates you'd go for this, but for families and couples, you deserve a divorce!!'

DAVID: Yep, we do need a divorce from places such as this.

PIPPA: There's a response from *le propriétaire*. It says, 'You paid cheap, you got cheap, what did you expect? Next time better book in a five stars hotel but it's more expensive!!! Nice trip and don't come back, even if you must.'

DAVID: *L'Équipe* are reporting this morning that Christian Prudhomme has got Covid and it says the Tour director will quarantine for seven days. I'm really pleased about this.

PIPPA: Is that because of the bollocking he gave you in Nice?

DAVID: Totally. How ridiculous was that? I'm going down the stairs to the car park at the start, minding my own business, he's coming up with three flunkies in tow, and he takes umbrage at the fact that my Covid mask doesn't cover my nose. He gets all stroppy, tells me to get my mask up, and I'm thinking you're the Tour director, not the Covid police. I wanted to tell him to fuck off, but it was a bit early in the race for that.

PIPPA: The funny thing about him getting Covid was that I'd seen him two days before in the VIP area in the Village Départ, standing there with various dignitaries. So presumably they've all got it now. Makes me laugh to think of the special *invitées* who came for their champagne and caviar and got Covid.

DAVID: Prudhomme used to be a journalist, then he became Tour director, and he pretends he hasn't changed but he has. They all do. Let me tell my Jean-Marie Leblanc story. [Leblanc was chief cycling reporter for *L'Équipe* in the early 1980s. We got to know each other pretty well during 1984, the year I lived in France.] I was writing a book about Sean Kelly, he was world number one back then and winning big races like Paris–Roubaix, Liège–Bastogne–Liège and, of course, Paris–Nice. I covered these races, and because I was constantly talking with Kelly, I knew more about him than any journalist on the circuit. Jean-Marie twigged this, and on days when Kelly won, he'd sidle over to me in the press room. He was friendly and charming, and I admit it was nice to have the man from *L'Équipe* befriend you.

The trade-off was I told Jean-Marie everything I knew about Kelly: the back story, that day's story, what he'd said at the start, at the finish, whether he was planning to ride the Giro. Jean-Marie and I had become friends. Then at the end of the year, there was a reception at a fancy venue in Paris for what were called the Super Prestige awards. I was there because Kelly got the main prize.

As I walked into a big room where people were sipping champagne, I saw Jean-Marie in a small circle, talking with some high-powered Tour de France bosses. I was pleased to see him, the only familiar face in the room. As he saw me coming towards him, there was suddenly an expression of total horror. He was in a suit, while I'd dressed like the freelance journalist I was. From his body language, the message was obvious. Please, please, don't approach me. To his relief, I walked past.

I've never forgotten that moment. Five years later he became the Tour director and had the job for 18 years. He reigned through the Armstrong years and never saw anything wrong. An emperor without clothes while Rome burned. That's how I remember my old friend.

PIPPA: Let me tell you about my Leblanc experience. Boiling hot day on the 1987 Tour, Poitiers to Chaumeil, through Limousin and into the Corrèze. Stage 11. It looked like the ideal day for a break to get away and then the race leader's team taking control. A day that you're hoping is going to be stress-free.

Instead, it was chaos from the start. GC [general classification] riders were trying to sneak into breakaways, others were chasing them down. It was almost impossible to keep track of what was happening. Riders attacked, others counter-attacked. The route itself had so many short climbs, winding descents, gravel strewn on corners and melting tarmac that made it feel like you were riding through treacle. Normally things settle down after an hour.

This day we went flat out for more than two hours. It was desperate. Guys strung out everywhere. Towards the end it got more hellish. The route narrowed into even smaller roads. The tension that had eased, returned. So the whole day was pure purgatory, physically and mentally. It was one of the hardest non-mountain stages I'd ever done and I was glad to get to my bed at the end of it.

Next day, still hurting, I was scheduled to do an interview with Jean-Marie Leblanc. He was one of *L'Équipe*'s top guys and he'd been a pro himself. I read his stuff most days, but that morning his summary of the previous day's stage basically said that nothing happened, everyone had enjoyed a rest day, boring. One long French yawn. Jean-Marie had been watching a completely different bike race to the one I'd ridden. I knew what I was still feeling in my legs. So he got an unexpected answer when he asked me what I thought of the previous day's stage.

He didn't take my analysis of his story very well at all. He seemed hurt when I asked if he'd been dozing in the press room after a heavy lunch with some good wine. I actually suggested this might be the reason his piece was so piss-poor. The interview didn't last very long after that, but Jean-Marie still managed to produce a full-page story the next day. He took his revenge by being highly critical of me in the piece. He poured the misery on. It was bad.

I'd thought that if we as riders could be judged on our performance, then we ought to be able to do the same to those writing about the race. He didn't see it that way. So, David, at least we agree about Jean-Marie Leblanc.

Chapter 6

28 June 2021
Stage 3, Lorient to Pontivy – 182.9 km

By now, you'll have realised that for journalists the Tour de France isn't exactly a five-star experience. Mostly this is down to the Tour organisation booking all the good hotels before the route is revealed. We're left with places they couldn't possibly countenance.

There are compensations. Sometimes accommodation that seems modest turns out to be better than that. Occasionally, we'll stay at the home of people who are attentive and generous hosts. Other times, the two- or three-star hotel is cosy and almost classy.

Take the Gîte à la ferme (farmhouse cottage), near Merléac, our third stopover on the 2021 Tour de France. Set in the heart of Brittany, Merléac is scarcely big enough to be considered a village. Just 463 people. The Gîte à la ferme was two miles from Merléac and not well signposted. Still, we managed to find it.

It was good. Three bedrooms, two bathrooms, living room, a nice kitchen with a coffee machine. It cost €109 for the night. And as you so often do in the middle of the countryside, we slept like logs and woke up rekindled.

Then, the clincher. The next day's stage began in Lorient and finished in Pontivy. From Merléac to Lorient would take more than an hour, and then another two hours to get to the finish. But if we went directly from Merléac to the finish, we'd be there in less than half an hour.

So, of course, we went straight to Pontivy, getting there at 11 a.m., more than two hours before the stage began. We had ample time to shoot the breeze over coffee and then take a long stroll through the town. We talked a lot about cycling. The race. Tadej Pogačar and Primoz Roglič. Ten months earlier, in the 2020 Covid-affected Tour, Pogačar astonished us with a brilliant time trial on the penultimate stage, which turned the race on its head. Roglič had what seemed an unassailable lead, but Pogačar's brilliance in that race against the clock and Roglič's own substandard performance changed everything.

This was complicated. They're both Slovenian and back home everyone supported Roglič. Pogačar, they thought, was one for the future, or at least he was until that tumultuous time trial. Saddened by Roglič's defeat, many could barely bring themselves to celebrate the man who defeated him. Though he never said a word, Pogačar felt that.

Before the 2021 Tour, Pippa and I both wrote pieces in which we had to nominate the rider we thought would win. We both picked Roglič, as if we somehow thought the kid's victory the year before had been a fluke and flukes are not repeatable.

It didn't take long for the second-guessing to begin, prompted by a thought that just wouldn't go away. In Pontivy, poor Pippa had to listen while I explained.

DAVID: Pippa, there was a documentary that came out last December. Don't know if you saw it, but it was called *Code Yellow*. Roglič's Jumbo–Visma team collaborated with a Dutch TV company to make it and it centred on the team's attempt to win last year's Tour. There's one scene that stood out. After the time trial on the second-last day in which Roglič has lost everything, he's talking with teammate Tom Dumoulin. He's devastated, Dumoulin is shocked, and suddenly they start casting doubt on Pogačar's performance. How could a rider who looks like 'a miner' on his bike go so fast, asks Dumoulin. Roglič says the speed at which Pogačar went made no sense to him. They didn't mention the word 'doping'. They didn't need to. It was there. Pogačar grew up watching and admiring Roglič. How do you think he reacted to *Code Yellow*?

PIPPA: The champion just thinks, *I'm going to beat you anyway*. They have a different mentality to everybody else. It's not, *I'll show you. You'll see how good I am*. It's more like, *I'm just going to wipe the floor with you*. Hinault was more like that than anybody else. He wanted to crush you every time. But all champions have it.

*　　*　　*

Code Yellow did raise the question of whether Pogačar might have cheated to win his first Tour de France. Two rivals more or less suggested he had, though without offering a scintilla of evidence. From what I'd seen of Pogačar, there wasn't any particular reason to suspect him. For sure, there were people in positions of authority in his team who'd doped during their careers, but this was the case for most teams.

Iñigo San Millán, an assistant adjoint professor in the department of medicine at the University of Colorado, was Pogačar's trainer and mentor at the time. San Millán grew up in the Basque Country of Spain, was a keen amateur cyclist in his youth and had worked as a team doctor with different pro cycling teams. Some of those teams doped.

He also worked with Garmin, the American team founded by Jonathan Vaughters which is now the EF Education–EasyPost team. Vaughters was a good source of mine during the Armstrong years and a man I trusted. I asked about San Millán. He said Iñigo was one of the most honest anti-doping people he'd encountered in the sport. In one team, San Millán explained to management his suspicion that two of the riders were doping. One of them came for the doctor and it ended in a fist fight.

DAVID: Pippa, did you ever see a doctor in a fight?

PIPPA: Mechanics, soigneurs, yeah. The doc, no.

DAVID: I got in touch with Iñigo, wanted to see what he was like. We've spoken many times and I've no doubt that he's anti-doping. I asked him about Pogačar. He said he thought he'd never put his hand in the fire for a bike rider but that he believed Pogačar.

PIPPA: Why would he say that? That's putting his entire reputation on the line.

DAVID: That's what I said. If this guy were to test positive, people will say you're a crook, Iñigo. He totally understood that. If he believes in Pogačar, he's entitled to say he does. So do you believe in Pogačar, Pippa?

There's a short silence as Pippa considers this.

PIPPA: You know, you said to me the other day that half of the journalists at the Tour de France are fanboys.

DAVID: I remember that, yeah. Fanboys.

PIPPA: Well, I'm listening to you and you come across as a fanboy.

DAVID: I see it as reaching an informed judgement and not pointing a finger without evidence.

PIPPA: Well, yeah, but still a fanboy.

DAVID: This pisses me off because it's like you're not entitled to have enthusiasm anymore. If you want to be cool, you have to suspect everybody.

PIPPA: Yeah, but you at least have to be sceptical.

DAVID: Here's how I see it. People say to me, oh you suspected Armstrong but here you are believing this guy Pogačar. The thing about Armstrong was the evidence was overwhelming. You needed to be a complete fucking idiot not to see it. Now, if you believe someone is clean, you're a fanboy.

PIPPA: Well, that's what you said to me. You said that half the people here will be fanboys. I come to the Tour and I'm not really a fan of anybody. I respect them and I might become a fan if they do something really impressive.

DAVID: Well, Pogačar did something really impressive last year. You were here for that. Did you believe what you saw?

PIPPA: I remember we both thought the story of that time trial was as much about Roglič's bad day as Pogačar's good day. Since then, Pogačar has obviously gone on and done really well.

DAVID: See, Pippa, I actually think you believe in Pogačar. I'm going to make a fanboy out of you.

PIPPA: Fangirl, David. And probably not.

*   *   *

Our stroll in Pontivy comes to a natural end in the finishing straight. Two hours before the arrival of the publicity caravan, four before the peloton. We stall 300 metres from the finish line. 'This is unusual,' Pippa says. 'The road has been going up a little and here, at 300 metres, it starts to go downhill. So close to the finish, this is the last thing you want. This is dangerous.'

We walk on. Today's stage is likely to end in a mass sprint, and as the road keeps gently dropping to the finish line, Pippa sees only danger. 'See how the road sweeps from right to left and then back to the right at the 150-metre mark. There's going to be a crash right here, wait till you see. And there's the reason for this stupid finish,' she says, pointing towards the impressive Château des Rohan overlooking the *arrivée*. They want the castle in the TV pictures of the finish, and that's why the riders are going downhill to the line. If they go in the opposite direction and have a much safer finish, the castle gets missed.'

It's her certainty that is impressive. Pippa truly believes a crash will happen, and that it will have been caused by indifference to the welfare of the riders.

Four hours later the peloton speeds into town. The riders at the front surge up the gently rising road and then, with 300 metres to go, they come hurtling downhill. Jasper Philipsen leads, with his Alpecin–Fenix teammate Tim Merlier on his wheel. Tucked in behind are Caleb Ewan and Peter Sagan. The four are going so fast now that those behind can't get near them.

Around that left/right section 150 metres from the line, Ewan's front wheel touches Merlier's back wheel and suddenly Ewan's bike slides from under him, taking down Sagan. This happened right at the spot where Pippa said it would.

Ewan suffers a displaced complex fracture of the right collar-bone and is out of the Tour. A titanium plate will be inserted in his shoulder to help recovery. In Pontivy that evening, people were saying cycling is a tough sport and these things happen.

This was something that didn't have to happen.

Chapter 7

10 July 2022
Stage 9, Aigle to Châtel – 192.9 km

It's early morning on the second Sunday in July 2022. The previous night Pippa and I stayed at the Hôtel de Savoie in Morges, a pretty Swiss town on the shore of Lake Geneva. Earlier that day we waited in Lausanne for the Tour de France to arrive. A short but sharp climb to the finish would shake up the peloton, giving the cream an opportunity to rise to the top.

Wout van Aert won, Tadej Pogačar was third, so we're talking *crème de la crème*. Journalists, bless us, find it easier to write about the bigger names. So that was good. My story was filed and, lo and behold, we got to Morges in time to have dinner. And the Hôtel de Savoie was a genuine three-star. Hallelujah!

This morning we take the A9 autoroute heading north and then east towards Aigle, where the day's race starts. Pippa's on my left, Lake Geneva on my right. After circling round Lausanne, the road hugs the lake shore, but on a ridge high above. The sky and the lake are shades of perfect blue, the views beyond stunning.

This hour from Morges to Aigle is what I love about the Tour de France, but I can't just sit there and savour it. I have to tell Pippa that it's mornings like these that make life bearable. She says nothing, though the silence has its meaning. I know from previous conversations that something about Switzerland irks her.

DAVID: Pippa, I sense you're looking out over this incredibly beautiful scene and thinking, *The Swiss don't deserve it*.

PIPPA: Correct. The Swiss have spoiled it. It's like Paris. Paris is lovely, but it's been destroyed by the Parisians.

DAVID: What exactly did the Swiss do to you?

PIPPA: It's what they didn't do.

DAVID: Just explain this, Pippa, will you?

PIPPA: Have you seen *The Third Man*?

DAVID: The movie? Orson Welles?

PIPPA: Exactly. Well, the best line in that movie is when Harry Lime says, 'In Italy, for thirty years under the Borgias they had warfare, terror, murder and bloodshed, but they produced Michelangelo, Leonardo da Vinci and the Renaissance. In Switzerland, they had brotherly love, they had five hundred years of democracy and peace, and what did that produce? The cuckoo clock.'

DAVID: It sounds like something you just made up.

PIPPA: No, no, no. David, the problem with the Swiss is actually much bigger than cuckoo clocks. There's no flexibility in the rules here. That doesn't go in Switzerland. The rules are the rules. No compromise in Switzerland. The rules apply to everybody and they're fine with grassing each other up.

DAVID: But come on, admit that this is a stunningly beautiful scene.

PIPPA: Everything is just too fussy. Take Swiss Army knives. Just in case things get bad, we're equipping you with a nail file and a corkscrew and a pair of tweezers for your nasal hair. What sort of army is that?

DAVID: Maybe one that thinks there's more to life than war. You cannot deny the view of that lake. It's stunning.

PIPPA: It is. I actually remember, though, that my gran used to come here on holiday.

DAVID: So where do these anti-Swiss feelings come from? Are you sure you didn't have some Swiss-related trauma in a previous life? A bad experience with a Toblerone?

PIPPA: No, I always raced well in Switzerland. The first time I did the Tour of Romandie, I was with the A-team, the guys who would go on to do the Dauphiné and then the Tour.

DAVID: This was when you were riding with Peugeot?

PIPPA: Yeah, I was there with Michel Laurent and Hennie Kuiper, those guys. I was support crew for those. And I ended up being team leader after the mountain stage, I was sixth or seventh in my first year. Christ, it was terrible weather.

DAVID: So hang on, now you're complaining about the Swiss having Scottish weather? Surely that would have suited you, a cranky Glaswegian, duck to water?

PIPPA: I didn't move to Europe to have the same weather.

DAVID: Well, you should have told Europe that. Surely you were used to it? As a kid, you must have ridden in plenty of bad weather.

PIPPA: No, because there's no point in training in bad weather. It's not training, it's survival. I might have been subjected to it in a race but I'd never train in it.

DAVID: This is all news to me. I never saw Robert Millar as a fair-weather cyclist. What about the times you went out training and it starts pissing an hour and a half after you've started?

PIPPA: If I was thinking that way, I'd never have gone out. It's like Ireland – if you thought about the possibility of rain, you'd never leave your house because it's always a possibility. And if you stay out for a while it's a certainty. It's not just a Scottish thing. I liked racing in Switzerland, I was always successful when I travelled here. The road surfaces are nice and the organisation is really good. I almost never had a bad race and I'd win climbers' prizes. It's outside of the bike races where I've had a problem. It's the Swiss.

DAVID: The Swiss? Weren't they the ones doing the organising of all those things that you liked? The Swiss are pretty common in Switzerland?

PIPPA: Yeah. Now you have it. Switzerland is overrun with the Swiss. Now, it's overrun in a very ordered way. No overrunning on the grass and all that. That's the problem – the general Swiss person. And I know this makes me sound like this ranting woman, but it's just one of those observations. The Swiss just don't seem able to relax.

DAVID: Are you getting a bit wound up? We'll cross the border back into France later this evening, and you'll able to say goodbye to Switzerland, at least for this year. You'll be free from all this upsetting efficiency, beauty and nice watches.

PIPPA: I'm happy just thinking about it.

* * *

I'm one of those people whom Robert Millar would have forgotten about as soon as he finished racing. I'd be surprised if he even remembered me from the among the pack that followed him, hoping for crumbs of wisdom to place between inverted commas in the next day's paper.

As such I didn't get to know Pippa York until she emerged from the long period of seclusion that preceded and included her transition. I see the finished product – a woman at ease with herself and her past, and good company – every single day of our time together.

I missed her transition, and it's only occasionally that I get hints as to what it must have been like for her. We're talking today and the subject comes up about how at ease Pippa seems. She reminds me in a gentle way that life is not all wine and roses.

PIPPA: The microaggressions can happen almost anywhere. People might shout, 'Oi, mate' when I'm filling up my car at petrol stations. In shops, cashiers have pointedly called me 'sir' when I'm buying clothes. Less so now, but you always thought they were doing it deliberately.

DAVID: But things have improved? You come to this race and you're welcomed almost everywhere. And those that don't welcome you, what are they worth?

PIPPA: I'll tell you a story. One time I was coming back to Blighty through Dover after a trip to Belgium. I had my things in the car. I wasn't dressed as a woman. By then I knew that I didn't need the hassle of not looking exactly like my passport photo. I got stopped at customs and I was directed to the search area. They had a look in the car and, of course, they found my women's clothing.

Of course, anything that's different from their lives disturbs them. They don't know why they're disturbed, they just have an innate resistance to anything or anyone different. So they start in with that passive–aggressive tone that people in uniforms seem to enjoy using. They want to know why I have women's clothes in my car. They want to know what exactly I'm doing. Why am I coming here? What is the purpose of your journey, sir?

DAVID: When was this?

PIPPA: This was when I was in mid-transition. I was carrying a letter from my therapist stating that I was transitioning. It was a letter of explanation that I really hoped I'd never need, but now I had to hand it over. The border control people read it. Each one was handing it on to the next one. Hey, get a load of this. Each of them when they were done reading, passed the letter on without speaking but briefly glanced at me with a look of disgust. There was no reason for them to detain me any longer, so they sent me on my way, with scowls. No 'Thank you for your co-operation.' Not even a 'Have a nice day.' 'Bloody weirdo' one of them muttered as they went back into their office.

DAVID: What did you do?

PIPPA: What could I do? Drive on. Another of those days where I ask myself, yet again, is this worth all the crap? And I answer myself sternly. It will get better. The further I go, the better it will get. Drive on. Still, it's fucking exhausting, though.

Bobby Melrose

In the 1970s, nobody was coming looking for you if you had talent. You just got old and cadged drinks in bars and told people how you could have been a contender. In the 70s you couldn't google 'how to be a pro'. There were no scouts, no hungry agents scouring the estates for the next big thing.

A kid had to get lucky.

When he got to 17, Robert was still improving. There was a young junior called Bobby Melrose. He was the best rider of his age and more mature than all his peers. Bobby Melrose won all the junior races when Robert was still 16.

Robert took his beatings. He started training properly. Proper focus. And soon he was able to race with Bobby Melrose. He was encouraged. Soon after that he was able to beat Bobby Melrose. He felt he was able to progress every year by a couple of per cent. He was at that age where you never imagine that eventually you might just run out of talent.

When he wasn't yet 18 he started scrawling his name into record books. In 1976, Scottish Junior Road Race Champion; the following year, the Davie Bell Memorial race over the Ayrshire Hills, the classic Tour of the Campsies mountain time trial and the Scottish Hill Climb Championship.

By 1978 he had serious velocity. He won the Drummond Trophy, the Tour of the Peak and the British National Amateur Road Race Championships. He was second in the season-long Star Trophy and broke the course record in the classic Tour de Trossachs time trial.

They watched him, the small cycling community. He wasn't clubbable. He was a loner. Sullen. What's eating Robert Millar? The world wasn't shunning the kid. The kid was shunning the world. Nobody knew why he lacked cheer but he had something they'd never seen before. He could churn out the same times, sprint after sprint. He seemed to show more potential week after week. He had a talent that Scotland couldn't contain.

He decided, when he was 17, that he was going to be a pro bike rider. When he told people his plan he might as well have been telling them that he was going to take his Meccano, make his own rocket and fly himself to the moon. Glasgow produced pro bike riders at about the same rate as it produced astronauts.

A kid had to get lucky. He got lucky.

He met two men who'd been to the moon. Billy Bilsland was famous in this world. He'd been a pro bike rider for three years with Peugeot and then on Raleigh with Peter Post. Arthur Campbell of Glasgow Wheelers was on a UCI technical commission and was at the top of the political tree in the UK. The two men had access to that world that Dickie Davies sometimes revealed. They had knowledge. And they were helpful, because they saw that here was a kid who had the potential to reach that level. He latched on to them.

The two older men coped with his intensity. They believed in him. They set out a plan for getting him to where he needed to be. They talked about having to train more and how to look after himself better. How to have a better attitude and how to fit into each level. How to deal with all the issues that come along. From under their wing he learned the lie of the land ahead.

They told him gently that if you're a complete idiot and you don't fit in to the structure, you won't get anywhere. He absorbed that with a certain reluctance, swallowing hard on his own broody teenage rebellion stuff.

Meanwhile, he'd go work in a factory. He wanted just enough money to buy better bike stuff, and to be able to travel to races in England. No more.

Weir's

He left school and went into a job in a local factory, Weir Pumps. His brother Ian already worked there. Robert started in the foothills of a four-year engineering apprenticeship.

It was a world he didn't want to be part of. He resented the normality. He hated the settling for things, the idea that friends found whatever they needed to function in that world, without looking any further.

Weir's was about two miles away. They manufactured pumps and big pipes for engineering projects. There was steam and hot water everywhere. He and his brother used to drive the two miles to work in Ian's Ford Anglia. There was a choke on the dash that had to be pulled out to coax the car into starting. The daily drama. You've got a car with a choke and the prevailing weather is drizzle. Well, the car doesn't always start. Some days Robert would cycle in if the weather was inviting. Rare days.

At Weir's the apprentices were given a certain amount of work each day. Robert could do his work in an hour, which left seven hours to kill. So then what do you do? You look at what the other guys are doing who have been working there longer. They slept.

Some days he'd be placed in the supervision of somebody who actually taught him something. And on those days Weir's might take four hours of his attention. And then the tutor would say, 'Right, I don't need you here anymore. Off you go.' That was the release to go skiving somewhere. Read the paper, see some friends. Or have a sleep in the hot pipes where the night-shift men had kipped.

The guys had made beds for themselves in the channels between the giant warm pipes. There they could hide. The guys from the night shift would originally have made the sleeping channels, but the day men could go in there and sleep during the day when they didn't have any work to do.

Like everybody else he went to work to earn money. He had no ambition concerning work, though. He didn't go to Weir's to become an engineer. More money equalled better bike stuff. Now and again, he'd still spend his pounds and pence on girls' clothes, but he noticed that this expend-iture diminished the more he gave of himself to cycling. The more cycling asked of him, the more he could justify not having to deal with the girls' clothes and what it all meant. Weir's, somewhere in the middle of all that, never had a chance.

They weren't paid much. Then you went home and you gave your mum whatever money she demanded of you. It wasn't a champagne and caviar lifestyle. But you got your sleep.

He did three and a half years at Weir's doing as little as possible before he packed it. He quit in 1978, the year of the Commonwealth Games.

A year away from being out of your apprenticeship?

They said he was stone mad. He'd decided, though, that if he was going to become Commonwealth champion, he needed to be a full-time athlete. He wanted that gold medal far more than he wanted to work in Weir's.

The world around him was appalled by his decision. His parents were devastated.

But the proponents of common sense said, *You haven't qualified but you're within touching distance. A qualification! Something to fall back on. You could finish this apprenticeship and sure it would make no difference to your hopes of being a bike rider or whatever.*

His attitude was, well, you don't know what you're talking about. Now goodbye, I'm away to be a bike rider. No whatever.

You're mad, son.

But you don't know anything about what I'm going to do, so …

Yeah, I understand what you want to do, son. But this job, this place. It will give you something to fall back on.

He told them he'd deal with that when it happened. But he had no intention of dealing with it. He saw no reason why he wasn't going to be a pro bike rider. He hadn't reached a level yet where he'd failed. He dealt with every increased workload.

Billy Bilsland – who knew more, and knew what it took – believed the kid had enough talent. Going away, though, said Billy, even with a bit of French and a bit of talent was tough and it was lonely.

Robert knew tough and lonely weren't going to be his problems.

He'd known from day one that this factory life, it wasn't for him. In the arrogant way of teenage boys and sports champions, he wrote them all off as just losers. He knew these people, he'd grown up with them, he even fitted into that world, sort of, but he could never see how doing what they did might give the same satisfaction as doing what he wanted to do. It was a young man's impatient conceit. It would take him years to understand.

He got to Canada and the Commonwealth Games. An Australian called Phil Anderson, one of the favourites, won the gold medal.

that other part

That other part of himself? He buried it as best he could. In time he'd be able to go years without dressing as a girl. He could invest so much of himself into cycling that there wasn't enough left for anything beyond a bike. He was submerged in getting better, totally immersed. He lost those moments that he'd always known. He interred them deep into a kind of subconscious where he wouldn't have to service the need. It might be rumbling away somewhere deep, but he wouldn't have to listen. He wouldn't feel the need to dress as a girl.

That took time, though. Years. Going from the age of 16 through to 19, the observer saw a young man rising quickly through every level of amateur cycling. He went from being the best in Glasgow, to going to races covering the whole of the UK. He was big news at national level in cycling. He'd be national champion at the age of 19. He still dressed as a girl then. When he needed to. When he was back home. When the coast was clear.

Only then, only in that space. Only where he had always felt the urge pressing him. When he was away, he travelled with his cyclist head on. He studied obsessively. This race. I need to be in the front here, here and there. These are the guys I'm going to need to beat. These are the guys I need to watch. I'll do what they're doing, and then I'll beat them. Then? Next race. He was a hawk on a bicycle.

He knew that the next step was international level. He knew that he was still messed up in his head. It seemed logical to him, though, what to do. He'd only be able to suppress things further by going to international level. Do more training. Do more dietary work. Be more single-minded. Leave home.

The harder you work, the deeper it gets buried. It went from being a twice-a-month habit to maybe two or three times a year. And then even less. It would come up now and again in his head, but he kept moving.

He kept moving at the expense of everything else. It cost him relationships with his family and friends. They all got to stand in the line behind Robert's needs in being a bike rider. They didn't count so much anymore.

If they don't like me, he told himself, *I really don't fucking care. Till I can be whatever I want me to be I'm not going to be whatever they want me to be.*

national champs

He'd reckoned the workload needed to reach each new level was within him.

He'd looked at national-level races, for instance. They were always three and a half to four hours long. No point in going for a sociable six-hour bike ride in a training group when he was training for a three-and-a-half-hour race. Quality training. Be the fastest over the three and a half hours. Move on.

He worked out that out for each level.

In 1978 he rode past Steve Lawrence, who'd beaten him in a sprint nine days earlier to win the Manx Trophy at the Isle of Man International Road Race. This time when Robert rode past Steve Lawrence it was to take the National Amateur Road Race Championship by five seconds. No Scot had ever won the National Amateur Championships.

There was seldom a race he didn't learn from.

He forgot about that National win quickly enough. He'd messed up in the Isle of Man, though. That caught in his craw. He'd led out and Steve Lawrence had blown past him. You could guess how much strength a guy had in his legs, but you couldn't rely on your guess.

A year later, 1979, the National Amateur Road Race Championships were held just outside Bradford. The race finished in a duel between Robert Millar of Glasgow and Joe Waugh, a skinny lad from the north-east who wore his hair long, had been to the Olympics in 1976 and would surely go again in 1980. In the end it all boiled down to the same deal as the year before. It was a flat sprint on the drag to decide it.

Joe Waugh had spent time in France but he was back some years. Robert had just come back from the ACBB in Paris to race. He'd gone up a notch and was the favourite as defending champion.

He hung in a chasing group all day and let Joe Waugh do the glory work out front. When the time came, Robert went across alone from the group, reeling in the road so that when Joe was starting to smell the finish line, he suddenly had company.

When Robert caught Joe, having come across that gap from the chasing group, he sailed past his rival. *Hello!*

Joe, game as ever, just got fastened onto Robert's wheel as he came past. *Hello yourself. Where do you think you're going, kid?*

And they fell in beside each other, knowing the race belonged to one or the other.

Robert assessed the situation. This was the era when a rider had to change gears via a lever on the down tube. Robert looked at his rival's set-up. Joe had a 12 to 18 cassette at the back. Robert's biggest gear was a 13. There weren't that many choices. Joe's bike would give him an advantage, all other things being equal.

I'm not leading out from here, Robert said to himself, although he half-fancied it. *I'll wait*.

And they just rode on, and he watched Joe for a while more. He remembered the Isle of Man as they rode.

Robert was ready, though, because he knew that in the battle of nerves, he was winning. Joe was beginning to understand that he was going to have to lead out when the time came to burst for the line.

Before that sprint finish, though, there was the last uphill of the circuit. Joe was hanging on now. At that time, this big, solid man was considered the better climber of the two, but he was only just hanging on. Robert Millar was murdering him. Joe knew it, and Robert knew it.

Robert rode at the front to the top, and he murdered Joe again on the false flat after they came off the real hill. Then he made Joe do a share of the work because he knew that Joe didn't want to.

And the time came, as Robert and Joe both knew it would. Two hundred and fifty yards to the line … two hundred and forty yards to the line.

A game of chicken. Joe has done a sight of work all day. Now he's slightly tired. He doesn't want to wind it up yet because Robert has just attacked him on the uphill. Joe suspects now that he's being played. So he waits.

They'd shared short shifts till they got to the flat. Now there's a tailwind. Robert thinks, *If Joe puts on that 12, and I've only got 13, then I'm done. There's no way I'm coming round him.*

But Joe is so knackered now. He can't lead out that fast.

Robert waits. He knows what's coming

As soon as your hand goes down to change gear, I'm going to jump you, Joe. Yeah.

Joe Waugh waits too, he waits till about 200 metres from the line. Then, his hand leaves the dipped bars, and drops to find the gear lever. Robert has barely been able to contain himself. *Come on, Joe. Come on. The gears, Joe. Change the fucking gears …*

It's time, and now Joe doesn't wind it up fast enough. He just can't. He shifts gears. His legs take a moment to adjust their cadence.

Poor Joe Waugh. The condemned man never actually gets to hear the fusillade of the firing squad.

As soon as Joe's hand twitches, Robert has hit him with this acceleration. Bam! He steals ten metres from Joe straight away. Then Robert slams his bike into the 13, and he keeps his stolen ten metres for as long as he can.

Joe is coming back and coming back. He's big, strong and game, and his heart has long been set on this day. But he runs out of room. He finishes on Robert's wheel. Second place.

They both know the story. By the time Joe started into his sprint, by the time he adjusted his legs to the new gear, by the time that half second had passed, Joe Waugh already needed the finish line to be 20 metres further away if he was to come past Robert Millar in time.

To the spectators it has been a pure thriller.

Cycling magazine reports the next week that before the race Millar had sought out race organiser Gerry McDaid. He'd handed McDaid his championship jersey from the year before. It was neatly pressed and folded. Millar asked that he be presented with this jersey again. It fitted well and he did need not a new jersey when he won.

When. Not if.

Chapter 8

Stage 6, Tours to Châteauroux – 160.6 km

This was a day on the flat roads to Châteauroux, the hometown of actor Gérard Depardieu and a place where Mark Cavendish feels at home. The Tour first arrived here in 1998, the year of the Festina doping scandal. Mario Cipollini won that afternoon. In 2018 the Italian was given a suspended three-year prison for domestic abuse. Châteauroux's fortunes as a stage-end town improved after that first experience. The second time was 2008, when Cavendish won his first Tour stage. That began an enduring relationship between the sport's greatest sprinter and Châteauroux. In 2011 Cavendish won again in the capital of the Indre.

The peloton finished today with a 5.4-kilometre tour of the streets of Châteauroux that ended with a 1,600-metre surge down the Avenue de La Châtre.

When Cavendish won in 2008 he put both hands on his head in an expression of incredulity, as if he couldn't quite believe he'd just won a stage of the Tour de France. Three years later, on the same avenue, he recalled the first victory by re-enacting the same celebration. Hands on head, the same expression of wonder – but no longer spontaneous. It seemed to me he wanted us to see the victories as parts of a whole, each victory a piece in the jigsaw of his career, no less than the pieces that had gone before or would come after.

To mark his third victory today in Châteauroux, he chooses once again to repeat the hands-on-head celebration. Now the incredulity is performative but no less endearing for that. Why should the fastest bike rider be surprised by another victory in a town he knows well? Afterwards he refuses to explain why he replayed the original celebration. He doesn't need to. It's his way of recalling the first.

Two days earlier, he'd won in Fougères. That was his 31st stage win at the Tour and his first since the 2016 race. Better than most athletes, he finds a way of expressing what it means to him. 'This race has given me the life I've had, and I've given it the life I had.'

There's a big crowd of mostly French cycling fans in town to welcome the race. Sensing Gallic love for Cavendish, I mingle and initiate conversations. Pippa, whom I've dragged into the throngs, has agreed to translate.

We meet Kevin Sorbian, who tells that a week before he'd put his bike in the boot of his car, his girlfriend Joanah took the passenger seat, and they left Florensac close to the Riviera. Sorbian, 26, had a 1,150-kilometre drive to Brest in Brittany, then a 3,414-kilometre cycle from there. This was his year to ride the Tour de France route, to do something he'd long dreamed of. Most weeks, he delivers pharmaceuticals to hospitals.

On each Tour day, he sets off four or five hours before the peloton and Joanah follows on in the car. They'd arrived in Châteauroux long before the race and, after changing, they'd driven back out on the route to see the peloton climb the Category 4 Côte de Saint-Aignan. You see more of the race while standing on a hill. They then jumped in the car and whizzed back to Châteauroux to catch the finish.

Alas, he and Joanah couldn't get there as fast as the peloton. What disappointment they felt was more than offset by Mark Cavendish winning. 'My first reaction was to be happy for him,' Kevin said. 'I don't care what country a rider is from, there's no difference. In France, Cavendish is very popular. The French people didn't really like [Bradley] Wiggins, [Chris] Froome, Team Sky – but we never think bad things about Cavendish.'

Kevin and Joanah are transfixed before the giant screen at the intersection where they stood, as it's replaying the sprint Cavendish had won so brilliantly. Jean-François Collin's eyes were on the same screen. Collin had watched from a position near the finish line, grateful that Cavendish had been in the green jersey so he could more easily pick him out.

Now watching the replay, he shook his head as if seeing it for the first time. '*Impressionante! Impressionante!*' he said to no one in particular. At this point Gérard Blondeau and Natalie Corbeau, who had come from 70 kilometres away to see the Tour, were returning to their car. 'We're really pleased that the Tour is again in the department of L'Indre and that Cavendish won again in Châteauroux. He's a great rider and very popular around here.'

*   *   *

We're late leaving the press centre. A Cavendish victory always means more words. 'I don't know that many,' I tell Joe Hare on the *Times* desk when he asks for 1,200.

It's after ten o'clock on a midweek evening and Châteauroux has already gone to bed. We're hungry. We hit upon the taco joint on Place Voltaire, alongside the imperious Église Saint-André de Châteauroux. 'Any chance?' we ask the guy putting chairs on top of tables. 'Pizzas OK?' he says. '*Parfait.*' We sit outside, overlooked by the neo-Gothic edifice, and we talk Cavendish.

Something had happened the previous day at the end of the time trial in Laval. I'd been watching from not far past the finish as Pippa had a chance meeting with the king of the sprinters. 'What was that about?' I ask. She's reluctant to explain but I'm not letting it go.

PIPPA: Did you really see us together?
DAVID: I was just 50 metres away. Of course I saw it.

The press centre was right by the finish at Laval. Pippa and I had separately taken up positions to see riders complete their race against the clock. It was early afternoon and Cavendish had just come past us. Beyond the TV pen stood Pippa on the far side of a steel barrier. Strict Covid rules were still in place and journalists had been warned to wear a mask when interacting with riders. Any kind of physical contact was strictly prohibited.

Cavendish caught Pippa's eye and wheeled off to the right to greet her. He stopped, leaned over the barrier and hugged her. A proper hug, and not a mask in sight. I could see them talk animatedly and for some time. It seemed like long-lost-buddy warmth. I tell Pippa no rider ever hugged me that way!

PIPPA: You saw where I was standing. As he went past, I shouted 'Mark', he looked my way and his face lit up. He came right over and then he said with a lot of emotion:

'Thank you for believing in me.' What could I say? I had tears in my eyes, there were people around us, looking, wondering what it was all about.

DAVID: And what was it all about?

PIPPA: At the 2019 Tour of Britain, I tried to interview Mark. He was going through a tough time and had not been selected for the Great Britain team for the UCI World Championship Road Race, which was in Yorkshire that year. He was up for the interview, but the team told him every request had to go through them. The team said no. I saw Mark's wife Peta and started talking to her. We ended up talking for an hour and a half about all the stuff that had happened over the previous two years, the problems with his health, with the team, all of it.

I said to Peta, 'It doesn't matter what's going on now because Mark has such a great palmarès built up over the years. I know from my own career that everybody remembers the good things you did, they don't remember the bad times. They ask me about '84 and the King of the Mountains jersey at the Tour. They don't ask me about the years I got dropped in the Tour of Spain and finished 30th on GC.' I was hoping Peta would say this to Mark.

DAVID: I'd be surprised if she didn't.

PIPPA: After that, whenever I saw Mark, I said, 'You're Britain's best ever cyclist. No one can ever take that from you.' I explained to him, 'What you do is so difficult, to sit on the back of that lead-out train, waiting there, getting more and more stressed' and so often finding a way to win. He's the greatest ever Brit.

DAVID: Chris Froome won the Tour four times. Doesn't that make him at least a contender?

PIPPA: Not in my eyes. It's because of what Mark does. He's not the product of a system. Sky and Ineos became this manufacturing plant where they got their training down to a tee, got their diet right, their equipment, their bloody mattresses, got all the parts that you need, and for a number of years it almost didn't matter who was leader of the team – he'd win the Tour de France.

DAVID: I mention Froome, but to be honest I'm on your side in this debate. What Cavendish has done at the Tour makes him the greatest ever British cyclist.

*　　*　　*

It's now customary for the best riders to reconnoitre the Tour's mountain stages and time-trial routes, and for the sprinters to scrutinise the last kilometres of any day with the potential to end in a bunch sprint. From 1997 to 2019, no one conducted as forensic an examination of the entire route as Jean-Maurice Ooghe, director of France Télévisions' coverage of the Tour.

Sometime in February, using a car and helicopter, Ooghe covered every kilometre. Along the way he made notes of the castles and churches he passed, the bridges and rivers he crossed. He looked to the alpine peaks surrounding the ski-station where the day's stage would end, and saw the pictures that would frame his team's coverage of the race. Between all the cameramen, sound men, drone operators, motorcycle drivers and helicopter pilots, he had a team of 200 people at his service.

Believing he'd lose viewers if he concentrated too much on the race, he widened his field of vision. When not much was happening in the race, there would be shots of children dressed in yellow gathered in a field, a switch from the front of the peloton to a woman on horseback, matching the speed of the riders as she galloped through a field.

TV takes the race and puts it at the centre of a country that's one of the most beautiful on the planet. During the 2005 Tour de France, a journalist from *Le Parisien* interviewed Ooghe and ran their story under the headline: 'Jean-Maurice Ooghe, the man who makes people love France'. Extraordinary TV pictures touch the emotions of viewers sitting on living-room couches in faraway countries, whether they're of riders hurtling down alpine roads at 90 kph in the rain or pouring water over their heads from their bidons while sweating and suffering in the heat. Ooghe once said his job was to give viewers two shows at the same time: the Tour de France and the Tour de la France. The second attracted viewers to the first.

Television changed the game for sportswriters, compelling us to see the Tour differently. No longer can we just tell the story of the race – our readers will have watched it on TV and seen more than we've seen. Herein lies the challenge, and it's one I've grown to love.

On a typical Tour day you get to the Centre de Presse two to three hours before the peloton arrives in town. You'll know how the stage is going – breakaways, no breakaways, the bunch still all together and not much happening – and to escape the dread of an uneventful stage you search out the press buffet provided free to the journalists by the host town. It's a quirk of Centre de Presse life that the quality of the buffet is the subject of a never-ending conversation.

For the print journalist, the challenge is straightforward. Whatever the day's story, it has to be told in a way that enriches what readers have already seen on TV. Can you make the day's winner more interesting than he seemed in his post-stage interview? Can you help readers to understand why things turned out the way they did? Have you seen or heard something that TV's multiple eyes and ears have missed?

Pippa has a remarkable understanding of team dynamics, not only because she was once part of their world but also because she's smart. We talk about how this team rode today and why that team reacted the way it did. On average we spend five to six hours in the car every day, so there's time to dissect the race, something we both enjoy.

Each day begins calmly with an unrushed breakfast. But, almost immediately, the day then becomes a series of ever-more urgent priorities. We need to get on the road. Sometimes we go to the start. Talk to some people. Don't hang around. Get to the finish. Watch the race. Attend the virtual post-stage press conferences. Get quotes from the stage winner and the race leader. Write story. Edit story. File story. Make a check call to the office in London. Find that evening's hotel. Eat if there's time or a still-open restaurant. Suck it up quietly if not. Sleep. Wake, knowing what you wrote yesterday is gone. Time to begin again.

It's been a ride. At the start of the 2004 Tour in Liège – the height of the Lance Armstrong stuff – my travelling companions said they couldn't have me in their car anymore. We'd shared a car on and off for 20 years, but if I was there they'd no longer have any access to Lance. Faced with that choice, it wasn't that tough a call for them. I was on the side of the road. Recent years have been better. I drove the 2016 Tour with my daughter Molly in the passenger seat. That was an idyllic four weeks.

With Pippa, the days feel shorter. She tells colourful stories about life as a professional cyclist. They leave me laughing or gasping in disbelief. Today is about Cavendish; his decency, his sheer likeability and that totally unselfconscious embrace of Pippa at Laval. But tomorrow there will be others.

I recall a slightly awkward scene from the ITV documentary called *The High Life*, which followed Robert Millar through the 1985 season. Millar had become the first British rider to win a major award at the Tour, so the documentary would have seemed like a good idea at the time. But Millar was a reticent, sometimes uneasy subject. He wouldn't, or perhaps couldn't, perform for the camera.

DAVID: There's a scene in *The High Life* where you and your friend Allan Peiper are filmed from behind as you ride along a country road. It's a training ride and you're just chatting. Allan's in full young guy mode. He wolf-whistles at a couple of Italian women that pass and comments that 'a lot of chicks down here in Italy don't wear bras, do they?' And from Robert Millar, riding alongside, there's just silence. It made me think: how did you survive within that culture?

PIPPA: Well, first of all you have to think about how odd that life is. We were all young lads who'd been obsessed with riding bicycles on our own or with small groups of lads since our teens. Thousands of hours. We weren't socialised or worldly. And then next thing we're pro cyclists and we're in events like the Tour de France, which appear quite glamorous from the outside. These events attract women. Some of the women aren't at the race for the gear ratios or power outputs or race tactics. They're drawn to young fit men who are oiled, sweaty, toned and lean. I suppose they saw the Tour as a display of masculinity. And those men are a bit famous. And they're passing like sailors through their towns and will be gone in the morning. There's a bit of glamour and the strong whiff of testosterone.

DAVID: So they were cycling groupies?

PIPPA: Well, no doubt there are other sports where groups of famous men come across groups of attractive and available young women. And within that culture the men often use the sort of language they wouldn't want repeated.

DAVID: The women I've seen around bike riders always appear quite accepting of the terms of engagement.

PIPPA: There were a couple of women who would come to just a few races and they'd hang around with a certain group of riders They weren't the typical young pretty girls that you'd briefly see at starts or finishes. These women were well dressed, well cared for, and they no longer qualified as girls. They'd turn up in certain places and be willing participants in night-time activities with the same group of riders.

DAVID: Well, there's one famous story about the guy they called Chopper. Do you remember him?

PIPPA: No comment.

DAVID: Well, what I heard, he was well endowed and hence the name 'Chopper'. Anyway, Chopper was a part of one of the groups until one time when the ladies you mentioned, I'm fairly sure these were the same women I'd seen around, turned up. No sign of Chopper.

At the request of the women somebody went to fetch Chopper. They found him downcast. Age had caught up and he was grounded.

'No problem,' said the messenger, who vanished for a minute and returned with some tablets. Just take a couple of these and come down to the room in about twenty minutes. Soon Chopper appeared. He did his party piece and then threw himself into the action until he felt a violent bang to his chest. And ambulance had to be called. An awkward scene for everybody.

PIPPA: That's basically the story as I heard it all right. You'd have thought that a bad time or a dicky heart episode would have put everybody off those kinds of activities, but it didn't. I always wondered why the women got involved because the guys had no respect for them. But that was the environment.

DAVID: Really?

PIPPA: Well, we were young. We grew up differently. It was a different time. The only females we saw were secretaries or waitresses, or working in the hotel reception. You never saw a female journalist or female boss of a team. You never came across a female CEO.

The sponsor? Always a man in a suit. The marketing director? Never a female. The only females we saw were in that kind of service industry.

And, it sounds terrible now, but the men, as a group, had little or no respect for those women because they were just a fleeting moment of your life. They were serving you as you got on with something that you thought was supremely important. The only dealings we had with women were transactional. It's understandable that guys behaved that way because we're talking about a pretty hardcore, macho world. Cyclists like to be crass. They like to be crude in their conversation. And who was ever going to pull them up on it?

DAVID: But you had a different sensibility, based on what you already knew about yourself?

PIPPA: Not anything that I'd have spoken about. I'd go to bike races, and I'd see a young woman there and think, well, that looks like a great life, being her. I might have been seen as one of the stars of the peloton, but I'd be thinking, *I'd rather be doing that*. Not being a groupie or anything, just living life as a woman and enjoying my day like she seems to be. Sounds simple when you say it. It wasn't.

It was quite hard to process. You'd go back to your hotel room after the race and think, *This can't be right. There's plenty wrong with me. Society classes me as wrong but the lads, chasing the groupies and boasting about conquests, they're just lads being lads.*

At that stage I didn't know that it wasn't wrong. In my head it was an issue that I'm going to have to deal with down the road. This is the crap that I've been given. Society wasn't much of a help. It just taught me that what I was – or am – was morally and socially unacceptable. People didn't do this. Athletes who spotted a woman watching the race judged the woman on her looks. They didn't think I'd love to be her, that I'd love to be a woman. And the people that did have thoughts and feelings like that, they were just freaks.

And everything I read, and everything I've encountered, reinforced that. So then for me to, you know, be a good person and be seen as a shining example of athleticism and ambition in this really macho world, to be thinking anything related to femininity, was just wrong. I'd be condemned to the depths of hell, you know, if I even spoke about it.

DAVID: It sounds lonely.

PIPPA: When I now think back, I try to put everything in the context of that period. The 1980s were the biggest part of my career. Thatcher in Britain and Reagan in America. You had Section 28 and the prejudice that arose from AIDS.

DAVID: Remind me, what was Section 28?

PIPPA: It was an amendment to a Local Government Act in the UK, voted in sometime in 1988, I think. The idea was that local authorities could not promote homosexuality or publish anything that promoted homosexuality. It basically meant that gay relationships were written off as abnormal. It pushed the idea, which we see making a comeback now, that being gay should be corrected and with no mention of them somehow there would be less of it. Very few people were saying: look, these things are biologically determined. People need support to realise that, and love for who they are and the reassurance that it's a completely valid way to be.

I wasn't a gay man, but I wore my hair a bit longer and I had an earring. And I got the gay slurs. Now there were lots of straight men who wore their hair long and had an earring, and it was fine depending on what job you were in, but in cycling – which was hyper-masculine – a lot of people assumed that if you were slightly different it meant you were gay. And back then, being gay in the cycling world wasn't OK. People would run a thousand miles. Sponsors would flee. So what was going on in my head took some working out. I couldn't sit the lads down at dinner after a race and explain the difference between sex and gender. I couldn't say that I felt attracted to women but that I also felt I wanted to be a woman. That was unimaginable. And I looked at what was happening to the gay community and thought, fuck, what will it be like when they come for me?

*   *   *

During these moments when Pippa relives what it was like living in Robert Millar's cycling shoes, I feel a mixture of sadness and compassion. She's been through a hell of a lot, but she has come through it. The grit that helped Millar get to the summit of an alpine climb before the others enabled Pippa York to get to where she needed to be. The moment I cherish is Cavendish seeing her standing by the barrier at Laval, and then rushing to hug and hold her in the way that he did. That said it all.

Chapter 9

6 September 2020

Stage 9, Pau to Laruns – 153 km

Every time the Tour pitches a tent in Pau, I get a nostalgia rush. It was on a Sunday evening here in 1983 that my travelling companion Tony Kelly and I shared a bottle of rosé to celebrate Sean Kelly and Stephen Roche's success at that point in the Tour. Kelly had taken the yellow jersey, Roche was leading the young riders' classification. That was the age of innocence. It wouldn't last, but not much ever does.

Pau continued to punch above its weight. During the worst of the doping epidemic something always seemed to happen when the Tour came to town. It was at the city's Palais des Congrés in 2001 that Lance Armstrong first addressed allegations raised in a story I'd written for the *Sunday Times* two weeks earlier. He was six days away from his third Tour win. Eleven years from The Fall. If you're wondering why it took that long, you weren't in Pau for that first defence of his reputation in 2001. Lance could have lied for America.

The mood in Pau is sombre this morning as the Ineos Grenadiers riders line up at the front of the peloton. In a short ceremony, Nico Portal is remembered. Portal, who died suddenly in March aged 40, had lived in this Pyrenean town for many years. A former pro, he was directeur sportif at Team Sky/

Ineos for six of the team's seven victories at the Tour, the soul of a team that at times seemed to lack one. His wife Magalie and their two children Lenny and Aïnoa were present and stood alongside Portal's former colleagues.

'I never met someone who Nico didn't have time for,' the rider Tao Geoghegan Hart said about Portal. 'We miss you champ,' Luke Rowe wrote on social media. They all do. I thought about what Portal might have said to the riders as they rolled out of Pau and headed south to the Pyrenees. I'm guessing he'd have smiled and, without raising his voice, said, 'Guys, we need to do something in this race, if only to remind the others that we're here to win.'

It's not far-fetched to imagine that Ineos's riders were inspired by the tribute to Portal in Pau. They rode well and after crossing two difficult Pyrenean passes, their leader Egan Bernal fought out the finish at Laruns with three top riders – Pogačar, Roglič and Mikel Landa.

By now, Pogačar is confounding us. We'd seen him unluckily lose time on the stage to Lavaur two days before, then ignore the advice of his directeur sportif Allan Peiper and launch a revenge attack in the Pyrenees the next day. It shouldn't have worked, but it did.

That should have settled him down. *OK, kid, you've made your point. Just stay in the wheels today.* But this kid isn't like any other. Second day in the Pyrenees, he tries to get away on the Col de Marie-Blanque but now the others are ready, Roglič especially. He chases down his Slovenian compatriot, making him see there's no point.

'Yesterday was one story,' Pogačar says after the race ends in Laruns. 'Today it was different. The guys on the climb had the same legs as me. I guess I couldn't shake them. For sure Bernal looked better today. He was really strong in the climb. I saw their faces. I knew I couldn't shake them easily.'

Recaptured on the murderous ascent of the Marie-Blanque, Pogačar shrugs his shoulders and thinks, *What next? Why not win the stage?* Something he's yet to do. There are five of them in the race to the line: Marc Hirschi is fast, Roglič is fast and desperate. Pogačar, though, is the fastest.

Crossing the line half of a wheel ahead of Roglič, he raises his arms and cups his head in his hands, the same celebration Mark Cavendish used when he first won at the Tour in 2008. Pogačar was then an enthusiastic nine-year-old watching on TV at his home outside Ljubljana. He loved Cavendish, so maybe that celebration in Laruns wasn't mere coincidence.

*   *   *

Another long evening in the press centre. Journalists do have one thing in common with the riders: for both, mountain stages take more time. We leave Laruns at 9.30 p.m., the sun isn't yet down but is about to say goodnight. We have an hour and a half's drive to Cazères-sur-l'Adour and we can't get Pogačar out of our heads.

DAVID: Pogačar's win today makes him the youngest stage winner since Armstrong in 1993, which is another story. But this guy Pogačar, he's something special.

PIPPA: Yeah, two days ago he got held up by a crash in the sidewinds and missed the break. You could see he was pulling all the time and was so strong that nobody could help him. That was a tough day for him and then yesterday we could see he'd totally recovered. He attacked twice on

119

the Peyresourde and got away the second time. That's
amazing for a kid.

DAVID: At the start yesterday, he told the journalists that he
intended to attack on the stage. He was obviously pissed to
have lost time in the crosswinds and people were going to
suffer. For a 21-year-old, that was some confidence. Hard
not to warm to him.

PIPPA: Today when they caught Pogačar I thought, *That's it*.
You've had a good day, kid. It was a slightly uphill sprint
and it looked like Roglič and Hirschi were strong enough.
So for Pogačar to beat them, that was really something. It
just showed unbelievable recovery.

DAVID: That is the incredible part, the recovery.

PIPPA: When you're pulling in the sidewind, you're in a
giant gear, having to ride 55, 60k an hour, then that
transition to the rhythm in the mountains is totally
different. He assimilated it instantly. That should take years
to learn. Already in this race, Roglič and Pogačar are above
everybody else. When you look at Pogačar he can time-
trial, he can climb, he can ride in the sidewind and sprint.

DAVID: I reckon we can say that we've seen someone that
we're going to be talking about for a long time to come.

*   *   *

We travel north on the D934 from Laruns. Mountain stages
attract more people, more traffic, and now we're part of a very
slow-moving convoy. The sun disappears, night falls and I bring
up a subject that's easier to speak about in the dark.

Some context. Robert Millar was a great cyclist at a time
when doping was an integral part of cycling. I covered the sport

at the time. Journalists didn't have evidence about the cheating, but that was mostly because we weren't looking for it.

The signs were there. Why was everyone so reticent to talk about it? If some rider failed a drug test, *omertà*, the law of silence, kicked in. Gashes suffered in crashes took an age to heal, a side-effect of chronic cortisone abuse. We noticed this, but questions went unasked. It wasn't until Paul Kimmage chronicled the story of his career in the groundbreaking book *Rough Ride* (1990) that the broader sporting public could see how bad things were.

Millar was good through this era. One of the best climbers, I suspected he had to have been part of that culture.

DAVID: Did you dope when you were Robert Millar?
PIPPA: Just as much as everybody else. I didn't regard it as doping. I considered it cheating, and I didn't cheat any more or any less than anybody else.

This isn't a shock. I remind Philippa again that I covered the Tour de France in the 1980s and reported on Robert Millar. Although I suspected there was a doping culture, I had no understanding of how it worked.

PIPPA: As a rider I'd never have admitted cheating. Back then you lived in a closed world and you couldn't discuss it with anybody. It was the thing they call *omertà*, where people didn't talk about it.
DAVID: What substances did you take?
PIPPA: Cortisone for the big races. I was lucky that I didn't react well to cortisone and was spared all the worries that come afterwards when you've used a lot of it in your career

– problems with bone density and ligaments, that sort of stuff. It was mostly cortisone at that time. Steroids had been in use in the previous era, but they developed a test for steroids and that died down.

DAVID: Did you take testosterone?

PIPPA: I never used much testosterone because I wanted to keep my hair. Sometimes you'd have low testosterone, and I now sound like I'm justifying its use and I'm not. It's kind of weird to think of who I was then, a woman unhappily trapped in a man's body and taking testosterone. As a person, testosterone was the last thing I needed. I didn't do much of it.

DAVID: How did the cheating start?

PIPPA: I didn't talk about it with other riders and they didn't talk about it to me. Still, you knew everyone was doing it. I never thought about it as anything other than cheating. I was cheating myself and I was being cheated by the other riders. If I'd felt I had a choice, I wouldn't have done it.

DAVID: Do you recall when you first crossed the line?

PIPPA: You'd imagine it would be a seminal moment, and it isn't. Probably happened when you were really tired, thinking you needed a little help to get over this, and that's how it would have been presented to you. I know [Lance] Armstrong said he felt he wasn't cheating because everyone was doing it. I knew it was cheating. If you want to be a Grand Tour winner, this is what you've got to do.

Back then it was called Kenalog and Kenacort. They were brand names for the corticosteroid, triamcinolone, the one that Armstrong was caught with, the same one that was given to [Bradley] Wiggins in 2011, 2012 and 2013. I was as ambitious as anyone, and things were different back then. There was no out-of-competition testing and it wasn't that difficult to get away with stuff. They [the authorities] weren't interested.

We edge forward in the darkening traffic jam, the last remnants of sunlight disappearing over the mountains close by.

DAVID: What exactly were you worried about in relation to too much cortisone?

PIPPA: Some guys on cortisone, their legs would get thinner and thinner and they'd still be strong and quite often they'd have a bloated face, a moon face. I realised fairly early that the amount of training we did, the pain we went through, it wasn't healthy. When you're under 30, you've no understanding of how long your life is going to last.

Some people thought it would go on forever, playing with medications, staying up all night. I see them now, they're very stiff, they can't stand up straight. There's a French expression, *coup du vieux*. You suddenly get old. One of the first things I ask the guys I rode with is 'How is your health?'

DAVID: How is your health?

PIPPA: I'd say my health is very good. I can stand up straight, I can walk OK. I haven't got any major health problems. Nothing much has changed in the last 20 years. I've recovered really well from being a pro bike rider. I never put on weight, if anything I tend to be underweight.

DAVID: You retired in 1995. By then the EPO era was in full swing?

PIPPA: You saw changes in the way races were ridden. They never slowed down, guys who couldn't get up a hill would ride you off their wheel on a climb. I did a little EPO. In my whole career I was given less EPO than [Richard] Virenque or Armstrong would have taken in a week.

DAVID: When did you become aware of EPO?

PIPPA: From 1991 it was there. It took a while to understand what was happening. A buzz went around – 'There's something new.' In that whole period, from 1993 onwards, to me the thing became a farce because everything depended upon how you reacted to EPO. I remember saying to a friend, I'm glad to be getting out of it. It was getting really unhealthy. I felt sorry for the young guys coming into the sport. Without EPO they couldn't be competitive. They had very little choice. EPO was available to every team from 1993. Every team.

DAVID: If someone on the inside convinced you that some teams in this Tour de France were doping, would you still watch the race?

PIPPA: That's a good question. I'd still watch, because I like to see bike racing. If it was the case that certain riders were cheating, I'd be disappointed.

DAVID: If you knew there were clean riders being screwed by people doping, why would you want to watch it?

PIPPA: Because there are things other than the result that I appreciate. The aesthetics, the tactics. I'd feel bad for guys being cheated and bad for those who felt they had to cheat. That would be their choice, and you can't stop people making bad choices. But I'd still watch it because I'd enjoy it for its entertainment value.

The reasons I watch pro bike racing are different from yours. If I knew some riders were doping, I'd forget the results and just enjoy the spectacle, the show. It doesn't

mean I'm in any way supportive of those who felt they had
to cheat.

DAVID: My problem with your position is it's the same as
saying you don't care that the clean guys are being screwed.

PIPPA: I'm not saying that at all. What you see as a
journalist is different from what I see. You may think
sport exists outside of real life, that it has to be all clean
and fair. Inherently, it isn't. It's not fair at all. Some
people have more talent, strength and health than others;
what's fair about that? We all want life to be fair, but it
isn't. You want to live in Disneyland. The rest of us settle
for the real world. My not watching the Tour would
change nothing.

I want to believe the sport has changed and tell Pippa there's
encouragement in the fact of so many young riders excelling in
the Tour. Pogačar won it at 21. In a sport where there's a deep-
rooted doping culture, surely the young guys wouldn't be able
to compete against riders who'd been refining their doping
programme for seven or eight years. She agrees the sport has
changed for the better, although we can't be certain that everyone is playing by the rules.

Nearing Cazères-sur-l'Adour, I tell Pippa about a comment
from a *Times* reader that accuses me of not giving Sir Dave
Brailsford due credit for his role in the success of Team Sky/
Ineos.

PIPPA: I've noticed that too. You don't seem to like him.

DAVID: My belief is that what Brailsford and Dr Richard
Freeman did when applying for a therapeutic use
exemption (TUE) so that Bradley Wiggins could be injected

with triamcinolone before the 2012 Tour amounted to cheating. Other doctors in the team knew this wasn't right, but they weren't consulted.

PIPPA: I remember that. It was meant to be a kind of grey area. Triamcinolone, Kenalog, Kenacort, whatever you want to call it. I can tell you the only thing grey about that drug is the colour of your skin after you've taken it.

*　　*　　*

There were things that happened back in the 80s that made no sense. A rider could be exceptional for a while and then utterly unexceptional. It would be said he'd lost form or been sick or had no motivation, but the highs and lows didn't tally with what was happening in other sports.

There was Beat Breu, a Swiss climber who had days and even short periods where he was unsurpassable in the mountains. Then there were longer periods of bad performances and not being able to compete at the front end of the race. He was known as the 'Mountain Flea'.

I covered the 1984 Tour de Suisse when Breu won the mountain time trial from Bürglen to the Klausenpass in 55 minutes flat. Sean Kelly was second that day, 19 seconds behind. Robert Millar didn't ride the Swiss tour that year. For Breu, a Swiss rider in his national tour, it was a landmark moment, his time setting a new record.

Seven years later, the same mountain time trial was again on the menu at the Tour de Suisse. Present for this one, Millar delivered an extraordinary performance. Approaching our destination late into the evening, after a long, slow journey, I chanced one final question.

DAVID: How did you do that?

PIPPA: I rode the time trial at 100 per cent. I caught Sean Kelly on the way up. Passed him, just inside the 1-kilometre mark. I was wondering which side to go past him – do I go past full speed in a bit or sprint past now? No, it's Sean Kelly, have some respect. And then, what the hell, I just went past him.

DAVID: You beat Breu's time? Twenty-seven seconds faster?

PIPPA: And the next day the people were saying, 'No, that's not possible. Nobody could beat Breu. Nobody takes 27 seconds off Beat Breu's record on Beat Breu's mountain.' But there was a howling tailwind that day. Nobody mentioned that. There wasn't any headwind. Yeah, all of it was a tailwind.

DAVID: Did you feel any of the riders who rode that day were suspecting you?

PIPPA: I don't know. Because, the thing is, I went so fast that the guys on my team, you know, the non-climbers, the big strong guys who were there for the flat, they almost got eliminated because they'd just ridden up nice and easy and they looked at the time and they said, 'We thought we were going to be eliminated because you went too fast. We looked at the time limit and we were just inside it.'

But then some guy writes in the paper that it's just not right that Beat Breu's record has been smashed out of recognition. He says that the whole thing smells. Journalists. They didn't mention that [Andy] Hampsten also almost beat the Breu record too. You just look at the equipment we've got seven years on. It's lighter. It's better.

The tyres are better, the skinsuits, the whole thing. We're not knackered. It's not like after a week's racing. But mainly there was that howling tailwind!

DAVID: Were you not doing something that day?

PIPPA: I wasn't.

DAVID: One hundred per cent clean?

PIPPA: Yes.

DAVID: Honestly?

PIPPA: On my children's graves, I rode 100 per cent clean that day. What's going to help me ride that mountain time trial faster? I wasn't good with corticosteroids. They affected my breathing and made me slower. The only thing that's going to make me faster is amphetamines, and I'm not knackered enough to need them. And EPO hasn't properly arrived yet, though it will soon be on the way. I was physically fresh, strong tailwind, light bike, and I can win a mountain time trial if I'm up for it and in decent shape. But people still say, 'Ah no, that's not possible.'

DAVID: So Robert Millar rode that mountain time trial on bread and water, but it's cycling and there's going to be whispering?

PIPPA: I've been in plenty of races, and we're going fast, and I'm thinking now is the time to attack. But I'm knackered. Many other riders are knackered, but I know if somebody attacks now they will go away. Almost always somebody does attack, goes away and wins that day.

Pippa brings up the 1991 Tour de France. When the race hit the mountains, Greg LeMond started suffering immediately. Gianni Bugno and Claudio Chiappucci had ridden the Giro, but they were so strong. Good climbers were getting left behind. While grinding it out on some climb, Millar noticed guys not needing to get out of the saddle on steep ascents. They could pull the big gears all day. Then they'd come back and do the same the next day. It didn't feel normal.

Pippa especially remembers the 15th stage from Albi to Alès.

PIPPA: The scales really fell from my eyes on the stage into Alès. Two days earlier we had this massive stage to Val-Louron. [Miguel] Induráin got away, coming down the Tourmalet. Chiappucci caught him and they stayed away. Chiappucci won the stage. Greg lost more than seven minutes that day. Next day was shorter, and then another huge stage from Albi to Alès, 235 kilometres. That day Moreno Argentin rode the last 40 kilometres on his own. Nobody could get close. It was incredible.

DAVID: As in, you didn't believe it?

PIPPA: As in, it wasn't cycling as I knew it.

*   *   *

It's near midnight when we pull up at the Aliotel in Cazères-sur-l'Adour. On the long journey from Laruns, where we'd seen the future, we mostly talked about the past. My overriding sense was that when Pippa talked about Robert Millar, it was as she remembered it. That she just doesn't see any point in sugar-coating.

We'd travelled north, leaving the Pyrenees far behind, but what we'd seen in the mountains showed that Tadej Pogačar, even in his first Tour, was a generational talent. He'd come to the race with his exuberance and ambition, a breath of fresh air.

Journalists of a certain age could look back and struggle to recall any rider with this level of talent. Only Greg LeMond got into that conversation.

Chapter 10

3 July 2021
Stage 8, Oyonnax to Le Grand-Bornand – 150.8 km

Three kilometres from the top of the Col de Romme, Pogačar attacks. Thirty kilometres from the finish, old stagers wonder if he's got a screw loose. They apply conventional wisdom to an unconventional individual. Ineos leader Richard Carapaz knows Pogačar is different and that you can't give him an inch. So he responds to the acceleration. The two go clear. Carapaz then realises his companion is stronger and refuses to share the pacemaking. Dying is one thing, helping to dig your own grave is another.

In the end, it doesn't matter. Pogačar surges and eases, surges and eases, until Carapaz lay his cards on the table, face down. If you want it that badly, take it. Pogačar takes it.

From there to the finish, he's alone and in his element. He likes grey murky days like this, and one by one he overtakes stragglers from an early breakaway. Mattia Cattaneo, Sergio Henao, Guillaume Martin, Wout Poels, Ion Izagirre, Michael Woods, they're all reeled in. His chain fixed in the big ring, he powers past them on the left-hand side as they glance with hopeless acceptance at his fleeting presence.

They'll remember how fast he went. It's spectacular. He catches all but one of the breakaways. The Belgian Dylan Teuns stays clear to claim a terrific stage victory. Pogačar takes no risks on the final descent to Le Grand-Bornand, and finishes with Izagirre and Woods, 49 seconds down on Teuns. Behind them, there's carnage.

Race leader Mathieu van der Poel finishes 21.47 down, Carapaz loses more than three minutes in the final 30 kilometres. Others suffer greater losses. Wout van Aert finishes 21st, 5.45 behind, Julian Alaphilippe is 37th, 18.55 behind, in the same group as Richie Porte and Tao Geoghegan Hart. Behind them the 80-rider grupetto includes Geraint Thomas, Roglič and Froome. They cross the line 35 minutes after the winner.

Pogačar takes the yellow jersey and now leads by 1.48 from Van Aert. Wearing the *maillot jaune*, Pogačar claims the Tour isn't over. Anything can still happen. 'Today we got the gap, tomorrow someone else will,' he says. 'We're really confident and motivated, but sorry, it's not over.'

It's understandable that he sees it in this cautious way. The journalists nod their heads. They've heard it all before. Sometimes the truth is unspeakable.

* * *

It's after 8 p.m. when we leave the press room at Le Grand-Bornand, an hour's drive to the Hotel Terminus at Saint-Gervais-les-Bains. We're eight days into the 2021 Tour and the race feels over. This is an occupational hazard. A long time ago I stopped kidding myself about the uncertainties. People say anything can still happen. Delusional. Thirteen stages and more than 2,000 kilometres in front of us, it shouldn't be over. But it is. Pogačar has already won. We need to talk about this on the way to Saint-Gervais.

DAVID: What do you make of it?

PIPPA: Everyone knew it was coming. His team were setting the pace on the Col de Romme. Good tempo. No one was talking. And then he went. Only Carapaz tried. Everybody else just stayed there, looking at their power metres or thinking about the rain. Now they're riding for second, third and fourth place. We laugh about Enric Mas, defending sixth place on GC, but that's what he was doing today.

DAVID: The first mountain stage in the Tour always has a big impact. When you won into Bagnères-de-Luchon in 1983, that was a really big day.

PIPPA: I was surprised so few guys went after Pogačar. Normally you get out of the saddle and if nothing happens, you sit down again. There was no reaction.

DAVID: As that plays out, I'm thinking, *That's it, the race is over and we're a third of the way through.* We still have three more Sundays and we know Pogačar is going to win. No suspense.

PIPPA: None. But this is normal. Riders lose five minutes in the first mountain stage, they'll recover a bit, but they'll still be 10 or 15 minutes down by the end of the race.

DAVID: That is one of the truths about the Tour. The rider who wins generally loses less strength than those who finish behind him. You know not everyone in the press room is convinced about Pogačar. A dominant performance like today's and they're talking about another version of Lance Armstrong. I say, 'Come back with some evidence and we'll have an interesting conversation.' What do you think?

PIPPA: I don't see any reason to question him. The way it always worked with doping was riders were given the chance to do what they could without pharmaceutical help, at least until their early 20s. They'd reach a certain level and then someone would come along, probably the directeur sportif or his number two and say, 'Look, if you want to get to the next level, this is what you need to do.' That was the starting point. The sport has changed and a guy like Pogačar can win his first Tour de France at 21. No one is going to have doped him at 18 or 19.

Three hours after the race, while Pippa was driving, I called Iñigo San Millán, who has worked with Pogačar since he joined the UAE team in 2019. Iñigo is a sports scientist and a cancer researcher at the University of Colorado but is now back in his native Spain for the summer break. He'd already been looking at the data from the day's stage.

PIPPA: What did he make of today's ride?
DAVID: He agreed it was a dominant performance but said the numbers weren't at the level Pogačar produced on his best rides last year. He said the biggest factor today was the failure of the others to mount any kind of chase. Their numbers, he said, were really average. He knew this because after setting the pace for Pogačar through the first four or five kilometres of the Col de Romme, UAE rider Davide Formolo was still able to stay in the GC group all the way to the finish. Iñigo has Formolo's data and so knows what the others were doing. His point was that Pogačar's rivals didn't see any point in trying to peg him back and basically gave up.
PIPPA: I noticed that at the time, the UAE guy who'd done the work to try to put the others in trouble then managed

to stay with the others after Pogačar had gone. That wasn't because he was great but because they were ordinary.

DAVID: Intimidated by Pogačar's presence, would you say?

PIPPA: Exactly. He attacks and the guys he leaves behind are wondering if they can make the podium. Iñigo's assessment of what happened makes sense. Then afterwards, the guys who didn't get out of the saddle when Pogačar attacked are saying, 'It's not over', which is a joke.

DAVID: In their heads it was over before they left Oyonnax this morning. They've come not to bury Caesar but to praise him?

PIPPA: They're hoping for him to fall apart but not doing anything to make it happen.

DAVID: It should be said that Roglič and Geraint Thomas had bad crashes earlier in the week and they struggled because of that. Normally, they might have led some kind of resistance; instead they finished in the final group of the day, 35 minutes down. So when journalists come to me looking for me to share their scepticism about Pogačar, I know I'm disappointing them when I don't. Where's the evidence? A good performance isn't evidence. You still think I'm a bit of a Pogačar fanboy.

PIPPA: I don't have to think about it. You are. You criticise some of the other journalists for being fanboys when they come to the Tour. I don't have that, because I've been there. I don't look at anything and think, *This is amazing*. I know there are journalists who come to the Tour and say, 'Everything's great.' You're supposedly not like that, except when it's Pogačar, which I find quite funny.

DAVID: You like this feeling of knowing my weakness?

PIPPA: All the stories you tell about Pogačar, I'm thinking, *Fanboy, fanboy!*

DAVID: I'm not denying it.

PIPPA: You're right, though, about the way he races. So much enthusiasm. If he didn't have that, he'd have just put on his rain jacket on the Col de Romme and did what everybody else did.

*   *   *

We get to the Hôtel Terminus in Saint-Gervais at around 9 p.m. On the Tour, Wednesday night, Saturday night, it shouldn't make a difference. This might be Saturday evening, but tomorrow's just another Tour day, in fact a notably difficult one as it's in the Alps. So much for the Sabbath being a day of rest. And yet there's a difference. It always feels like we should make an effort on Saturday evenings, find a slightly better restaurant. In Saint-Gervais we do. Over dinner, Pippa and I get talking about what happened to Robert Millar after he stopped cycling.

PIPPA: I didn't stop riding as a professional until I was 37. I returned to the UK because by then my marriage, which had been falling apart, had ended. I wouldn't say the marriage ended because of the gender issue but because we stopped looking after each other. The gender stuff had nothing to do with it.

It's hard for professional athletes mentally when they finish a career, but the end of my career coincided with a marriage break-up and knowing that I had to deal with issues I'd been running from for a long time.

DAVID: And how did you cope?

PIPPA: Well, I came back to the UK and I entered into a spiral of depression. I had a lot of depression, four years of it, before I accepted that I needed professional help.

DAVID: And how were those four years? As a rider Robert Millar seemed very self-contained and resilient. If people were asked to guess, they'd have said, 'Millar got everything he could out of himself, he'll move on fairly smoothly.'

PIPPA: By the autumn of 1999 I'd reached a low point with who I was and how my life was going. Antidepressants didn't seem to be improving how I was coping, and I was getting more and more frustrated. They were dreadful years. Just unrelentingly dreadful. I ended up not in a good place at all with myself, relying on antidepressants. And it was just getting worse and worse, to the point where I thought, *There's no choice here, I'm going to have to deal with this transition stuff*. So then I sought professional help.

DAVID: Are you thinking at this stage that you want to do this, or you absolutely need to do this?

PIPPA: I wouldn't say I wanted to do it. It became a need. It's like a pre-ordained thing. You're not going to resolve the issues – the whole unhappiness with who you are – until you reach a level where you discover what might make you content. There are some people who transition and they've had counselling, and that keeps them happy. They can dress as the opposite sex and that keeps them OK, until the next time they need to do it. For others, they might need some kind of hormone replacement therapy, and that will calm down their unease. Others end up living as a woman, with all the things that go with that. As I've

137

said, when you start on this journey, you've no idea where it's going to end.

DAVID: So when you started, what was involved?

PIPPA: First there was psychotherapy and psychiatry, then it was onto hormone replacement. You try to figure out how far you want it to go. There are stages to it – you might be OK with just counselling, and if you're not, then it's medical therapy and that might keep you content, but if not, if you're going to fully transition, then it's surgery and stuff. When I decided that pretending I didn't have a serious problem wasn't a good idea, I researched the options for help with my gender issues. I needed a proper medical assessment, but given my situation and the attention I'd be subject to, discretion was of the utmost importance. NHS waiting lists were too long, so I chose a private provider a few hours north of where I was living. Local wasn't an option.

I won't name where, because as it turned out the whole set-up was about taking as much money from patients and the level of counselling was dire. It's bad enough having to pay for treatment that could be provided by the state, but you'd think that it would at least be professional and not an insult to those seeking help. After the first few visits I realised I was getting nowhere, the questions were getting more bizarre and the comments concerning my presentation became upsetting. I couldn't figure out what my sexuality had to do with any gender dysphoria, but somehow the people I was talking to were stuck on the idea that if I was properly transexual, then I'd be attracted to men. But I wasn't. I hadn't been abused as a child either, so that explanation of my deviation from the norm couldn't be blamed on any kind of trauma. I began to wonder what I was meant to say or wear, because if I turned up and wasn't wearing a skirt or dress, then that seemed to be judged as my not trying hard enough.

Their pricing for providing private prescriptions for a tiny dose of oestrogen was exorbitant, and so after reading their assessment of my personality and getting more and more frustrated with the counselling, I gave up on what I thought might be the start of transition. Obviously I wasn't trans enough.

*　　*　　*

That was where our conversation ended that night. The next morning, I went for a run. Pippa looks upon her travelling companion's advanced years and indulges this thirst for running as you would an eccentric uncle. But a curious thing happened that Sunday morning.

There was hardly a sinner about, very few cars on the road. In the distance a man on a derny was coming towards me, a bike rider in his slipstream. Soon they were alongside, then speeding past. As the rider flashed by, I could see it was Dave Brailsford, team principal for the Ineos Grenadiers cycling team. What struck me was the speed. For a 57-year-old, he was shifting along.

We needed to get a move on as well. The drive from Saint-Gervais to that day's finish high up in the Alps at Tignes would take us two and a half hours.

DAVID: Can we pick up where we left off last night?
PIPPA: Yes.

DAVID: So what came after those first and frustrating efforts to begin transition? Were you discouraged, tempted to leave it for a while.

PIPPA: New Year and the start of the next millennium came next. At the best of times I don't particularly like the winter in England, and this was no exception. Somebody suggested I go see Dr Russell Reid in London. I had nothing to lose. He was the best-known private doctor specialising in trans healthcare, so I was hopeful he'd give a proper diagnosis. I phoned and got an appointment for a few months down the road. It's like the state system. There's waiting lists and delays because there's such a limited number of people specialising in the field.

DAVID: How did it go with this doc?

PIPPA: From my first meeting with Dr Reid to the end of the medical process took three and a half years, which isn't particularly fast when you consider it would probably have been possible to do it in half that time. It was on my second appointment that I was prescribed oestrogen at a very low dose, and then on every subsequent visit we'd discuss how I felt. Was I coping with the effects? Did I want to up the dosages? There's a few myths about male to female transitioning, an idea that you turn up and it's instant access to hormones and surgery. Even when you use private healthcare, the reality is very different. It takes a lot of time, and there are checks and balances for each change in your treatment.

DAVID: In other words, nobody does this on a whim? Some people seem to have the notion that transitioning is a fad, with some element of attention-seeking?

PIPPA: It's very measured and monitored. Along the way they tell you that you can stop when you feel comfortable with where you are. There are no obligations. Nobody's pushing this on you. You started so you have to finish? It's nothing like that. Your oestrogen doses are increased slowly, male hormone levels are checked each time, even though they drop to female values very rapidly and you go through a second adolescence.

That's quite awkward, given you've already experienced it once before. There are tiny moments of euphoria too; I got them when I increased my oestrogen intake and I'd feel content for a short while, maybe a week or so, but then I'd get used to that level and the dysphoria would return – not to the same extent, it would be slightly improved, but that's when I knew I had to wait for my next meeting with Dr Reid to see if I had settled or if I ought to increase the HRT again. All the time the physical and mental changes were happening and it was a matter of processing them, asking myself if I was happier, was this what I needed to do, was I coping?

You ask yourself those questions and they're asked of you by others.

DAVID: And you went into it with no certainty that this was going to make you happy?

PIPPA: None.

DAVID: You're walking into unknown territory?

PIPPA: With each step, you're going into the unknown. You finish with counselling and you think, *I am who I am now*. Then you realise that's not enough. You decide, I'd like hormonal treatment, and then that makes you feel a lot better. And again, you want more because you're on a

141

small dose and it doesn't make enough of a difference. It just affects those pathways in your head that would have been active if you'd been born female. Now they're all activated. You're thinking, *This is good, I'm happy with this but I'm not happy with how I look. I need a different level of hormone intake to make those changes.* And then you go to that level, and then the bits you're left with, which are male and you're thinking, 'Well, I don't really need those.'

*   *   *

It was raining and uncommonly cold when we got to Tignes. It struck me that Pippa's transition has been challenging in ways that others can never truly understand. Each change was the forerunner to the next, and it went on for almost ten years. She started at 40 and, more or less, got to where she wanted to be at 50.

Life for Tadej Pogačar was simpler. He won yesterday's race to Le Grand-Bornand putting himself into a lead that, because it's him, seems unassailable. That effort cost him, and on the road to Tignes he got his teammates to ride steady. Let the breakaways go and we'll see later in the afternoon. Vigilance without anxiety.

'Yesterday the weather was bad,' Pogačar said. 'Today it was much worse. It was super-cold, a lot of guys really suffered, and I'm just happy to be over it and to now have a rest day. I did a small attack at the end to close a little gap. I thought if I didn't go, everyone would attack sooner or later and I'd have a problem. In the end it was OK. It's all in a good place.'

There will be bad days for Pogačar in future and his demeanour won't change much. Now we're seeing him take the smooth. When it comes, he'll take the rough in pretty much the same way. All in a good place.

Interlude

In another life I arrived at Charles de Gaulle Airport as a skinny wee kid from Glasgow. I had scratchy French and I carried too much gear. Nobody came to meet me. I humped the gear into the Citroën of an unimpressed taxi driver and with my threadbare French I smoothly directed us to the wrong destination.

And so I'd started a new existence.

I arrive at Bangkok International Airport twenty-two years later as – let's understate this wildly – a changed man. I think to myself that I'm not here to start a new life. I'm here to accept the hand that I was dealt at the start of my life. I'm here to make my life align with who I am.

There's somebody here to meet me, a small, dark-haired woman with a happy face. She's holding a sign with my name on it. Her name is Tair and she's the wife of Dr Chettawut.

I'd decided to come to Thailand because they had the best surgeons in the world. If you wanted to argue that they were not the best surgeons, I'd reply that they certainly had the most experienced surgeons. They had possibly the best outcomes and the aftercare was excellent.

I'd chosen Dr Chettawut after much research. He was a young surgeon who'd trained with the best of the Thai surgeons. He was a disciple of the best. He was just starting out on his own and to my mind that meant he was going to try his hardest. He'd also have the latest techniques. 'Cutting-edge' wasn't a phrase that I wanted to use at the time.

Dr Chettawut, I hoped, would be keen to make a good impression as he wanted to build his reputation. Sexual reassignment surgery isn't one of those things that you want messed up. I didn't need any complications. I wanted everything to work so that I didn't keep getting urinary tract infections or have the fuss of stitches coming undone just after surgery or even long-term.

I'd made my choice and I'd paid my deposit as a private patient. I was here and I had no thoughts of turning back.

Tair ushered me quickly through the airport. I remember arriving in Paris and the city making such an impression on my wide Glaswegian eyes as I took the taxi from Charles de Gaulle. Since then I've been arriving in cities for many years, and new environments don't make the impact that they once did. Bangkok was modern and slightly chaotic, but my thoughts were elsewhere. We drove through the city until we pulled up at a discreet little clinic in a quiet area.

From the outside the building gave little away. I could have been walking into an optician to have my eyesight checked. We were just on a normal street in central Bangkok and the world was going about its own hectic business. There was nothing to advertise the fact that this was a surgical clinic; the only hint of purpose was a simple white board with a medical cross on it.

It's May 2003 when I get to Thailand, but the process leading up to this journey began the previous December, when I legally changed my name. Among other requirements before you make the last – or ultimate – stage of transitioning, you have to show six months' proof of existence in a female state. So I'd changed my name to Pippa York six months earlier. It was a small adjustment, but …

The journey to Bangkok began a long, long time before.

145

Since I was five years old I've had, to say the least, an ambivalent position with regard to my gender. I didn't know what my gender really was through childhood in Glasgow. I was drawn towards dressing as a girl. I felt more comfortable with simply being a girl, in so far as I could manage it. Later, as an adult, I knew that it was something I was going to have to reckon with whenever my cycling career ended. It took a long time to figure out what form that reckoning would take.

But now, on the threshold of full transition, I began to wonder about things that had seemed certainties. I'd become hesitant. During those six months I wasn't sure that I was actually going to go ahead with surgery.

I'd been nudging myself along slowly but my brain was raising little flags. I moved house in March 2003 so that I could live as Philippa without any intrusion. I moved from the Midlands as a male and I arrived in Dorset as a female. No connections. Nobody who was going to peer at me and ask, 'Is that you, Robert?' I could start my story again on a fresh page. In Dorset, I realised that only Linda knew me and my story. Then I began to second-guess myself. Well, why are you putting yourself through this really invasive surgery?

I did my research through the winter, wondering where it would lead me, if anywhere. It's not exactly window shopping. It's not like choosing a dentist for a filling. You hear horror stories. People give you warnings. It's a major deal. It's a lot of time under general anaesthetic.

I'd undergone facial surgery the year before. That was a marathon operation and the recovery had taken a long time. So, why am I contemplating another major surgery, putting myself down for maybe another four or five hours on the table? Nobody in Dorset is going to know what I've put myself through.

In the end I signed up anyway. If there was one thought pushing me on it was this: you've come this far up the mountain, you may as well push on to the summit.

It was a joyless decision in the end. I didn't hate my body as some people in my position do. I had no hatred for Robert Millar. The things he did couldn't have happened without that body. I wasn't going to celebrate dismantling all those systems. There was no pleasure in taking apart the engine of Robert Millar's excellence.

But nor did I see anything as sacrosanct. I simply had a different relationship to my body than most people. I'd used my body as a tool during my career. It was just an instrument of cycling, like a plumber's wrench, a carpenter's hammer. I whittled it. I honed it. Starved it. Nourished it. I broke it and had it repaired. I got everything that I could out of it.

My working life was lived through my body – I saw it as something that I'd worked with or used till I no longer needed all its services. That's a different relationship than most people have to their own flesh and bone.

Also, I didn't hate having male bits. I just looked at those parts as added components that I'd been given. They came with the machine. The bits worked and functioned along with all the other components. My body was just that, functional, an instrument made up of working parts. I had gender dysphoria. I didn't have body dysmorphia.

So even when I signed up for the surgery, I thought, *Well, I don't really have to do this*. The deposit was 10 per cent, but even with that you could get some of it back. In the end, though, I got on the plane to Bangkok. I'd come that far and the people I spoke to about it all said that my thinking would change once I had the final operation. I needed to find out what was over there on the other side of that summit, but I wouldn't understand what it was until I got there.

*   *   *

Dr Chettawut is young and fresh-faced and reassuringly bright looking.

I've only corresponded with him by email to date, but in person he's warm. His first task is the examination. He needs to see what exactly he has to work with. What I have now, pre-surgery, this body, all comes into play in terms of how I'm going to turn out.

I'm totally matter of fact about it. As is he. I'd learned from multiple crashes in bike races and visits to hospitals that the bits I have – or had – are no different to what any nurse or doctor has seen on countless other people. I'm not squeamish or shy about that stuff. I'm not here in Thailand to be judged on my physical attributes. Dr Chettawut surveys me as a job of work, a problem of materials to be refashioned through his expertise.

When he finishes surveying me, he nods.

'Yes, that's fine.'

It had never occurred to me that it might not be fine.

People who've supported me through the process all said the same thing: you get to the point where you're living as a woman and nobody knows you're anything else other than a woman. When you get to this point, you're kind of doing it for yourself. You have your support around you, but you're on your own.

They might have been speaking metaphorically, but it's also literally true. I've come to Bangkok on my own and I'm completely OK with being alone. I understand why I'm in Thailand. This isn't something to share with somebody. I never looked forward to the journey thinking, *Oh, this will be a community project and it will be fun to share it with somebody.*

I can fully understand people who need somebody along with them. Younger people will go with their mother or sister or brother or whoever. They'll need that because they haven't been used to being on their own in that sort of environment. And they're young. But I left Glasgow and landed in Paris alone as a kid, and I've been arriving alone in foreign places for many years.

About one thing, I am sure. This is my decision. Mine alone. There's a notion that some sort of modish trans club exists whose slogan is 'Hey, come in the water, it's lovely!' That others are egging you on. Certainly, for me, this wasn't the reality, and I don't believe it is for anyone. It's much more serious than that. Nobody transitions frivolously.

At every stage along the way you're challenged. How do you feel? How do those people whom you love feel? What has the impact been internally and externally? What do you want to do now? Do you want more hormone treatment? Do you realise the consequences? Are those around you being OK? Are you feeling sure?

There's no encouragement. No peer pressure. No one nudges you forward.

There were times I didn't know if I was going to be all right at the next level of oestrogen treatment. *Is the next stage the one where I'll arrive at the point of just being content?* I don't know. I can't know till I get there. *Will I have that little bit of euphoria when I step up? Will I suffer a sinking heart when it all calms down again and I slide back to feeling miserable. Will I wake up one morning depressed because I realise that I need more, because I need to go further.*

And if I need to go to the next step, there's a six-month minimum in between each step. A long time out to be used for reflecting.

It's not a question of OK, next week I'm going to be a woman, so take a last look at me while you can. It takes a whole lot of time.

And now the last step is here.

It's not a simple thing either. It's not a full-stop or a dotting of the i's and a crossing of the t's. It's a major rewrite.

You realise when you do the research that there are things that can go wrong. You could end up with, say, a colostomy bag for the rest of your life. You might have lingering problems with internal stitches that don't heal properly. You can die on the operating table. It's a general anaesthetic, it's a major surgery and it's majorly invasive.

So you don't go into this thinking, *Well, if nothing else this is interesting. It will be a story to tell. I'll give it a whirl.*

In the last few weeks, though, something new has become clear to me. My body has been doing some talking.

I began my hormonal treatment over three years ago. Almost instantly that treatment turned off the flow of testosterone in my body. After six months I was at the testosterone level of a natal female. This affects the way the brain functions. So I've now been in a state of non-existent testosterone. I've been inhabiting a male body, but one with low testosterone. If that happened to you as a man, you'd be miserable, aching, depressed. I went through all those things.

To prepare for this surgery, however, I've had to stop taking oestrogen – that's the advisory in case of blood clots. And when I stopped with the oestrogen, I experienced a slight increase in testosterone. I got menopausal sweats and started waking up in the night, agitated.

150

I'd gotten used to being the way I was. I'd thought I was OK. The testosterone increase was a reminder of how much would change after taking this final step. How I'd feel about myself, how I functioned, would be different. But still I wanted to go ahead.

The essential genital surgery I am to undergo in the morning will take about two and a half to three hours. I'm having breast implants tomorrow too. That will take an extra hour or so.

I decided to have everything done under one general anaesthetic. The genitals and breasts were the only things that I hadn't already altered in order to make my life easier. I could have left the breast implants until later, but it makes sense to do it while I'm here and still relatively young and fit. Apart from that, there was a shopping list of other things that could be done, from buttock contouring to clitoroplasty to vulvoplasty to feminisation laryngoplasty to having the pitch of your voice heightened.

I considered having the voice work done – somebody removing my anterior thyroid cartilage, collapsing the diameter of my larynx, and shortening and tightening my vocal folds. Ultimately, however, I decided it was a step I wasn't comfortable with. I'd had my Adam's apple shaved down back in the UK. It's a local anaesthetic procedure. The Adam's apple is just a growth that occurs through adolescence. It wasn't traumatic, but it was enough.

Surgery is scheduled for 36 hours later. That means one day to kill at my hotel. I've chosen a hotel that has a five-star rating. It costs US$20 a night. The difference between three stars and five stars is the difference between $15 and $20. So I pushed the boat out. The hotel's on the main road beside a giant shopping centre. I spend the next 36 hours trying to make sense of what's about to happen.

Rue de Sèvres, 1979

On a grey February afternoon of steady drizzle he boarded a British Airways flight to France. Charles de Gaulle Airport was so futuristic he felt that he'd travelled through time as well as space to get to France.

There was no mighty fanfare of trumpets to herald his arrival on the 'continent'. He was greeted by dry weather, a freezing cold wind and nobody. He later learned that this was one of the tests they gave. They wanted to see if you were sufficiently grown up to deal with things like airports in foreign cities.

Bowed down with his own belongings, he struggled to the taxi rank. One of the ubiquitous boxy Peugeot 504s trundled along and deigned to accept his custom. The driver sat patiently at the wheel as the boy packed everything he could into the car.

Welcome to *la belle France*. Welcome to the Athletic Club de Boulogne-Billancourt. Welcome to the brutal life of the aspiring professional, where there are more hopefuls than places available for the hopefuls. He asked to be taken to the Rue de Sèvres, the address of the ACBB *Service des Course*, the team HQ. Ah, the wonder of driving for the first time into Paris from Charles de Gaulle! Down the A1, under the various runways, past all the bog-standard industrial units and factories. Then the Périphérique, where the level of chaos ramped up a level or two. He'd never seen people so gaily improvising the rules as they drove. There were bonus points for aggression, speed and rudeness. Braking was for sissies. Indicators were for fussy tourists.

The taxi driver negotiated the bedlam using cussedness and cusses, all the swear words that Linguaphone cassettes didn't teach. Memo to self: Learn to curse in French immediately.

They – boy and driver – got off at Porte Maillot, negotiated more madness at the Arc de Triomphe, drove down along the banks of the Seine, crossing the river at the Pont de la Concorde. He spotted the Tour Eiffel in the distance.

This Parisian life is the glossy magazine life. Swanky streets, elegant people, busy cafés spread on the pavements under the shadow of fairytale buildings.

You're not in Glasgow now, kid.

The taxi finally pulls up at the given address. Elegant too. Well, this doesn't look too bad at all.

The big, solid wooden doors suggest the presence within of a fabled institution. Ancient and discreet. There's no signage for ACBB. He rings the bell, which brings forth the concierge. In French films the concierge is almost always a woman. This lady fits the central casting profile.

She looks at Robert Millar with his suitcase and his bike bag. He can tell that she's going to be haughty about admitting him.

'*Oui?*'

'*ACBB?*' he says, self-consciously trying to enunciate each letter in his Glasgow French.

No response. Shit. *Merde!*

'*Equipe de vélo …?*'

'*Non,*' she says.

'Rue des Sèvres?' he says.

'Oui. Mais …'

Apparently, this is the Rue de Sèvres that traverses the 6th arrondissement. It's not the Rue des Sèvres in Boulogne-Billancourt, a teeming suburb a few miles to the west.

Oh.

The concierge finds some pity in her heart. She phones for another taxi. Robert holsters his broken French for now and just shows the driver the address by pointing it out on a letter he carries. Half an hour later he's outside a sports centre in a significantly less swanky part of town.

He's spent his budget for the day. He's tired and hungry. He consoles himself with the thought that at least he's arrived. Now he'll have a decent bed to sleep in and, most likely, something to eat.

Wrong and wrong. Here's a windowless room off the main sports hall. Two basic beds from a prison movie. 'Sleep here,' says the guy who a minute ago had scooped him up from the pavement outside. 'The team car will arrive for you at seven in the morning.'

That's all.

'Good night.'

He walks to a corner shop that he's spotted not far away. He buys a bag of crisps and a can of fizzy orange. Glasgow cuisine. He downs them on the slow walk back to the night's accommodation.

acébébistes

The ACBB Peugeot 504 estate car has its livery on the outside, just like the professional team cars. Today the car is filled with the new season's recruits.

The long drive south begins. The small Glaswegian boy wedged into the car notes for the first time that when driving down towards the Côte d'Azur the sun seems always to be shining. In that simple way, the Côte d'Azur is quite different to the Firth of Clyde.

The training camp is like an early attempt at a reality TV show. The ten recruits will be whittled down to just four or five survivors by Easter. It's now February. There's no acclimatisation or orientation. There will be no dispensation or mitigation. Only competition. You win races and you stay. You lose and you go home.

He won some races, though. He finished near the front in most of the others. He was one of the lucky few.

After the Côte d'Azur selections torture, it was back up to Paris. The real season began. More whittling. The early races were testing affairs, but when the one-day classic races began, life became a sharp uphill.

Each weekend they departed Paris to race somewhere, usually about a hundred miles away. Sometimes the courses were mainly flat, sometimes they were hilly all day. In the early races, sometimes the course would be flat and then there would be a killer hill at the end that decided things.

The one-day classics were a level up again. The fight just to be in the front was fierce.

The good thing about being in ACBB was that people were intimidated by the team's presence. Most of the other riders made their way to the races as individuals, driven there by parents, friends, wives or girlfriends. Their club's entourage sorted out the bike while the rider got ready to race. Some of the bigger clubs had a team car, but it was generally something old and jaded.

The ACBB, however, was essentially the nursery club to the Peugeot pro team. When ACBB went to a race they looked and behaved like a professional team. '*Acébébistes*' was what the others called the ACBB riders. The *acébébistes* raced on Peugeot bikes and they arrived in Peugeot team cars, not one but two estate vehicles. From time to time, if they'd entered almost the whole squad in a race, they also brought a van, and bikes and riders poured out of it like ancient Greeks from their wooden horse.

They sometimes rode wearing a swathe of the black-and-white chequerboard symbol of the Peugeot pro team across their jerseys, and, just like the pro team, a team car followed the race all kitted out with spare bikes and wheels.

The ACBB rode like the professionals that they intended to be. They had the best race plans, the strongest riders, the best coaching and the greatest numbers. They won races. When they didn't win there would be an enquiry next day in the *Service des Course*. And for all the seamless presentation of unity, their fiercest rivalries as *acébébistes* were with each other, in their continual internal dogfights for pro contracts.

For inspiration, Robert liked to walk down to the *Service des Courses* and gaze at the framed photographs that hung there, portraits of previous graduates, a golden thread to be followed. He'd gaze at the faces or study the jerseys that they'd worn and donated to the club. Mickey Wiegant, who ran ACBB, had previously been a pro team manager, working with some of the biggest stars of the sport. Occasionally these guys would drop in to say hello, names his imagination conjured with: Jacques Anquetil, Bernard Thévenet, André Darrigade and so many others that he'd heard tell of, their race leader jerseys – from every major race you could imagine – challenging you to win one of your own.

The team had lightweight wheels that were kept back for special occasions and frames that only were used for one or two races a year. When Robert was being supplied with these bikes, the best equipment he could imagine, he always thought of those who'd used them before him. ACBB had better equipment, planning and pedigree than most national federations. He respected the tradition and he longed to add to his story to it.

The bearpit nature of amateur races, events where everybody was competing for the chance at a career, gave the weekends a whiff of danger to go with the drama. There were frequent crashes. Everybody so desperately needed to win, but there could only be one winner. So what would you do? How far would you go? Just how bad was your want?

Robert Millar was more desperate and less afraid than anybody. He willed himself to be competitive in every sprint. If a bunch of five went pell-mell for the line, he expected either to win or to lose to somebody exceptional. If there was a corner close to the finish line, he expected to be first into that corner. First in was first out, and least afraid was usually first home. Robert took a lot of first places because he wasn't afraid of falling off and eating either gravel or humble pie.

That was a conscious decision. In a race he had to win, was he willing to risk crashing to the ground on the last corner? Could he handle his body scraping violently on the sharp gravel or bouncing on the cobbles, his bones fracturing, the wheels of other bikes unable to avoid him, the next weeks or months written off to injury? Yes. Bring it on. Yes. He was ready for that. Yes. Yes. Yes. *Faisons-le!*

From the corner to the finish, they weren't going to come past Robert Millar. That whole mix of arrogance and reckless self-belief that he had as a lean and hungry youngster brought him wins that year in French amateur classics like Paris–Evreux, GP de Lillers, GP de Grasse; a major stage race win in the Route de France; a big time-trial win in the Chrono Madeilinois; and the Merlin Plage, a trophy for best amateur of the season in 1979. Best of all, perhaps, was his fourth spot in the World Amateur Road Race Championships in Valkenburg – were it not for a pulled foot right near the finish he'd have been on the podium.

the high life

By the end of April it had become clear that there were two riders from the 1979 crop who were likely to earn a pro contract and one other who just might graduate. Phil Anderson of Australia and Robert Millar of Scotland were the two likely lads. Loubé Blagojevic, a French boy with a Slav-sounding name, was the one hopefully hovering. They called him 'Blago'.

Blago won Paris–Ezy, a race in which Robert finished fifth. The French lad went on to win the Tour du Parc du Haut-

Languedoc, but after that the pieces seemed to fall off his campaign. At Paris–Roubaix Blago was out in front and looking good for the win, when disaster struck – he punctured. Then he fell off his bike while chasing to come back after the repair work, with Phil Anderson riding on in cold blood and winning the race instead.

Over the rest of the year poor Blago just faded. Misfortune kept on finding him. There were more punctures, falls and time lost to other riders. There were crashes or just times when he was badly positioned at the decisive moment.

Was it bad luck or just how things run for a young rider? Who could say? From the end of the classics onwards, Phil Anderson and Robert Millar lived at the front of every race they entered. Poor Blago just gathered what crumbs got left behind.

Foreign riders were popular with the ACBB management, but not with the French riders in the club. Away from home, the foreign boys grew up more quickly than their French counterparts, becoming self-reliant once they'd recovered from the culture shock. They hardened, and grew the calluses and tough hides needed for life as a professional. They were highly motivated too, never wanting to return home crestfallen. The only dark cloud was their lack of fluency in French, preventing them from arguing for better conditions. So they just got on with things.

Robert Millar was typical of the breed. Outside of competition he looked after himself for food, entertainment and little moments of enjoyment. He had the commitment, focus and some talent, possessing the inner strength to deal with the workload and the serenity to handle the boredom.

Food was the universal bugbear. The same flavourless pasta being served endlessly at team meals meant having to ask the team manager for an advance to buy the occasional treat just to break the monotony. Any advance on the prize money being accumulated would be deducted from the tally at the end of the year.

Alternatively, the young riders could compete in night-time circuit races in the hope of winning the prize money on offer. Primes – or intermediate sprints – usually offered cash rewards at various points during the race for being first over the line on a certain lap. Instant cash prizes meant having money to spend without having to ask the team for an advance.

In the summer months, as the daylight hours stretched out, there were circuit races in the suburbs of Paris. The ACBB boys went along too, approaching them as training rides that were helpful to keep their high-end speed topped up.

The thing about winning cash prizes at these events was that everyone else liked that idea too. So money could be quite hard to win. One evening, Phil Anderson and Robert Millar, bored and hungry, set their minds to winning some of the primes. They'd use the instant cash to treat themselves. They didn't care about the end result of the race; they just wanted that sweet prime cash money. As the race developed, they fell into a strategic pattern. Robert led out, Phil followed and won the sprint. Robert leading and Phil following turned out to be the perfect formula. They won all of the sprints that night.

This success sat poorly with their rivals, whose stomachs were equally taut. As the evening wore on, disruptive tactics came into play. Riders would go wide at corners to box

Anderson and Millar in, and there was some hefty barging directed at the pair. Rivals generally tried to cause upset, fair or foul, but it made no difference. Millar still led out and Anderson still won the sprints. Ker-ching!

Finally, an older Polish guy, a little gnarly, approached the pair. Why not ride with himself and his friends? Help with the final placings.

OK, why not?

So Robert and Phil went on with winning the sprints, and at the end of the race, having taken their turns at the front, they left the Polish guys to mop up the best places at the finish. Race done, they went to collect the cash for the primes. Then the trouble began. The Polish guys were all in their thirties and built like brick outhouses.

The Poles made their income from a mafia-style arrangement where they shared out the prime money between themselves. They were from different clubs and different areas, but acting in concert the prime money was usually their domain. Nobody had ever dared to challenge them. Until tonight.

The Poles now expected the ACBB boys' winnings to be shared out with them. Anderson and Millar felt the arrangement was different. We keep the primes. You keep the finishing spots. The primes cash is ours. The official prize money is yours.

The tone of the discussion deteriorated fast and matters became heated, with riders shaping up to each other. A beating became a very real possibility. Suddenly, Claude, the ACBB team manager, appeared. He interceded and sought a fool's pardon for his boys. These two greenhorns don't speak the language so well, he pointed out. Let's make it up to you in the future. Maybe we can sort you nice Polish bike-mafia chaps out from the end-of-season prize kitty at the club?

Robert Millar and Phil Anderson left with their cash, but their little enterprise was at an end. Claude decreed that there would be no more midweek circuit races. The boys shrugged. On his next free day Robert went to the Champs-Élysées and got himself a peach Melba ice cream to be consumed on the spot and an expensive packet of decent pasta for later. Heaven.

By the end of the season, between them, Robert Millar and Phil Anderson had won most of the races worth winning. They both signed for Peugeot at a slightly higher rate than was normal for new pros, while Blago loitered in the *banlieu* for a while longer.

Robert Millar took a last look at the photos on the hallowed walls in Rue de Sèvres and wished himself a place in that company. All that and the peach Melba had happened since February. You want to tell us about the high life, kid?

Troyes boys, 1980

That first year as a pro he lived for the early part of the summer, June or July, in the outskirts of Paris. The French rider Pascal Simon was also in the Peugeot team at the time. He was two years older, quietly spoken and reserved, but he made time for the young *étranger*.

'Don't live near Paris,' he told Robert. 'It's too congested, too full of people. And when you come to race, you're stuck in a traffic jam. This happens every weekend. For training, it's not great. Just millions of people.'

'Where do I live then?' said Robert.

'Come and live in Troyes.'

So Robert Millar moved 160 kilometres east from his rented flat in Paris to the Champagne region in the northeast of France, because that's where Pascal Simon lived. Bernadette was Pascal's wife and her dad was a policeman who worked in Troyes.

Pascal was proved right. Troyes was indeed a location better suited for a pro bike rider. The pair trained together when it suited them to do so. They shared rooms while they were away racing, finding each other's company congenial, and they'd talk endlessly to each other about everyday things.

Robert stayed with a local family who'd created a modest apartment at their house just outside of the town. They lived downstairs, Robert was upstairs. He lived on his own and he was fine with the loneliness. He made himself think that it was quite normal, just another toll to be paid.

Before he left Glasgow, Billy Bilsland and Arthur Campbell had told him that often the hardest thing to deal with was the long periods on your own, with no family and few friends. But Robert didn't mind; being an outsider wasn't a new experience for him. He wasn't fluent in French yet, but he could understand cycling's language and what he was being told to do in races. He just couldn't say much in response.

That was OK too. Loose words would never be a Robert Millar thing.

words not spoken

Robert's mum Mary Millar died on 30 July 1981 of carcino-matosis. She was in her 40s.

Robert was riding with Peugeot but he wasn't riding the Tour de France that year. He got a call from home telling him the news. He knew that his mum had been unwell but the thought had never crossed his mind that she was that unwell. She'd always had poor health.

Afterwards, when he thought about it, he never remembered the call from home being at all emotional. Just his sister Elizabeth saying, 'Mum's died.' He replied flatly, 'OK, I'll be back for the funeral. Do we know yet when it will be?' And his sister said, 'Well, she died a month ago. We've already had all that. You know, the funeral and stuff.'

His first thought was, *What the fuck?*

His first words were, 'What do you mean? Why didn't you tell me?'

'Oh,' said Elizabeth, 'we didn't want it to get in the way of what you were doing.'

And he just thought, *But it's my mother. It doesn't get in the way of what I'm doing.* He thought those words, but he said nothing.

He was still living in Troyes at the time. Long-distance calls in 1981 were expensive and difficult, but there was a phone in the house where he stayed. There were numbers for Peugeot that his family had been provided with.

So he left it at that. Too many words had been unsaid when he hung up on the call from his sister. It was done, and funerals cannot be redone. His grief was mixed with shock at the lack of empathy from home, but he never asked any more questions about it.

He went back home to Glasgow when the season was done. It was late in November or maybe early December and the weather was terrible. He was cold there, and still too many things went unsaid.

Chapter 11

13 July 2022
Stage 11, Albertville to Col du Granon – 151.7 km

Five kilometres from the summit of the Col du Granon, an inner voice reminded Jonas Vingegaard that second was no good. He'd been there, done that. It was time to take another shot at race leader Tadej Pogačar. Vingegaard stretched his torso upwards, making himself seem taller than he was. Out of the saddle, he pressed hard on the pedals, and soon there was daylight between himself and his rival.

Daylight for him, a dark abyss for Pogačar, who had teammate Rafał Majka alongside. Eager to close the gap to Vingegaard, Majka went a fraction harder, then stole a glance over his right shoulder. Pogačar wasn't there. That was it. The greatest young rider since Eddy Merckx was about to suffer the greatest reversal of his brilliant career.

From that point to the top of the Col du Granon it played out like a funeral where the deceased was still – just about – alive. Pogačar unzipped his yellow jersey to let in the soothing mountain air. He wilted so badly that riders who'd been left behind regained the lost ground and overtook him. Geraint Thomas, David Gaudu and Adam Yates could barely bring themselves to look his way as they passed.

Vingegaard and his Jumbo–Visma teammates sought their rival's breaking point and found it. Like the matador with a bull, they taunted him on the Col du Galibier and then went for the kill on the Col du Granon. Talk about the toughest alpine climbs, and the Granon is in the conversation: 2,413 metres above sea level, 11.3 kilometres at an average gradient of 9.2 per cent. Vingegaard said that with three kilometres to go, he just wanted it to end.

We can only imagine how it was for his poor rival, toiling behind him.

*   *   *

At a sports hall converted to a press centre in Briançon, Pippa and I watch the battle play out. Halfway through the race, the narrative of the 2022 Tour de France has been written. The young champion has fallen. Long live the new champion. A sense of shock hangs heavily in the room. Pogačar's attacking style has endeared him to journalists. There's plenty of respect for Vingegaard, but nothing like the same affection.

We had better get used to him, though, because he's going to be with us for the foreseeable future. Pippa and I have an hour's drive to our hotel in Embrun, and, of course, we're talking about what we've seen.

DAVID: On the Galibier, Vingegaard and his teammates did the equivalent of taking Pogačar down a dark alley and giving him a going-over. But even allowing for Jumbo tactics, I thought Vingegaard was stronger today?
PIPPA: Yeah, he was climbing better than Pogačar, but the softening-up tactics meant the margin at the end was

bigger. I think it hurt UAE not to have their directeur
sportif Allan Peiper in the car.

DAVID: Wrapped up in the race, you forget that Allan is
back in Belgium battling cancer.

PIPPA: Allan would have looked at those attacks on the
Galibier and told Pogačar to let Roglič go because you're
not racing Roglič. Vingegaard is the guy you have to stay
with.

DAVID: There's a rivalry between Pogačar and Roglič, two
Slovenians, and Pogačar couldn't let him go. He gets into a
local fight, takes his eye off the global war.

PIPPA: Yeah, it became personal.

DAVID: At a pre-Tour press conference, I asked Roglič if he
and Pogačar were close. He said, 'We didn't hang out
before last year's Tour and we haven't since.'

PIPPA: When Roglič and Vingegaard attacked in turn on the
Galibier, Roglič was already a few minutes down on
general classification. The message from Pogačar's team car
should have been, 'Let Roglič go.' If he had, Vingegaard
would have just sat there on his wheel. Others would have
then come back to them and given Pogačar some help. But
in the heat of the moment he rode like a junior. You can't
do that.

DAVID: Did it remind you of Hinault in '86?

This was the 1986 Tour de France and Pippa, then Robert
Millar, was leader of the Panasonic team, wearing number 31.
No one who watched that race or rode it was a neutral. Greg
LeMond or Bernard Hinault, you couldn't support both. It was
the most intense, the most personal and the most controversial
battle in the Tour's history.

The American *wunderkind* against the French champion, New World against Old, pupil against teacher, innocence against hard-headedness. The backstory was straightforward. With help from LeMond, Hinault had won the previous year's Tour. It was his fifth, and it put him on the same number as Jacques Anquetil and Eddy Merckx.

In the moment of that victory, Hinault said he'd repay LeMond the following year by helping his young teammate to win.

DAVID: You weren't a Hinault fan?

PIPPA: No, and I doubted he was going to ride for LeMond in '86 because I'd never seen him ride for anyone but himself.

DAVID: You're right, but that's what made Hinault a great bike rider.

PIPPA: He'd done Greg over in '85. Greg was riding better than him in that Tour. I was there for that. I respected how much Hinault could hurt me in a race, but I didn't admire him. He wasn't likeable. He had to dominate you and – if he could – humiliate you. He liked to make you look weak.

DAVID: In relation to '86, I've a certain sympathy for Hinault. He's allowed to go all out in the time trial and wins it by 44 seconds. He knows he's stronger than Greg and he can't stop himself in the Pyrenees. After the first mountain stage, he's got a lead of five minutes 19 seconds. That was it. Race over.

PIPPA: Hinault would say he attacked to eliminate riders like me, which he did, but he was eliminating Greg as well. He played it craftily. In the group, Greg was saying to us, 'I don't know what's happening. I don't know why they're doing this.' I'm thinking, *They're doing this to do you all over again, mate*, but it wasn't my place to tell Greg, so I said nothing.

DAVID: Then the next day, he attacks again. But, to use your expression, he rides like a junior.

PIPPA: He's got this huge lead, he doesn't need to add to it. But he's Bernard Hinault and he scents blood. On the descent from the first mountain, he goes once more. The rest of us are now racing for places on the podium. Greg had a full panic going on. 'Will you guys ride?' 'No,' we said, 'we're not racing him.' There was no point.

DAVID: On the road that day he's two and a half minutes ahead, taking his overall lead to almost eight minutes. His La Vie Claire team wanted him to ride conservatively, just protect the 5:19 advantage. Hinault had his man on the ropes and wanted the knock-out. Then, suddenly, his lead began to falter. Not because anyone was chasing him. He just lost power. You guys caught him in the valley before the last climb to Superbagnères. Do you remember?

PIPPA: He was in a state. As soon as I saw him, I thought, *Right, payback*. On the biggest stage he'd tried to humiliate us. Anyway, we liked Greg a lot more than him. In Hinault's eyes we were all useless. It wasn't often you had the chance, but when it came, I wanted to hurt him. I was willing to ride half of that mountain just to get rid of him. We were all happy to see his demise. He was so angry he'd cracked and that everyone took advantage of his moment of weakness. I wouldn't go as far as to say Hinault hated foreign riders, but he definitely had a dislike of them.

DAVID: Still, he should never have lost that Tour. Could have been the only man to win the Tour six times.

PIPPA: People say Greg beat Hinault in '86. He didn't. Hinault beat Hinault. He had us all beaten, Greg included, but that wasn't enough. His need to crush us meant he destroyed himself.

DAVID: Pogačar isn't at all like Hinault, but on the Galibier he made a Hinault-esque mistake, biting off more than he could chew when getting into that slugging match with Roglič and Vingegaard. On the Granon he paid dearly.

PIPPA: As soon as they hit the Granon, it's hard straightaway. Vingegaard's thinking, *I'm not hurting*. He sees Pogačar's face and knows he isn't good. So he attacks.

DAVID: I don't think we quite realised how good Vingegaard is. For the first time, he's made us reconsider the question of who's the best Tour de France rider. Before today, everyone would have said Pogačar. Now, you've got to think that maybe Vingegaard is the man.

PIPPA: True, today the balance of power shifted. I can't see Vingegaard not winning this Tour.

DAVID: From that point to the finish, Jonas Vingegaard defended his yellow jersey. Pogačar recovered from his nightmare on the Col du Granon and rode well all the way to Paris, but without landing a blow on an exceptional rival.

*　　*　　*

Three Tours, almost 12 weeks, 10,000 kilometres in the car, Pippa and I did a lot of talking. Sometimes conversations focused on the day's events and our memories of bygone Tours; others dawdled along, without much rhyme or reason. On our first Tour together, after the fifth stage, we travelled from Privas to Pranles, a tiny commune in the Ardèche.

Our bed and breakfast was called Domaine du Clap, which perhaps didn't augur well. Pippa raised her eyebrows as I tried to say the name came from happy residents applauding before they left. As it turned out, Domaine du Clap was one of the better pit stops. Our accommodation was in an old and historic chateau overlooked by nearby hills, one of those magically secluded places in France where the only sound is birdsong.

After breakfast, we stayed at the table and talked. From things Pippa had previously said, I knew her mother's death and funeral had caused her much unhappiness. Maybe talking about it would help.

I was 19 when my mother died in 1975 and remember many of the details around the funeral, especially the way my siblings supported each other. On the day after the burial, we went for a long hike in Waterford's Comeragh mountains, something we'd never done before or haven't done since. It's a cherished memory. Pippa's experience had been very different.

DAVID: I wanted to talk to you about your mum's death and the impact it had on you. You said your family didn't tell you she'd died until a month later?

PIPPA: I just thought about what kind of relationship we have in our family, that they think this would be OK, that I'd be OK with this. And then I wondered whether I came across as so selfish and self-absorbed that my own family thought it best not to interrupt me. It shocked me that they hadn't warned me: 'Oh, you know, she's really ill. It would be good if you can come back. You know, to see her before she dies.' I didn't fall into any kind of depression, but it certainly affected me. I had a difficult period for probably two months or so before coming round and asking, 'What am I doing here?'

DAVID: Even to be told that she died yesterday and the funeral is going to be in two days?

PIPPA: Yeah, something like that, or she had died unexpectedly. But when somebody has been ill for a long time, it's not unexpected. So, you know, they could have said something like that. It's going to be soon. Come back. In the case of my father, when he was dying, that's what happened.

DAVID: There was no point in having arguments with your sister or your brother or your dad about it.

PIPPA: Oh, no. I think, you know, the deed is done, what can you do? I was so shocked at the lack of empathy that I never really asked any more questions about it.

DAVID: How would you have described your relationship with your mum?

PIPPA: I thought it was OK. I was closer to my mum than I was to my father. And I was horrified – and am horrified to this day – that they could just let that happen. I don't know if it's because we were brought up to be independent and not rely on each other, but it just seemed really strange.

DAVID: I'm guessing you wouldn't have been talking too often with your sister or your dad about your mum?

PIPPA: No, no. I almost never called them, no.

DAVID: And they wouldn't have called you?

PIPPA: They'd never call me because it's at that time when it cost a fortune to do international calls.

DAVID: You got on better with your mum than your dad. Why was that? Did you have lots of conversations with your mum?

PIPPA: No, I just felt closer to my mum than to my father, because my father quite often worked away. I think we were all just closer to our mother. It's that generation – your father's seen as the sole strong, authoritative person in the family, your mother's the one that smooths the corners of the relationship that you have. And she's looking after you most of the time.

DAVID: As a young pro in Europe, at a time before mobile phones, it would have been easy to get detached from the folks at home?

PIPPA: Yeah. I was already detached before my mother died. I'd only go home in the winter or whatever to see my family. But even then, there was a kind of detachment. Contact was really sparse. So I'd go back in the winter, and it would be dreadful. I'd be thinking, *Why have I come back here?* And then, eventually, I just stopped coming back. Because it felt like, not exactly wasting my time, but I was just not doing anything when I was there. I didn't feel any closer to anybody. And I didn't feel like I could prepare properly for the next season. And there was the travelling, you know, a day there, a day back, and I'd end up knackered for a week, and yeah, it was just a poor use of my time. Or that's how it felt.

DAVID: Was it that your family just didn't see the importance of telling you immediately that your mum had died?

PIPPA: No, I don't think it was that. I think they thought that my career as a pro cyclist was more important to me than my mother dying. That's what came across to me, you know. Of course, I then looked at myself and thought, *Well, have I given them that impression? Am I that poor a person?* And maybe I was? I don't know. You can't judge yourself. They didn't want anything to interfere with my career. And I'm thinking, well, it's my mother. I can understand the part about how they didn't want to interrupt my career because I was so dedicated to it. But I'm not going to have another mother.

DAVID: Was it the case that your single-mindedness gave them the wrong impression?

PIPPA: Yeah, I think it was that.

DAVID: Ultimately, this all relates to you more than your family?

PIPPA: Yeah, to the protective image I'd cultivated, the shield around myself so that you could say stuff to me and it's not going to hurt me because I'm not letting you inside. What you say can't get past the shield. I was living in a little bubble. You'd have seen it when you came to races.

DAVID: I've said it so many times down through the years, it was like Robert Millar had a sign on his forehead, *chien méchant*, beware of the dog?

PIPPA: Yes, it looked like I'd bite you. So a lot of people stayed away. And then obviously my family, they've also seen that. Jesus.

DAVID: As if they thought, better not go there. Even when your mother dies, better not go there.

PIPPA: Even in those circumstances, they're thinking it's not worth it. That's one of the really poor things; people think the person doing the bike races is you, that the person on the bike is all there is.

DAVID: You mentioned this to me before: if you lose a race you're not going to go home and be horrible to your wife.

PIPPA: Yes. I'm not gonna go home and shout at my kid because I lost a bike race or act differently if I won a bike

race. I was competitive, but that was work. I'd give myself
half an hour or an hour after the bike race to process what
happened. And then after that, I didn't want to talk about
it. I didn't take it home with me. I didn't come in and make
a big fuss. I just didn't. At home, I didn't have cycling-
related stuff in the house. Because I wanted to separate
work from what I wanted to be my normal life. So I didn't
have trophies. I didn't have pictures of myself riding, and
you could come to my house and you didn't know what I
did for a living. Yeah, because I needed that. That
separation.

DAVID: So did you go back to your dad when the time
came?

PIPPA: Yeah, I was in the Tour du Pays Basque, in the
Basque Country. I was in Bilbao and I got the call. And the
next day I was on a plane back to the UK.

DAVID: Had he died, or was he dying at that time?

PIPPA: He was dying. That was his last few days.

DAVID: What year was that?

PIPPA: That would be 1991, '92. I think it was the first year
I was at TVM. So I'd left Z. My contract wasn't renewed
and I went to TVM. And yeah, I was in the Basque
Country. And I got the call saying he was dying. Best to
come back. Or they didn't know if I could come back.

DAVID: And was he well enough when you got home? Did
you see him alive?

PIPPA: Yeah, he was well, well enough. On morphine. So if
he recognised you at all it's a case of in between the
morphine shots. So yeah, barely, you know, barely able to
recognise you and barely, barely functioning.

DAVID: And did he die soon afterwards?

PIPPA: About two days later.

DAVID: And did you come back for the funeral?

PIPPA: No, I couldn't come back. My contract said I only got one day's compassionate leave – you get a day for a parent dying. Seriously, that's what it said in my contract. I think you maybe got a half day off if you lost an arm or you had your eye poked out. Seriously, all that stuff was written in the standard contract from the Federation that you had to sign. It gave a list of the days off you were allowed for serious accidents, ill health, people dying. You got a different kind of allowance for each person.

DAVID: When you remember your mother now in your mind's eye, what do you see? How do you remember her?

PIPPA: Now, there's a hard question. I don't remember her as the person that became ill. So you've just made me cry.

A long pause.

PIPPA: I don't really want to answer that.

Pippa gets up from the table and leaves for her room. So much hurt had been unintentionally caused by the family's decision that it would be better to let Robert get on with his career and not have to worry about getting home for his mum's funeral. Forty years later, the scar is still there.

We've got a three-hour drive, but as we're going directly to the finish, there's no rush to leave Domaine du Clap. By the time Pippa comes to the car, she's her old self. I know enough to not even ask if she's OK. How upset she got at that moment isn't mentioned.

Chapter 12

Thirty-five kilometres from Megève, the route was blocked by climate-action protestors from the group Dernière Rénovation. They sat in the road, with two female protestors having chained themselves together. One wore a white T-shirt with the message, 'We have 989 days left.' For riders getting ready to tackle the Col du Télégraphe, Col du Galibier, Col du Granon, the Galibier again, Col de la Croix de Fer and Alpe d'Huez, 989 days seemed too far away to worry about.

At the Centre de Presse in Megève, I meet a photographer. He's been coming to the Tour for a long time and he asks who I'm travelling with. I tell him. Back in the press room a few minutes later, I seek out Pippa.

DAVID: Did you see that photographer?
PIPPA: What a dick.
DAVID: Yes! I've just had a very irritating conversation with him. We talked about you. I told him I was travelling with you. He said, 'Oh, you're travelling with Robert Millar.' I said, 'No, no, I'm with Pippa York.' He then says, 'I knew him as Robert Millar and he'll always be Robert Millar to

me. That's how I refer to him.' So I wanted to get to you before he did, to give you a heads-up.

PIPPA: I've already had this conversation with him, probably before he met you. And I've had the same conversation with him back in England. I went to the Tour of Britain in Bath. I'm hanging around, waiting to interview somebody, I can't remember who. I did my interview and I'm close to the last getting away, standing talking to this couple about bike racing. And that photographer comes up to me and starts talking.

DAVID: Did you know him at that point?

PIPPA: Yeah. He knew I'd transitioned because I'd seen him at a couple of races. He comes up to me, and he's talking away about this and that. And he calls me Robert. He says that's the original and all you've done is mess with yourself. And we know that it's not true. It's not real. So this random version this guy has of me is supposed to be more authentic than my own knowledge of myself, of how I need to express myself. The couple that I'd been talking to are taken aback. They say to him, 'Wait a minute, her name's Pippa now.' And he says to them what he said to you: 'I knew him as Robert and that's what I'm going to call him.'

DAVID: That's exactly what he said to me.

PIPPA: And the people said, 'They're Pippa now, use the name they want to be known as.' And he went, 'No, I'm not doing that.' I'm thinking, *What a dickhead*. And I don't want to say it to his face because it will just make me look bad to those people.

DAVID: The two people were upset?

PIPPA: They were really angry. They were English people from Bristol, they'd come to see the end of the Tour of

Britain. And then he says, 'Oh, you know I'm running a cycling event for old pros. Sean Kelly will be there, we'd love you to come.' And I'm thinking, *Wow, you've just insulted me*.

DAVID: I said to him, her name is Pippa now, why can't you call her that?

PIPPA: It's what I call ignorance. The people in Bath said, 'How can people say that to you?' And I say, 'It's not the first time. People say all kinds of stuff.'

DAVID: It surprises me that you don't get really upset by it.

PIPPA: I used to. I'm just trying to process it now. I do get upset but I don't show it. I'll try to judge what's behind it. Was the person drunk? Sometimes people are just being idiots. People like him who do it to my face, that's just ignorance.

DAVID: Ignorance maybe, but still, it's extraordinary arrogance too.

PIPPA: It's presented as: this is what you were, and this is what you will be. It's still the case nowadays – they'll put up that 'before and after' picture so there'll be a comparison for people to look at and see. Oh yeah, sorry, but I can see you're still a man. They have no understanding that you failed at being a man. You haven't been able to be a man. You might have functioned really well in one or two areas when you were a man, but the rest of the time you failed. And what you really needed was to change into what you now are.

* * *

We leave the press centre at Megève around 8.30, with a 120-kilometre drive south-west to Échirolles taking us to the PoMo Hotel and Restaurant. On the Tour, it's not the distance that determines the length of the journey but the roads and the traffic. Set deep in the Alps, there's no easy way out of Megève. The first 33 kilometres are painfully slow-moving and will only improve when we funnel onto the N90 at Albertville.

In two days the race will go to Alpe d'Huez, perhaps the most iconic climb in the Tour. I saw this climb for the first time in 1984, which was the first time I covered the race from the opening stage to the Champs-Élysées. How different things were back then. Riders stayed in school dormitories, and if some rider had the misfortune to fail a drug test or be sanctioned for an illegal manoeuvre in a sprint, tour director Félix Lévitan would march into the *salle de presse* to give us the news.

It was also the year that Millar won the polka dot jersey for the Tour's top climber – the first English speaker to win this award. On the journey to Échirolles, I ask about the 1984 Tour.

DAVID: You did well that year?

PIPPA: I was fourth, but Hinault, Fignon and Greg LeMond were the three in front of me. That wasn't bad. Plus the polka dot jersey. I had some good days and some days when I was less good, but nothing catastrophic happened. Through the race I kept better control of the natural weight loss that occurs during the Tour, though I definitely finished the last few days underweight.

DAVID: Did anything prepare you fully for what the Tour would take out of your body?

PIPPA: I think that when you're young you take things as they come, but you know it's quite shocking to see what was once your competitive racing weight basically become your out-of-season weight. I had a good mentality, though. Occasionally I'd train with other people and they'd murder me, but then when it came to the actual race they fell apart.

DAVID: But looking at you as a rider, I got the impression that Robert Millar was quite meticulous about diet, training and weight. Ahead of your time?

PIPPA: Maybe. I became obsessed after some disappointments in 1982, and I focused on who I was as an athlete, what my priorities were and how I was going to go about achieving them. If I wanted to be a Tour de France rider I needed to improve, and that's what I did.

DAVID: I can remember looking at Robert Millar and thinking nobody could be lighter.

PIPPA: When I was an amateur I was racing at around 62 kg. But when you turn pro and they weigh you, they'll shake their heads in alarm and tell you 62 kg is the weight you might want to come back at after the off-season – if you've really enjoyed yourself. So in 1984 I began the Tour at 56.8 kg, and that came slowly down to 56.2 kg after ten days. I tried to keep it there, because after that you lost power on the flat. When we came out of the mountains with still three or four days to go to Paris, I was 55.8 kg.

DAVID: I think of what Robert Millar did in 1984. Polka dot jersey winner, and fourth behind Fignon, LeMond and Hinault. Between them, those guys won the Tour de France ten times. There are good years and there are great years. Millar finished fourth in an outstanding year.

Back on the road to Megève, the Dernière Rénovation protest came and went without causing much commotion. Any sporting event that plays out on public roads is going to be vulnerable, and the Tour is generally sympathetic to people's right to protest. They stop the race and restart it as soon as the police re-open the road. As for the protesters, they know they can disrupt the Tour but not stop it.

Chapter 13

19 July 2022
Stage 16, Carcassone to Foix – 178.5 km

We're at a lovely restaurant called Restaurant Le 1900 in Lagrasse, a beautiful village in Corbières. Feeling rested.

DAVID: What was that story you were telling me earlier about that former teammate you rode with, way back?

PIPPA: If it's the one I'm thinking about, you can't name him.

DAVID: No, we won't name him.

PIPPA: He was at Peugeot – this would have been in my second year as a pro. We're at an Italian one-day race. He's a sprinter, he's our favourite for the day. So we do the race, we're coming back and we're going through the border. This is back before the free movement days and you always had to stop at the border. They might check your car and they might not. They expected you to make a donation of some piece of cycling kit. So there would always be a collection: shorts, jerseys, tyres, that kind of thing to ease the passage over the border. Otherwise, they'd make you fill in all the paperwork. There was a mutual understanding.

DAVID: Were these Italian cops?

PIPPA: Italian customs. Fifty metres later you had French customs. Both worked exactly the same deal. The Italians were first this time, so they got the best pick. When we were crossing from France to Italy, the French got first pick. We'd give casquettes [peaked caps] and tyres on the way into Italy, jerseys and shorts on the way out.

So we get through the border and we then fill up the car, because the French being the French don't want to buy anything outside of France, even petrol. I'm in the lead car with the second director, his name was Bob something, he was a Belgian. The race wasn't very important, so Bob had taken charge of this expedition.

There are two cars and we've stopped to get petrol for both cars. Phil Anderson is sitting beside the directeur sportif in the front car. I'm in the back, in the middle, the worst seat because you've got a body either side of you and everyone is sweating.

And our man who won't be named comes and he opens the door beside Phil, opens the glove box of the car and takes out a package, a brown envelope, in which there was ...

DAVID: A gun!

PIPPA: Correct!

DAVID: Why is a cyclist carrying a gun?

PIPPA: Why? Well, he's bought this gun in Italy and he's bringing it back into France. Obviously he hasn't paid by cheque.

DAVID: So you're thinking he may not have purchased this from an authorised dealer.

PIPPA: I suspect not. Old Bob, the director sportif, looks at the gun, looks at his cyclist and almost has a heart attack.

He's driven through two border checkpoints with a gun in his glove compartment.

DAVID: Was the gun left in the car?

PIPPA: No. He took the gun with him for whatever he intended to do with it. He'd put the gun in the car that he wasn't travelling in. Just in case. Poor old Bob said nothing. What could he say? One of my riders bought a gun and I drove the gun through two checkpoints. This was the kind of thing that happened in those days.

DAVID: Whatever became of the guy who bought the gun?

PIPPA: Who knows?

*   *   *

Talking to Pippa York as we chat away the car time, it's noticeable how often the names of Robert Millar's various directeurs sportifs crop up. I take a little consolation in the thought that it wasn't only journalists who felt the salty side of Millar.

Peter Post was the daddy of the team bosses in the 1970s and 80s. His team won lots of races, and with that came respect and fear. He stood at six foot two inches out of the saddle and during his career as a rider he was nicknamed 'de Lange' (Big Man). The name suited. He could be charming, but by nature he was authoritarian. If you wanted a difficult life, you only had to get on the wrong side of Post.

I wouldn't have taken him on, but Millar was different. I like Pippa's Peter Post stories because they offer us a portrait of the cyclist as an outsider, doing things that no rider from the UK had done before. Millar never genuflected before anyone's altar, even Post's.

Pippa remembers the fourth stage of the 1987 Tour de Romandie. Post liked to bring his team to Switzerland; good roads, good organisation, classy place for a classy directeur sportif. Millar was the only non-Dutch rider in the Panasonic team who got into the break of the day.

Near the finish there was some negotiating among the group as to who would lead out into the sprint. While they dithered, Beat Breu, the little Swiss flea – whom Post had worked with previously with TI Raleigh – came from behind to overtake all four and steal the stage. Disaster.

The bollocking from Post was destined to be the worst ever.

DAVID: Post would have seen that as your error and given you no credit for actually getting in the break?

PIPPA: Definitely not. To Post at that moment, I'm useless because I haven't won. He'd get very agitated, and when he was really wound up he was spitting words out in Dutch. I was multilingual when it came to swear words, so I caught the drift of the insults. He always did these bollockings in front of the team – that way you'd be properly humiliated. 'That Breu, he's a real rider,' he'd say. 'No wonder he beat you.' I could feel all my teammates shrinking in their chairs.

'You're saying he's a great rider,' I said, 'so why did you let him go?' His face went red. He was completely shocked that I'd answered back. 'I'm paying you too much money,' he said.

And he didn't speak to me for the rest of the race. The guys told me I couldn't speak to Peter like that. I told them I hadn't signed up to be a soldier in the army. If I was getting a bollocking I didn't think was fair, I'd say, 'Hold on, I don't think that's right.' I was told you couldn't say that. 'Why not?' I'd say.

DAVID: Peter Post died in 2011.

PIPPA: Yeah. A lot of riders who rode for him went to the funeral.

DAVID: Did you?

PIPPA: Fuck no.

not tonight, Zsa Zsa

Occasionally nowadays, a bright young pro fast becomes the centre of his team's plans. In the early 1980s a young pro served his time before he progressed. He clawed his way to respect by doing whatever was asked of him. Going back and forward to the team car, fetching clothing or rain jackets? No problem. Giving up his feed bag because someone had missed theirs? My pleasure, monsieur. Waiting for riders who'd had a puncture? Why, of course. That's what I'm here for. Serve the greater good by riding on the front chasing a breakaway into a headwind for 100 kilometres? Part of the job. If it were asked of you, it was assumed it would be done. Do more than you were asked, and nobody noticed. Do less, and there was trouble.

This was the world that young professional Robert Millar discovered in the early 1980s. One of his first appearances for his team Peugeot brought an early lesson. They were down on the Côte d'Azur for a few one-day races in France, some over the border in Italy. This particular race was in Italy. Peugeot's plan was to control the race in the final hour to set up the win for their sprinter. That was the idea, anyway ...

When the peloton splintered there were no Peugeot riders at the front. The guys in the second group almost made it to the lead group, but they fell away. Meanwhile, the star sprinter was even further behind.

Millar saw none of this. The older guys had sent him back down the road to the team car with long-sleeve jerseys and other bits of clothing that they no longer needed or wanted to carry up the hills. This was just before the crucial climb started, so he'd spent the whole ascent trying to recover ground on the bunch. He was doing this on a narrow road with nowhere to pass.

He ended up in a group that just rolled, tired and defeated, to the finish line. When he reached the hotel, the management inquest had already begun. The noise coming from a room at the end of the corridor told him that it was ongoing, and it wasn't pleasant.

Millar had finished in a forlorn group with his teammate Frédéric Brun, who'd been a pro for two years already. Now they were walking together up the hotel corridor. They thought they might perhaps skip the post-mortem, but a sour-faced soigneur directed the pair down the corridor towards the bloodbath with an ominous nod of the head.

In they went, like lambs to the slaughter. Everyone was seated except for team boss Maurice De Muer, who stood in the middle of the room, holding forth. Nobody had showered. The riders sat stewing in their own sweat and grime. The effort had drained their faces. Millar and Fred Brun hurriedly found seats slightly out of De Muer's immediate gaze and sat down to listen.

De Muer was five foot zilch and they called him 'Napoleon'. He was midway through a systematic evisceration of the riders, but being late didn't spare Millar and Brun. They had the additional torture of waiting for their own disembowelment while the others suffered.

One by one, De Muer asked the riders how they thought they'd done. Before they could even reply, De Muer answered for them. 'I'll tell you! Fucking disgrace! You were pathetic! Embarrassing!'

As he worked through the line-up his ranting grew angrier and more operatic. Millar, new to this, feared for his safety, but he was intrigued to see if Napoleon could continue ramping up his rage without actually exploding.

Eventually, it was Fred Brun's turn.

'How were you feeling?' Napoleon said to Fred.

Instead of going straight into his rant, Napoleon refuelled with a sip from his bottle of water and waited for a response.

Fred, unsure what to do, finally filled the silence.

'Not too bad,' he said.

Maybe he thought that his relative youth might save him from the same awful fate of his peers. Wrong.

'Not bad?' screamed Napoleon. 'Not. Too. Effing. Bad? I don't pay you to be effing not bad. Fuck you! If I wanted not too bad, I'd get someone cheaper, someone dumber, someone who wouldn't be not so fucking bad.'

His fury subsided slightly, then resumed his offensive.

'Not too effing bad,' he repeated over and over. Every time he said the words, Napoleon would glower at somebody he'd already tortured.

'Unbefuckinglievable! Not too effing bad!'

At last his mad eyed settled on Robert Millar

'You,' he shouted. 'How did you feel?'

'Shit,' Millar heard himself say. 'Really, really shit.'

Had he been asked a minute earlier, Millar would have said that, well, the others had sent him back to the team car at just the wrong time and that he didn't have a chance. Now he noticed a slight break in the weather of Napoleon's face.

'That,' said Napoleon, 'is what I want to hear. I don't want "not too bad" riders. I can get not too bad riders anywhere. Effing not bad. You're either good or you're shit. I don't want to hear that you were not bad, because if you were not bad then why weren't you in the fucking front? Effing not bad. Of course you felt shit.'

'How were you?' he said to the final rider, who crept in and sat next to Millar.

'Very shit. Totally, totally shit,' came the reply.

'Good boy,' said Napoleon, and his shoulders slumped.

He was spent and he knew it. He left.

They sat for a moment, enjoying the respite that came with the silence. Somebody suggested quietly that maybe Zsa Zsa, the glamorous wife of Napoleon, had been giving the boss a hard time.

'Quite the opposite,' said somebody else. 'Napoleon hasn't been giving her a hard time. Not too effing hard anyway.'

And laughing like schoolboys they dispersed for their showers.

another fine kermesse

The term 'kermesse', from the Dutch word *kermis*, denotes a mass that's said on the anniversary of a foundation of a church or parish. The mass is said in honour of the patron. In Belgium, especially in northern Flanders, kermesse festivals are common, and the highlight is often a kermesse cycle race. If a criterium race generally takes between an hour to 90 minutes to complete, a kermesse can run to two or three hours.

A decent pro might ride the kermesse circuit on the way up and hope to have made enough money to avoid kermesses when he's back on the way down again.

In March 1982 Robert Millar had become ill and he didn't recover quickly. He stumbled through the classics season, feeling weak, then rode the Tour de Romandie in average form. In the team training camp in the Alps he did what he was asked, and a little bit more too. Ditto the Dauphiné, through the Midi Libre and the Tour de l'Aude. But when he found out after the French Championships that he wasn't in Peugeot's team for the Tour de France team, he was broken.

So, in 1982, instead of riding his debut Tour, he ended up doing as he'd done the previous years and went to Belgium to ride kermesse races for two weeks to keep his conditioning in some kind of reasonable shape.

It was a risky business. Falling off in these races wasn't uncommon. Less experienced riders often made mistakes and would encounter challenges that they didn't have the skills to match. Kermesse races usually meant riding through wind, rain and cobbled streets against hardened kermesse riders who didn't really want big-time pros around.

So you took your chances in the kermesse for very little money and a decent chance of crashing.

It was a hot and dry day, his second week in Belgium. He was getting better at surviving the special demands of the races but today felt endless to him. He'd made it into the first group, but fatigue was pulling at his hem. He was hanging on and having to miss his turn at the front now and then. Now, he'd just done a shift in front and was coming back down the line. He happened to look round to see what was going on behind him. In that instant when he looked over his right shoulder, the rider who was the last man in the group pushed him from the left to shove him back into the group.

Unfortunately, he pushed Robert Millar into the rider in front of him. Robert flew over his handlebars and hit the roadway at some speed. It was a rough surface. Of course it was. He wasn't wearing gloves. Of course he wasn't. The landing ripped his hands to pieces and his back to shreds. End of the kermesse.

The medical people at the race patched him up just enough to let him drive the 40 minutes back to where he was staying. The drive was agony. Home was yet another 400 kilometres away. Robert could neither hold the steering wheel nor sit with his back against the driver's seat. He spent three days just lying on the bed in his rented room. He cleaned his own wounds out twice a day until he recovered enough to drive home. Every kilometre was torture.

He wore gloves thereafter.

the reset

He spent July recovering from the fall, as the Tour de France captivated its audience. He spent a week alone in the Alps just riding up and down mountains, pedalling and thinking until he felt halfway human again.

Then they sent him to the hellish late-summer races that nobody else wanted to do. The Tour de Limousin. Four flavours of misery in late August. Corrugated roads. Gravel-strewn corners. More sheep than spectators. Thirty-five-degree heat.

His contract was up at the end of the year. He felt that his appetite might be up by then too. He skipped the World

Championships at Goodwood in early September. No point in going along just to make up the numbers.

So, instead of the World's the team dispatched him to the Tour de l'Avenir, which began the following week. To his surprise he finished second to the American Greg LeMond. At the time LeMond was deemed to be better than everybody else by some distance. To finish second to LeMond was to finish first among all those not called LeMond. Robert felt that he was competitive uphill, and he'd raced well against the Colombian climbers who showed for the race, guys like Rafael Avecedo and Luis Herrera.

On reflection, he figured that the week alone in the Alps had saved him from becoming an ex-pro bike rider. Those retreats became something to which he'd return whenever he needed space in his head to figure the world out.

That winter he decided that 1983 would the year to find out if he'd reached the end of his talent. Maybe there was a rich seam of natural ability to be mined. If not, if he'd come as far as he could, he made up his mind that he'd settle for a career at the level of domestique. Racing was what he loved and even being a humble, hard-working grunt back in the pack was more attractive than a normal job.

He ramped his training up by another per cent or two. Ten weeks of weights instead of eight. Mudguards onto the training bike so he didn't skip riding on rainy days. No more excuses. He did an hour of weights after every ride. Three days hard riding. An easy day or a rest day. Three more days hard riding. A reduced week every three weeks.

More stretching meant fewer injuries and an improved riding position. His diet became more restrictive. From time to time he adhered to a strict vegetarian regime when he was approaching major career objectives, but now vegetarianism became his norm. This wasn't an ethical or moral decision; he'd just noticed that without meat his body functioned better and recovered quicker.

He set about putting a healthy mind into his healthy body. He learned about visualisation and how to use it in training as well as races. He studied the techniques of dealing with stress. He identified what he was good at and what he wasn't good at. He reinforced the strong points and coped with whatever he couldn't improve.

Regathered and reset, he was ready to go on.

little old lady in black

He was third at the Dauphiné in 1983, later promoted to second after a positive test for teammate Pascal Simon. As with his second place in the Tour de l'Avenir the year before, he now knew he could climb big mountains. The performance at the Dauphiné earned him a place on Peugeot's Tour de France team.

Still, it was his weaknesses that leased living space in his head. He remained a work in progress.

He didn't like bumpy descents, or downhills that were super-fast either. Oddly, when they were wet he felt OK about them. On wet days, if you come off the bike flying down a mountain you slide better when you hit the ground.

Someone once told him that every rider has a speed in their head that's acceptable. Exceed that speed and you become afraid. Racing often took him there, to that place of fear. Racing pell-mell down a mountain is a different thing to riding down a mountain. Some days they'd reach the bottom and riders would be laughing. Too loudly. Too hysterically. They'd survived intact. They were high on relief, fear and adrenaline.

So ...

His first Tour de France, and there was more of everything. More than at any other race. More crowds, more media, more competition, more noise, more stress, more reward and more adrenaline. Bombast and grandeur dripped from the skies. It was a year of notable rookies, Millar, Laurent Fignon, Pedro Delgado and Stephen Roche all wide-eyed and hopeful.

Twice he'd come off on cobbled stages of that year's Tour. Each time the riders in front crashed and he joined them on the ground. Positioning errors! A fall on the road to Roubaix cost him 17 minutes. He figured out that he needed to be strong enough or brave enough to be further forward in the bunch.

A couple of days after the Pyrenees they were riding through a small village not far from the middle of nowhere, the kind of place where if a street lamp stopped working it made the local paper. It was desert hot and his feet were hurting. Mosquitoes had feasted on him the night before. The novelty of the Tour had worn thin.

There was about half an hour to cruise before the last scrambles of the day began. The peloton had been a little tense due to a bothersome wind. There was a slight uphill into the village. Robert took the opportunity to move up a few places on the left. As they came into the main square he could see that the villagers had trestle tables laid out. They'd put bunting up. It looked like the riders were interrupting a village fête, but small towns often marked the Tour's arrival like this. A community meal, music and dancing. Things to mark a day of days.

They rode past happy people who'd been waiting all day for this glimpsed moment, full now with wine and cheese and whatever delicacies they'd made. The sun was beginning to dip and the world felt good.

He saw an old woman sitting outside her front door away from the fuss. She was dressed all in black, as tradition would have it for the old ones. Probably someone's grandmother, if not great-grandmother, he thought, judging by the lines on her face. She was laughing with the abandon of a young girl, though; her face, caught by the sun, was awash with joy. The great spectacle, Le Tour, had come to her door. It was unlikely that she'd ever see this great streak of colour fly past her door again, but she was all the happier for being too old to take such days for granted.

He was a part of this great flying circus. One of the cast. He realised that his job, if he could, was to make it all as entertaining as possible.

Chapter 14

14 July 2022
Stage 12, Briançon to Alpe d'Huez – 165.1 km

Over the top of the Col du Galibier, 2,642 metres above sea level, Tom Pidcock attacked. His thinking was that others wouldn't want to take risks on the descent. Without some dare-devilry, they were never going to stay with him. Watching him descend is one of the joys of the Tour. He flies into corners, accelerates out of them. Smoothly. A natural.

Such is Pidcock's skill, it never looks dangerous. He caught Chris Froome, who'd already escaped, and though the four-time Tour winner descends well, he had no wish to get into a downhill race with Pidcock. 'I definitely backed off a bit, because he was pushing the limits,' said Froome.

As Pidcock went past, it was like the future overtaking the past. Pidcock would soon slow, however, as the advice from the team car was that with Froome alongside, he'd do better in the valley. So they became a tandem and, sharing the workload, they caught the breakaways up front. On the first slopes of Alpe d'Huez, something happened that foretold the rest.

Pidcock had taken food, sucking the life from a gel, and rather than stuff the wrapper in his pocket, he spotted a refuse bag pinned to a pole by the side of the road. Racing uphill he aimed the wrapper and in it sailed. Stephen Curry on a bike.

He won the stage by 48 seconds. Near the finish line he shook his head before raising his arms. 'It's certainly one of my best experiences in cycling, it was unreal,' he said afterwards. 'When you're slaloming through people's flags, arms and God knows what, you can't experience that anywhere else, other than on l'Alpe d'Huez in the Tour de France.

'It's made my Tour. Even if something happens and I get dropped every day, I don't care. A stage win at my first Tour, it's not bad.'

*   *   *

After our work was done, Pippa and I had a long and winding journey through the Romanche valley to Grenoble. From Bourg-d'Oisans it's just a 50-kilometre drive, but it's not a road that allows for overtaking and, of course, this is 14 July, Bastille Day. It feels like all of France has come to the Tour. What the heck, we've seen something a little special from Tom Pidcock, and like so many of our journeys this one is shortened by conversation.

DAVID: What do you think? Pidcock was brilliant on the descent from the Galibier?

PIPPA: That's an understatement.

DAVID: One of the best descents you've seen?

PIPPA: In the circumstances, to be going round the outside of guys who are also going really fast and not look out of control, that's really unusual.

DAVID: You were a pretty decent descender? First stage that you won on the Tour, you were away on the descent from the Col de Peyresourde down to Bagnères-de-Luchon.

PIPPA: I was average. I wouldn't have been able to follow Pidcock. Not many would. I'd have had to go way beyond my comfort zone. When you're on a descent, you're already out of your comfort zone, you're scared, and once you go deeper into that, a moment comes where you think, *I have to stop this.*

DAVID: Frédéric Vichot was probably the best descender of your generation. Would he have been able to stay with Pidcock?

PIPPA: Yeah. Vichot would, he was that fast.

DAVID: The perception in the press room used to be that Vichot was a nut job?

PIPPA: Not really. When you tried to follow him, it wasn't dangerous. There was no emergency braking because he flowed downhill. He was the same standard as Pidcock.

DAVID: Pidcock got away today because he was well down on GC and not seen as a threat to the yellow jersey guys, but on the other hand he climbed Alpe d'Huez as fast as any of those behind him.

PIPPA: That's impressive.

DAVID: Does this performance show Pidcock can win the Tour?

PIPPA: I think so, but he's got to stop messing around with mountain biking and rein back on the whole cyclocross thing in winter and spring. The crossover between those one-hour races and riding on the road isn't going to help him in the second or third week of a grand tour.

DAVID: I remember reading a quote from him where he said he felt he was born to be a mountain biker.

PIPPA: If he was riding for a Dutch team and not Ineos Grenadiers, they'd say to him, 'We're not paying you to do mountain-biking. Your salary is at a level that means you have to be winning grand tours, or looking like you're going to win them.'

DAVID: Ineos agreed to pay him €3 or €4 million per year, and have allowed him to do cyclocross and mountain biking, so that's on them?

PIPPA: Of course. They're desperate to keep him. He's got them by the curlies.

DAVID: Talking to one of the Ineos team directors, the story is that Pidcock isn't going to fully commit to the Tour until 2025. A pity.

PIPPA: Yeah, because the only place the best guys are going to distance him is on a severe uphill finish, and it won't be by that much. Vingegaard and Pogačar are better climbers, but if there's a descent to the finish, Pidcock's going to leave them behind.

DAVID: How do you describe his career to this point?

PIPPA: It's already spectacular in terms of results, but it could be better. He came in straight at the top. Reminds me of Stephen Roche when he arrived – a new pro, first year on the road, goes to Paris–Nice and Sean Kelly only just beats him. It's the same level of natural talent. But Stephen wasn't doing all the other stuff that Pidcock's doing.

DAVID: I've the sense that he has a smaller engine that Vingegaard and Pogačar. What do you think?

PIPPA: He's got the ability to win a grand tour.

DAVID: But a Tour de France against the best guys? Can you see him winning that?

PIPPA: No. He'd need Vingegaard and Pogačar to have bad years.

*   *   *

Our drive from Bourg-d'Oisans was even slower than we feared. This happens every year on this particular day. Tour organisers honour Bastille Day by making sure the day's stage is worthy of the national holiday, and the people come in their tens of thousands. It seems they all want to leave at the same time and on the same road. We inch forward on the D1091 through the villages of Livet, Rioupéroux, Salignière, Les Clavaux, Gavet, Séchilienne.

In the early 20th century this was a thriving industrial region, hydro-electrical plants everywhere, thousands of jobs in electricity-dependent industries, but then as the industrial age in France was overtaken by the information age, the hydro-electric plants closed and the Romanche valley declined. Every time I've travelled through this valley in daylight, I'm struck by the number of villages that live in the shadow of the mountains.

To take our minds off out snail-like progress to Grenoble, I start a stupid game with Pippa.

DAVID: If big cities were bike riders, who'd be who? I think Geraint Thomas would be London: pretty clean, solid, enduring.

PIPPA: And in decline? Anyway, that's a terrible thing to say about a Welshman. Paris? Who'd be Paris?

DAVID: Wout van Aert, definitely. Classy but with attitude. What about Pogačar? What city for him?

PIPPA: New York, though I've never been to New York.

DAVID: No. Can't see him as New York. He's more Sydney. Modern, looks great, likes to think of itself as down-to-earth but with a deep-rooted confidence. That's Sydney. That's Pogačar.

PIPPA: Sydney Pogačar actually sounds like an interesting name.

DAVID: Primoz Roglič? I'm thinking of Prague, an Eastern European city that transcends its geographic location. Roglič has an Eastern European mentality but a Western outlook.

PIPPA: OK, hit me with it, David. What would Robert Millar be? If you say Glasgow, I'll cut up rough.

DAVID: No, Glasgow is too predictable, and you're definitely not Glasgow. Let me think for a minute.

PIPPA: Yes, think. You'll have to be careful. An entire friendship hangs in the balance here.

DAVID: I know. I know. I walked myself into this.

PIPPA: Remember during the Lance years when you became so toxic that you were left at the side of the road and people didn't want to drive with you? This time, as you're thumbing a lift, you won't even be able to think that your suffering is noble.

DAVID: Seriously, I think Robert Millar is Berlin. Troubled backstory, not sure whether it wanted to look east or west, but in the end things got resolved and it's now one of the coolest cities in the world.

PIPPA: I have to say I'm flattered. Berlin, I like that. I think if you were a cyclist you'd be Torremolinos.

DAVID: Torremolinos?

PIPPA: Yeah. Torremolinos.

DAVID: That seems a bit underwhelming, Pippa? Why Torremolinos?

PIPPA: Well … popular back in the day. Not so popular for a while. Then a bit of a comeback.

DAVID: But Torremolinos? It's not really a city, is it?

PIPPA: And you're not really a cyclist, are you?

Chapter 15

Michael Matthews attributed his victory to a conversation he'd had last night with his wife Katarina. Together they talked through the stage. This goes to show that people need to speak more with their spouses about their work. Michael and Katarina had been shooting the breeze about his Tour so far: two second places but no victory. *Not good enough*, thought Katarina

She told him he needed to gamble. He needed to do the unexpected, to be unpredictable. In other words, to be a man. Michael thought that his better half had a point. So, from the start at Saint-Étienne this morning, he tried to escape the sanctuary of the peloton. Michael would have been forgiven for stopping at a payphone before lunch to call Katarina, just to tell her that her ideas are harder in practice than in theory. The would-be breakaway wasn't going to succeed the first time he tried, nor the second, but eventually the gambler got his reward. After 50 kilometres today, 23 riders broke free. Michael was one of them.

They were free, but Michael wasn't entirely happy. Unlike many of his rivals in the group, he didn't have a teammate riding shotgun. Then the word came from the team car.

Nineteen of Michael's 22 fellow escapees could climb. That was important, because at the finish in Mende there was a 3-kilometre climb that might, in places, be too steep for Michael, but would be meat and drink to the 19 climbers.

What was he to do? Katarina's words rang in his ears: 'Don't be afraid to take a risk.' So 50 kilometres out from Mende, Michael counter-attacked from the group, and only three riders could go with him.

On the early part of that climb to the finish in Mende, Michael got rid of his two remaining breakaway rivals. Alberto Bettiol then came from behind to briefly overtake and go ahead of him, but Michael rallied to achieve a notable victory.

Occasionally, things just fall into place at the Tour. That Saturday in Mende, the Centre de Presse was 500 metres from the finish. And, hallelujah, our hotel was just five kilometres away in the centre of town. More than that, the Hôtel du Pont Roupt was pretty smart. It even had a sauna. Forty years of Tour de France hotels, this was a first, even if we didn't have time to use it.

Over dinner in our hotel that night we talked about Katarina Matthews' contribution to the outcome of the day's race and somehow, of course, the conversation wound its way back to Robert Millar

DAVID: One thing that made me curious about you, Pippa, and I suppose it's a sign of our age, but you grew up in a time when transitioning was almost unheard of, and so you ended up having this other life that had extraordinary parts to it career-wise, the kind of things many of us can't imagine for ourselves, and you also had the ordinary, conventional stuff. You got married.

PIPPA: You seem surprised?

DAVID: Maybe not surprised, but curious. How did you meet? And how old were you and what career stage were you at?

PIPPA: I met Sylvie in 1981. I was in my second year as a pro. I'd moved to live near Troyes because I was friends with Pascal Simon. In Sylvie's family there were three daughters and they all followed cycling. Pascal's brother Jerome, who also became a pro, was attached to the middle sister, who was called Nadine. And there was an amateur rider called Jean-Paul, and he was attached to the older sister. I started going out with Sylvie, who was the youngest daughter. She was about three years younger than me. So I'd have been 22, 23, and she'd have been 19 or 20. We got together, we split up for a bit and then we got back together again. She had an accident, she hurt her back.

DAVID: Riding a bike?

PIPPA: No, she wasn't a cyclist, none of the sisters were. Which suited me quite fine. Because although she followed cycling and used to go to races with her sisters, I didn't actively seek out somebody that was into cycling. Because I don't want to come home to find the world I've just left waiting for me: how did the race go?, all of that. I didn't want to have to explain stuff about my work.

DAVID: So, how would you describe Sylvie?

PIPPA: Sylvie was pretty, intelligent. And quite independent. So I quite liked that she had that independence, beyond the kind of physical attraction. She was fairly strong-willed as well. And I liked that. I like people with a bit of character. I don't like to hang around with people that just agree with you all the time.

DAVID: Which is the basis of our relationship!

PIPPA: Well, it's definitely not your prettiness, David. Anyway, Sylvie and I got on fine at first, things were OK.

DAVID: When you asked Sylvie to marry you, did you think, I'll get married to Sylvie and everything will be easier on the dysphoria front?

PIPPA: I think that I thought I'd be a normal person. Because you feel so different, you crave normal situations. You look for stability, at least in your external world. As for the internal part, you just try to cope with the turmoil. The outside world didn't see any of that, because you fit into all the social structures around you. But on the inside, it's a complete mess. I wanted to feel normal, I wanted to be normal. And I wanted to do things that made it seem there was normality to my life. But being a pro cyclist isn't a normal existence. And then with the dysphoria stuff going on, it just adds to the complication.

DAVID: If you're going out with Sylvie, the other riders aren't wondering, is there anything different about you?

PIPPA: No, you just want to fit it into the whole culture of male–female relationships. Yeah. Perfectly presentable girlfriend.

DAVID: Did you feel Sylvie was a good person?

PIPPA: Yeah, she was a good person. Naturally quiet. I liked that. Having said that, Linda is naturally talkative. I like that too. Very, very different. And it's quite strange that I found an attraction in Linda that has lasted, even though you'd think I was more suited to the quieter person.

DAVID: You always thought it would be somebody relatively quiet?

PIPPA: I thought it would be somebody relatively quiet. A quiet partner in the background, supportive, a steady hand on the ship that was sailing into stormy waters.

DAVID: And were you absolutely intent on keeping your dysphoria a secret from Sylvie? You'd never have mentioned that, when you were a kid, you had this desire to dress as a girl and buy girls' clothes?

PIPPA: No, I'd never have mentioned it. So then, when eventually it was discovered I had women's clothes in my possession, for Sylvie it must have been a bit of a shock. But that wasn't the reason why our relationship went downhill. It had gradually eroded, like things do. I don't know if we grew apart or if I became more difficult to live with. I started to shut down emotionally. I turned off that whole system, the emotional system.

DAVID: Why?

PIPPA: It wasn't related to my career but to my personal issues. I started to shut down all that kind of stuff. And then, because Sylvie is quiet, there were awkward silences for days, even weeks, between us. We just didn't speak. In hindsight, when you stop communicating with each other, then it's only going to go one way. Sylvie wasn't getting any support from me, and I wasn't getting any care from her. So, you know, the whole thing goes badly then.

DAVID: And Sylvie would never have said to you, 'What's wrong?'

PIPPA: No. That wasn't her nature, and I wouldn't have been in a mood to explain what was wrong.

DAVID: That would have been quite difficult for her?

PIPPA: Oh, yeah. It was.

DAVID: Would you accept more of the responsibility for it going downhill?

PIPPA: No, not really. I think each of us had our own challenges. I'm the youngest of my family and she was the youngest. And I think in these circumstances, you both come with a different mindset. She was different to her other sisters, much quieter than they were.

DAVID: How did you feel about getting married?

PIPPA: I got married in December 1985, when I left Peugeot and went to Panasonic. We went to live in Belgium. It was a whole new world for Sylvie outside of the family unit. And it went quite badly.

DAVID: Had you thought that getting away from the family might be helpful?

PIPPA: I didn't think anything beyond my own selfishness. As in, this is where I need to be workwise.

DAVID: Would Panasonic have wanted you in Belgium?

PIPPA: I really don't know why I went there. Maybe to prove that I could be a Belgian cyclist for some stupid reason. I look at it and I think, *Why did I go to Belgium? Why didn't I go the other direction?* I lived south-east of Paris. I don't think there was any reason, just an instinctive decision: I'm going to live in Belgium.

DAVID: Where in Belgium did you choose?

PIPPA: We lived in a place called Wielsbeke, which is near Waregem. I ended up living there because there was a guy I knew that ran the carpet factory who was into cycling. So he arranged to find me a house to rent and smoothed my passage through the local mayor's office for my paperwork and arranged car insurance and all the other stuff that can be difficult when you go to another country.

DAVID: How did Sylvie feel about going to Belgium?

PIPPA: I don't know. You'd have to ask her. She got bored. She got a job in the carpet factory. I don't know why she went to work there but she did. I think just to pass the time, you know, because she'd be stuck at home without anybody to talk to.

DAVID: She'd have missed the family support network?

PIPPA: She did. Already after the first year of Belgium, she was probably struggling a bit. And then the second year, she knew she'd had enough. And she'd said she'd had enough. And I'd probably had enough of Peter Post by then, that I too wanted to get out of that.

DAVID: Given the dysphoria, and the stuff that was unresolved in your head, could you really have had a marriage that worked?

PIPPA: Probably not. It would be quite easy for me to take three-quarters of the blame for the failure of the marriage. But I don't feel that would be fair on me. People will ask, 'Oh, did your marriage end because of dysphoria?' No, it ended because we stopped looking after each other. The reasons for that are complex, and maybe the dysphoria came into it, but I honestly don't know if Sylvie had a problem with my dressing in female clothes because we never discussed it. So what happened between us remains unresolved and we will never explain it to each other. Looking back, I was married but emotionally I wasn't invested in it.

DAVID: Did a part of you think, *When I'm married to Sylvie, that will take care of my gender dysphoria?*

PIPPA: Yeah, in some way, that was the hope. You think, *I'll get married, I'll settle down. I'll have a family life and that will cure me. Forget all this nonsense about transition, you're not going to do that. It's not possible, try to forget about it.* You try to bury it by being 'normal', having a normal life. But obviously you've so much stuff in your head, you can't be normal. That hurt my relationships with other people. I couldn't be emotionally attached.

DAVID: When did your son Edward arrive?

PIPPA: Edward arrived at the end of the second year. So Sylvie got pregnant in 1987 and Edward was born in '88. Our relationship started to deteriorate when we were in Belgium. And I think that was just because I hadn't realised that for her to step outside of her family unit wasn't going to do her any good. Because for me, I was fine outside of that environment.

DAVID: What impact did Edward's arrival have? Were things better for a while then?

PIPPA: I had that funny feeling that things would get better, because Sylvie had something to occupy her. When a woman has a child, they often become really focused on that child. A lot of the husbands or the partners who get neglected resent that. I felt a little resentment that I was getting even less of her attention. I think that just added to the difficulty of the whole thing. I wouldn't say it went downhill immediately, because you're constantly tired and focused on looking after a small baby. But then, you know, when your child gets to three and becomes a little bit more interesting, you realise that you and your partner haven't looked at each other for the last three years. We haven't been the couple that we once were. We've been the people that looked after the baby. You haven't looked after each other anymore.

DAVID: All through this, Robert Millar didn't talk to anyone about his marriage? Who was your most common roommate?

PIPPA: Pascal Simon at Peugeot.

DAVID: You didn't tell him anything about your marriage?

PIPPA: I'd never have mentioned my marriage to Pascal. I'd never ask him about his. It just didn't happen. Bike racing, cars, tomorrow's stage, stuff men talk about. And the usual crap. Who's cheating with whom? Who's going to this team, that team? The peloton isn't a place for emotional support.

DAVID: In terms of the ending of your relationship with Sylvie, when did it really come to a head?

PIPPA: Oh, probably, I'd say the end of '94, the start of '95.

DAVID: You've been ten years together at this point and you're getting kind of towards the end of your career?

PIPPA: I'm getting towards the end of my career, and I'm getting towards the end of my marriage, which I don't think is a consequence of me being at the end of my cycling career. It just happened at the same time.

DAVID: What happened after the marriage ended?

PIPPA: I came back to the UK in '95.

DAVID: Did Sylvie become aware of your dysphoria?

PIPPA: Yeah, she did.

DAVID: When?

PIPPA: Let me think, probably 1990. So we'd been married about five years.

DAVID: She found clothes?

PIPPA: Yeah, she found clothes. A 'What's this?' discussion took place.

DAVID: Was that very upsetting for you both?

PIPPA: Yeah, it was. If I think about it, yeah, it was fairly upsetting.

DAVID: And how do you respond when Sylvie asks what's this about?

PIPPA: Just to tell the truth. I need to do that now and again, for my own sanity. This was a bit like it was with my father, you know. There wasn't really a discussion of, 'Is this going to go any further?' Or, 'Is this just some kind of sexual thing?' or whatever. There was never this discussion. And that's one of the things that's quite apparent about the whole transsexuality thing: people, those who are really close to whoever's thinking about transition, it's a difficult topic to bring up because they don't want to believe that it's going to happen.

DAVID: Is it that for Sylvie or your dad to have a full discussion about it would be to validate it, to normalise it?

PIPPA: Yes, so that doesn't happen. There's no proper discussion. And they don't want to think about it. Not if the outcome is going to be that you change sides. People can't imagine what you're going through.

DAVID: Did Sylvie tell her family what she discovered?

PIPPA: I don't know. I don't know if she told her parents. I've never asked her and I probably never will because we've split up now and that part of my life is over. Even now, when it came out that I'd transitioned and I'm living as a woman, I've never had any contact with her. No conversation where she's said, 'What happened to you?' or, 'I knew this was gonna happen.' There's been none of that.

DAVID: No little message to wish you well in your transition?

PIPPA: We did wish each other well in our lives after we split up.

*　　*　　*

Our resting place in Mende was the Hôtel du Pont Roupt. It was one of the better ones, a three-star hotel that really was quite classy. We ate in the restaurant and the food was great. I thought about what Pippa had said about her marriage to Sylvie and realised afterwards it was possible to feel equal sympathy for two parties in a failing marriage.

Mende itself is the kind of town where you get there and marvel that France has so many wondrous places you never knew existed. The Tour, though, is a race of one-night stands, and after breakfast we're soon on the road again. Two hundred kilometres to Carcassonne. It was Sunday, traffic was light and the weather majestic. We'd travelled for an hour on the A75 when I broke the bad news. 'Pippa, I'm sorry, I've left my mobile phone at the hotel. We're going to have to turn back.'

She said no problem, and calmly swung off at the next exit. Two hours added to our journey. Thank goodness Robert Millar wasn't driving.

Chapter 16

15 July 2021
Stage 18, Pau to Luz Ardiden – 129.7 km

During the 2021 Tour a story appeared in *Le Parisien* quoting two anonymous sources accusing Team Bahrain Victorious of doping. Both admitted they had no evidence. The French anti-doping police, based in Marseille, decided to come and see for themselves. After a four-hour search, the police left.

'I didn't sleep at all,' Sonny Colbrelli, the team's sprinter, said. 'We don't deserve this. In our world, if you ride strongly, they say you're up to something. If you ride slowly, you're a nobody. They turned everything upside down. We all collaborated. We all underwent an analysis of our hair too. They didn't find anything.'

For the Luz Ardiden stage, the Centre de Presse was 25 kilometres away in Pierrefitte-Nestalas, a village of some 1,100 people. As is clear from TV pictures, things get congested in the mountains, especially when the race finishes at the summit. Four or five hundred press cars lumbering to the top adds to the chaos and increases the danger. So the press centre is often down in the valley, or out of harm's way in some nearby town.

Pierrefitte-Nestalas is one of those places. In our marquee Centre de Presse we attend remote post-race press conferences, connected by a video link to the riders at the finish. There are the usual questions for the yellow jersey and also an interesting interview with Matej Mohorič, the Bahrain rider, who talks about the French police raid on their hotel the night before.

Pippa files her story for Cyclingnews, I get mine off to *The Times*. From the press centre to the Hotel Astoria Vatican in Lourdes is just 22 kilometres, but the traffic is painful. For 55 minutes we inch our way towards Lourdes, using conversation to keep our minds off the evening meal we both crave.

DAVID: When I heard about the police raid, my first thought was, 'There must be something in this. Why are they targeting Bahrain? No smoke without fire.'

PIPPA: I thought about the story that first appeared in *Le Parisien*, the one that led to this raid, and straightaway thought of one particular team boss who's known to whinge when his riders are beaten by riders he considers inferior. To people like him, the fact that Mohorič, Pogačar and Roglič are all Slovenian is suspicious. He wonders how a small country can produce three outstanding riders. To me, that attitude is xenophobic.

DAVID: What do you think about Bahrain?

PIPPA: I believe Mohorič when he says there's nothing to be found. Things have moved on in the sport. I don't think teams have doping programmes anymore. I also feel half of the press room is looking for a doping story, or expects there will be one.

DAVID: I don't see that?

PIPPA: Maybe that's just me. People do expect the issue to come up.

DAVID: If it comes up, it has to be dealt with. If there's a police raid, it has to be reported. The reason I don't agree with you about the journalists is that the numbers in the press room are down, and many who are there now work for specialist cycling media outlets and they want to believe the sport has changed for the better.

PIPPA: It's the nerdy ones now.

DAVID: A bit of that, for sure.

PIPPA: The way Mohorič explained it, was I tempted to disbelieve him? No. But I thought what he was saying fell on deaf ears. I can believe what he was saying, but I don't think everybody else can.

DAVID: I felt people in the press room were sympathetic to him and what happened to the team.

PIPPA: Yes, because it was three in the morning when some were getting to bed. To Mohorič, it felt like a personal attack on him and his teammates. I understand that.

DAVID: I spoke off the record to one of the Bahrain backroom team and he said he'd asked the policeman leading the raid why they were targeting Bahrain and the cop said they'd read the piece in *Le Parisien* where the unnamed French team manager and the unnamed rider made their accusations. That was their intelligence.

PIPPA: In the Tour, the sponsors attach themselves to the race because the publicity is so big. And the police come from Marseille, make a raid, knowing the publicity for them is huge. If they turn up at the Tour, it looks like they're doing something in the war against doping, even though there's a good chance we'll never see any prosecutions or hear about it again.

DAVID: Last year they raided Arkéa–Samsic and I remember having the same feeling – 'Ah, there must be something going on there. Why else would the police turn up at the hotel?' But we're a year down the road and there have been no charges and we're left to conclude that nothing was found, but we're not told this. Do you think the French police would be allowed to turn up at the Paris hotel of Atlético Madrid or Liverpool or Inter Milan the night before a Champions League match against PSG?

PIPPA: Not a chance.

DAVID: Is it possible the Tour de France organisation doesn't complain because it likes the intrigue that a police raid adds to the race?

PIPPA: No doubt, it adds to the story. Then it becomes, 'Are they cheating?' Are these exceptional performances, or are we being done over again? Can we believe what we see? This is all part of the intrigue at the Tour.

DAVID: The good news, of course, is that our hotel in Lourdes is just a short distance from the Sanctuary of Our Lady of Lourdes, where sick and disabled people have been coming for decades to be cured by the healing waters. I appreciate that your great-grandma, a proud Protestant who used to celebrate the 12th of July in Glasgow, is probably turning in her grave at the thought of you in Lourdes, but I think you should come with me to the shrine. Growing up in Ireland, Lourdes was a big thing.

PIPPA: Nah, I'm not a believer.

DAVID: Did I tell you the story about the Irish guy who had a bad accident, damaged his spine and claimed £1 million from an insurance company because he was left in a wheelchair? The insurers felt sure he was exaggerating his injuries and put a private investigator on the case. It ends up in court and the judge awards the guy his £1 million. Walking away from the courtroom, the investigator tells the guy in the wheelchair that he's a fraud and he, the investigator, is determined to follow him wherever he goes. 'In that case, you'll be coming with me to Lourdes in two weeks' time where you're going to see an incredible miracle.'

PIPPA: During my racing career, I stayed in Lourdes a number of times. Do you know what I've never understood?

DAVID: No idea.

PIPPA: If Lourdes is so miraculous, how come there's a pharmacy on every corner?

DAVID: Oh ye of little faith!

*   *   *

A year after the police raid on Bahrain Victorious, there were further raids on the team before the start of the 2022 Tour de France in Copenhagen. Police searched the homes of riders, as well as their hotel rooms in Copenhagen. They provided photos of the pills they confiscated. It emerged the police had found the drug Tizanidine during their initial 2021 search, and there were traces of the drug in hair samples taken from three riders.

Tizanidine is a medication to treat muscle spasticity resulting from spinal cord injuries or multiple sclerosis. It's taken to relax muscles. However, under the World Anti-Doping Code, it's not a prohibited substance. Whether it's right to use a prescription drug for off-label purposes is another matter, as is whether Tizanidine has any performance-enhancing value.

Olivier Rabin, scientific director of the World Anti-Doping Agency, is far from certain that it does. In an interview with

L'Équipe he said that WADA would re-evaluate the drug, while adding that the side-effects of the drug, which include dizziness, drowsiness, hallucinations, vomiting and stomach pain, wouldn't make it an obvious performance enhancer.

In February 2024, it was reported that following the 2020 raid on the Arkéa team during that year's Tour de France, Fredy Alexander Gonzales Torres, a Colombian doctor, had been charged 'with possession of a prohibited substance or method for use by an athlete without medical justification, in the case of equipment, tools, products and devices allowing the implementation of perfusions and/or intravenous injections'.

At the time, Gonzales Torres was doctor to the Arkéa team leader Nairo Quintana and was expected to stand trial in September 2024. Nothing was reported in September, leading one to conclude that the trial has yet to take place. By the time Gonzales Torres has his day in court, almost five years will have passed since the raid on the team hotel.

The Centre de Presse is just 22 kilometres from Lourdes, but with the traffic we progress at a funereal pace. We weave our way through the town's narrow streets and it's almost 10 p.m. when we get to the Hôtel Astoria Vatican, a good name for a hotel in this place. Every time we pass a pharmacy, Pippa chirps up, 'Oh, look, there's another.'

Her staunchly Protestant great-grandma would be proud of her.

*   *   *

After our overnight stay at the Astoria, we consider our options over breakfast the following morning. This is a daily occurrence. We can drive to the start at Mourenx or go straight to the finish at Libourne. Three days from the end of a Tour already decided in Tadej Pogačar's favour, we take the easier option. Three hours will get us to Libourne.

Without knowing exactly why, I'd felt that when Robert Millar's career ended, he'd continue to live in France. He spoke the language, he'd spent almost half of his life there, so why would he go back to the UK? On the drive to Libourne, I enquired.

DAVID: What made you leave France and settle in England?

PIPPA: Because I realised in France that if I was going to transition, it wasn't going to happen in France, because the care system and the medical system for that to happen were worse than in the UK. The situation regarding gay rights, trans rights, was worse and, socially, it was even more of a taboo subject than in the UK.

DAVID: Would you have said that at this time [1995] the UK was a trans-friendly country?

PIPPA: Oh no, no. But France is a Catholic country, and even though French people talk about the sexual stuff that happens between adults, at least back then it was quite a straight kind of dynamic. They were good with heterosexuality, but all the other stuff that exists, they didn't really want to know about that.

DAVID: Some guy having a mistress, that was fine?

PIPPA: Fine, but some guy having a same-sex relationship and being in a heterosexual marriage, that would have been a complete scandal.

DAVID: Would the thought of transition have been constantly on your mind through the early 1990s, when your marriage was on a rocky road?

PIPPA: Yes, I'd say from probably the last couple of years in the 80s. As I was leaving France in 1995, it had become apparent that I was going to have to deal with this. As far back as my 20s I decided I was going to deal with it after I'd finished my career. My career was coming to an end and I knew I was going to have to face up to what was going to happen to me. I knew I needed professional help. And that was one of the reasons why I went back to the UK. The services there were poor, you know, not appropriate, but they were certainly better than France.

DAVID: Did the idea of transitioning fill you with dread or hope?

PIPPA: I didn't know. I had no idea what was going to happen to me when I went for medical help. I knew from the point I'd reached in my life that I couldn't go on with the anguish and depression that I had. When I arrived back in the UK, it took another five years to really get it started. Dressing as a female wasn't enough and wasn't in any way lessening the inner turmoil. So then I needed professional help to find out what my options were and if there was a treatment. How would that work? What are the stages you need to go through?

DAVID: Casting the net a bit wider, how were you as a parent to Edward, and to Lydia, the daughter you've had with Linda?

PIPPA: I still try my best, but I just don't feel like a good parent.

DAVID: Why not?

PIPPA: I don't feel I have enough empathy with my children. And I don't know if that comes from my own kind of background. I feel like I'm a slightly below average parent.

Good, in some respects, quite useless in others. And it's quite hard to say that because it makes me sad, but I don't feel there's any way out of it.

DAVID: Have you always felt like this?

PIPPA: I've come to realise that's what I've been like.

DAVID: If you see the problem, you can address it?

PIPPA: No, I'd still judge myself as a below average parent.

DAVID: Was it possible to maintain a good relationship with Edward, given the stuff that was going on in your life?

PIPPA: I don't think he knew. When I told him that I was going to transition, I don't think he really understood because he was very young. When I decided to transition, he was coming to his adolescence. There's no resentment from my transition. Any resentment is going to come from other things that happened, as he grew up and the marriage fell apart. I've said to him, you know, that the marriage ended because we stopped looking after each other, not because I did this or your mum did that.

DAVID: What made you choose Edward as a name?

PIPPA: Sylvie didn't want a French name because she's quite independent and rebellious. I had no problem with the name. I didn't choose it because of Eddy Merckx. The choice was between Edwin and Edward. And I thought I don't know anybody called Edwin, and that it sounds slightly poncey to me.

DAVID: Do you not remember Edwig Van Hooydonck, Lanterne Rouge in the Tour de France?

PIPPA: That would have been another reason not to go for Edwin. Too similar to Edwig.

DAVID: Didn't Van Hooydonck twice win the Tour of Flanders?

PIPPA: Of course I remember him. He's the one that was behind the invention of knee-warmers. The first rider one to cut up his leg-warmers and turn them into knee-warmers. And we all went, 'Oh boy, why did you cut your leg warmers?' and he just said it feels better. Then we all discovered he was right. So he invented the knee-warmer. He was six foot plus. His leg-warmers were so long you could put them on an elephant's trunk.

DAVID: And now you can buy knee-warmers?

PIPPA: Now there's knee-warmers in every length, every material, waterproof, warm, cold, the whole thing. In our day it was just a pair of leg-warmers.

DAVID: There you go, I never knew about Edwig's role in the history of knee-warmers.

Interlude

On the day of the surgery I pack my suitcase in the way I packed so often when leaving for a bike race. My hotel room will be waiting here when I return in a few days. Tair comes to fetch me and takes me from the hotel to the hospital.

We do the paperwork. I sign in. The last paper I sign is the form releasing the clinic from responsibility for what may happen to me. If anything goes wrong it's my responsibility. It says so right there on the paperwork: 'Things may go wrong. You may die.' I'm at peace with that.

I sign my name and I wait, and after a few minutes somebody in scrubs comes to fetch me.

I'm led to pre-op. Happily, Dr Chettawut looks wide awake. He has a long day ahead of him, with two operations to perform after he's done with me. I'm happy to be his first task.

I'm given a gown and they place me on a gurney. By now I realise, to my surprise, that I'm terrified. As they wheel me down a corridor I lie on my back staring up at the fluorescent ceiling lights passing above me. We enter a lift and I feel us rise slowly to the floor where the operating theatre is. I'm wheeled into a prep room and left there for about five minutes.

Everything then seems to hit me at once. The years from looking over at the girls in the schoolyard, the early days of dressing up as a girl, the years of educating myself gradually about what my feelings were and why I had them. Years of suppression. Years of depression. Years of hormone treatment.

Here I am now, and I still can't believe this. I'm really scared. I'm shaking. Sweating. My brain feels like I'm in a slow-motion bike crash. Muffled, distorted shouts, my stomach jumping, my guts twisting. The feeling of falling. I'm going to hit something soon, so brace yourself, for fuck's sake.

If somebody comes along now and asks me again, there's a very good chance that I'm going to say, 'No, I'm not sure. Look, I'm out of here.'

I've never felt so frightened.

A year ago when I had my facial surgery, which was a longer operation, it took over eight hours – I wasn't at all scared about that. I was so calm. I wasn't thinking about waking up being beautiful or especially nice-looking. But I was certain and confident. I knew when I was in San Francisco that I wanted to pass that scrutiny that every trans person feels. When people looked at me in the street, even if I was ugly, that didn't matter to me. I knew I'd rather be an ugly woman than a nice-looking man.

At the time I'd thought, *I can spend this amount of money on a really good car or I can spend it on a better face. Which will serve me longer? Which is more important to me? When I'm sitting on a bus and a load of teenagers get on and they look over at me, do I want them to think that I was previously male? Recently male? Or do I want them to glance over and think,* There's a woman, *and not give me a second glance?*

Now I'm lying on the gurney in the prep room in Bangkok and I'm still shaking. Actually physically shaking in a way that I've never known in my life, before or since. Am I experiencing this because I've already grown used to passing that scrutiny? For a while now there have been no more second glances. I realise now how much that meant to me. This surgery is different because it's something that I've talked myself into. Nobody knew that I had male genitals and nobody will know that they have been subtracted. Am I going under general anaesthetic just for myself? Is it too far?

The people who are to do the anaesthetics breeze into the room. They're masked and they don't speak any English. They focus on arranging all the drains and tubes for putting the different chemicals into me. They start about their business straight away and, once they're busy, I suddenly feel OK. It should have been more frightening having these wordless people going through this strange invasive routine, but I was OK with it because for them it was routine.

I'm wheeled into the operating theatre. Dr Chettawut and his assistants are there.

'Are you OK?' he asks.

I say, 'I'm OK now, thanks.'

The anaesthetic will flow into my arm at various stages during the next few hours. The last thing I remember is the guy saying to me, 'You're going to feel like there's cold in your arm.' He wants me to count to ten. One … two … three … four … five … six … sev …

* * *

I wake up. It's over. I'm in a bed in a recovery room. Four or five hours have passed.

I seem to have a lot going on between my legs. A major wound, for one thing. Soreness. Swelling. And? It dawns on me what else I'm feeling down there. Jesus, I have a big nappy on. Talk about being born again.

The first thing, though, was a question for myself.

Right, now what?

Because it's done. Now what happens? Now what is my life going to be?

Before asking, *Did it go well?* or *Am I OK?*, I was wrestling with that question. *Now what? What happens to me?*

The scale of what had just happened crept over me while lying on that recovery bed. I hadn't thought about what I was supposed to feel when I woke up. Was I meant to be happy or jubilant? No. I wasn't feeling either of those things.

Just the question going around my head. *Now what? How will this work? What is going to happen?* There's no more process. No next level. It's done. And dusted. Or at least, properly cleaned up.

I wasn't yet ready to wonder if all the new bits would work. I was just sleepily shocked. Nothing prepares you for what happens when you wake up after that strange sleep.

Perhaps it's different for people who've hated their body and hated having male genitalia. It might be a major thing for them. But, I say again, I never hated that body. It allowed me to be a bike rider, and being a bike rider allowed me to pay for waking up in this bed in Thailand. It allowed me to solve what the writer Jan Morris called 'the conundrum'.

I stayed in Thailand for 23 days after my surgery. I was there for almost a month in total. I stayed five days in the hospital in a private bed with private care. They checked the dressings every day and put new ones on. They checked for infections and they checked all the stitches. For the first couple of days the dressing was changed twice a day, then once a day towards the end.

I went back to the hotel after five days. On about the fourth day post-op I'd had to stand up. As anybody who's had general anaesthetic knows, if you've been lying in your bed for a long time, your legs don't work. And in my case, I didn't know what else worked or how.

I'd been rejigged. New plumbing.

When I stood up after four days, the legs didn't work too well. The nurses had to help me to the bathroom. I sat down on the toilet and tried to pee. Previously I'd been using a catheter, just dribbling (willy nilly, you could say) into it. Now a bit of forcing is needed. It doesn't come easily. I'll have to learn to rework the muscle that closes the urinary tract. That was OK, though. It all worked.

I stood up and got a couple of steps in before the nurses needed to help me back to bed. By the fifth day I was able to get out of the bed and walk to the bathroom with the nurses watching me in case I fell over. Then they allowed me to go back to the hotel.

I'd been in this post-operative limbo before.

In San Francisco I'd loitered for almost a month following my eight to nine hours on the operating table. You can't get on a plane for a while after having that level of work done on your head – they'd been moving the bones about in my face, I had internal stitching and stitches in my scalp. You don't fly with major wounds, the change of pressure on the plane makes it inadvisable. So I rested and healed for a month.

Mr Douglas Ousterhout was my surgeon in San Francisco. He'd been carefully chosen too, picked because he was a pioneer of facial feminisation surgery, the art of transforming the faces of transgender men and women to better match their gender identity.

Plus, a little bit of fun trivia, Mr Ousterhout lives in the house in Pacific Heights where the movie *Mrs. Doubtfire* was filmed.

Remember that movie, in which Robin Williams transformed himself from a divorced dad into an elderly female with a vaguely Scottish accent? Would my transition be as simple as it seemed in *Mrs. Doubtfire*?

Another odd thing was that Mr Ousterhout turned out to have an interest in cycling. I had a sort of single-minded view of what I was doing there, and then this curiously avuncular man popped my bubble, asking, 'Did I know Greg LeMond? What's he like? Had I ever met Lance Armstrong ...?'

The care in San Francisco had been excellent but Thailand didn't lag behind that level in any respect. If you go to a good surgeon, you get excellent care and the chances of anything going wrong are minimal. I've met a few people since then who've also been to Dr Chettawut. They've all said the same thing. No problems. All went well.

I got no infections during the entire time I was there. After about ten days in the hotel a stitch burst and they restitched it instantly. It wasn't anything internal, not a major issue.

I thought about Linda a lot. In Thailand I spoke to her probably every two or three days as my support. There was nobody else that I talked to. I knew, though, that my being in Thailand was quite difficult for Linda. For her too, the operation came at the end of the process. Or the beginning of the end.

She had to deal with the change part as well. The finality of it was bigger for Linda. She hadn't signed up for any of this. She hadn't spent decades thinking about this. None of it was as straightforward for her as it was for me. She hadn't felt compelled through the different stages of transition. She'd come along, supporting when she could, but obviously wondering where would it end. *Where would we end up?*

There's a whole discussion in the trans world about the fact that you have to allow everybody the time to deal with it. People close to you have to grieve, they have to get over the anger that they've got. People will be supportive, but nobody's happy with it. They don't want you to be unhappy but your transition is painful for them. There's an element of 'Are we there yet?' to their questions. Sometimes they worry that if they'd made you happier, perhaps you'd never have felt this need. *Will you regret the next step?* they worry.

In Thailand I wasn't happy with the actuality of just being there. The operation was something that I'd accepted rather than something that I'd chosen. It was a part of the process. If I could have avoided it, I would have. If I could have been born female, I'd have greatly preferred that. The choices that I've made have all been about how to deal with it. Having to make those choices hasn't been an altogether happy experience.

Sometimes things were quite strained between Linda and me. By the time I left Thailand I wasn't sure how it would all work with her. I was hopeful, but I couldn't feel certain. I thought that we'd be OK, but I knew it wasn't going to be straightforward and easy. I knew that she harboured resentment for all this. I fully understood that. It takes a long time for everyone. The need to recognise the grief of others and to give them the time for a grieving process is a responsibility we all carry. You can't just browbeat somebody through it all. *Why can't you just bloody well be happy for me?* That won't work.

Linda fell in love with a man. She fell in love with Robert Millar. And Robert Millar has changed in a way that Linda never imagined when she fell in love. We've moved very slowly through the process, but there's a finality to it now; we've reached this moment where I've just been surgically separated from the last landmarks of manhood.

To me, with my hard, functional view of my body, after three years of hormone treatment those bits were never going to work properly again. For Linda they represented something else beyond their function, I'd think. For me, as I've said, my body was a tool.

For Linda, it was a more integral part of the person she fell in love with.

So the final step will be quite a struggle. I expected all along that it would be hard but I'd had the advantage of a lifetime of thinking about it all. Linda came along stage by stage, wondering if each progression would finally solve things for me.

And now what is Linda left with of the man she fell for? The same soul, the same essence, except I hope a more peaceful one, more aligned with itself. Happier. The same heart that still loves her.

I hope that the body she's left to look at, although it's packed with different hormones and decorated with more discreet bits and bobs, will come to represent a correction to her. If I was born male by sex and feminine by gender, this in the end was the only correction I could make. I'm less of Robert Millar because he is no more, but I'm more of myself. It is, I hope, that self – myself – that she loves and will still recognise in my altered body.

In Thailand it's a relief that the process is finally over, but there's been no euphoria along the way. This isn't a stage that's been won with arms upraised. It's another part of a very long climb.

*   *   *

For those weeks in the Bangkok hotel, the nurses came every day to check on me. They did the dressings and they made sure that I could perform dilation. Making sure your new vagina remains in a vagina shape is important, otherwise it will just heal up, and that's not a discussion you want to be having when people politely ask you how things are. So you have to learn how to dilate, and that takes up a surprising amount of time.

I was generally exhausted. Day to day I was just sleeping a lot and eating a little. I was just taking soft foods for a while. Most of the time when I was awake was devoted to looking after my wounds and to learning dilation. My main memory, though, is just of always, always being knackered.

I was only waking up when the nurses would arrive full of professional cheer. Maybe I was having something to eat and then coming back to the room and dealing with more dressings and more dilation and then falling back asleep. I'd sleep in chunks of two or three hours, then wake up for half an hour only to fall back asleep again.

I'd order room service quite often – two dollars to have your food brought to the room. Why wouldn't a woman spoil herself? I'd get up in the morning, pad about a bit to make sure I kept my legs active but then have second thoughts about dressing and heading down for breakfast. Hello? Room service?

It took maybe two weeks after the surgery before I didn't feel completely drained every day.

Dr Chettawut visited me two or three times, otherwise the nurses reported back to him every day. After about ten days I was able to leave the hotel and walk to the shopping centre next door just for the exercise. I'd sit down when I got there, five minutes' rest, then I just walked back again. It was only in the last week of my time in Bangkok that I had the strength to walk for an hour.

Eventually I stood and looked at myself in the mirror for the first time. There was no emotional reaction. No grief. No whooping. Just me, alone in a hotel room on the other side of the world.

So this is what I look like now. This is how my body is. Here's where the journey ends.

I hadn't been handed a smooth, pert vagina of the kind that you'd see in a porn film. I'd known that before I allowed myself to gaze downwards. What I saw when I looked down there was still a surgical site. Everything was swollen. Red. Lined with stitches. Nothing looked pretty. Frankly, it looked like something that had got run over. I suppose that was the initial shock.

*   *   *

I recovered well enough over the three weeks to get back on the plane. There's a thing that they call the donut ring that you get to sit on in order to be a little more comfortable. As it's not all healed down there in the undercarriage area, your sore bits get suspended over the hole in the donut.

I didn't have a donut ring to sit on. I'm not sure I wanted one. So I waited in Thailand long enough to know that I'd be able to sit down for a long time without the journey home being really uncomfortable. For all my precautions it was still quite an uncomfortable ride. I had to get up and walk about quite often.

As I recovered, however, I realised that as a person I'd become a lot more calm. In the month before the surgery when I gave up taking oestrogen, the return of testosterone to my system had given me problems. With my testes removed in the surgery I felt I was back to the female state again. There was a certain – welcome – change in how I felt. In my modified state I was a more peaceful person. People had told me that I'd feel that way, but you never entirely trust people who don't know you as well as you know yourself.

The situation with Linda, who did know me very well, wouldn't resolve itself for maybe another six months. It's not possible for me to speak with certainty about her feelings on this. She's entitled to give her own account of what she went through, but it was a lot. That's her story to tell, but watching her, yes, I'd say it probably took another six months for her to settle to the changes in our life.

It was difficult for us both, but since the physical changes my life has definitely become easier. I don't have that sense of limbo. I don't have the sense of life still being pending. This is me.

Some people transition and they reach a point of contentment where they don't have to have any kind of surgeries. That's OK because they've reached their contentment level. I only got there after the surgeries and all the processes. I went to a place that I'd hoped existed but I wasn't certain about.

All the surgeries were private. I paid for everything myself. I don't want to put a figure on it, but it cost more than the first house I bought. So not cheap. The facial surgery cost more than a nice car, but I went at a time when the pound to dollar rate was really bad. I looked at it as an investment. I was going to have this face for the rest of my life. I wanted it to work. No comebacks. The same with the genital surgery. I wanted it done right. No infections. No things that don't work. When I go for a pee, I want to be able to stop and start peeing.

It's a long journey that has no ending, but you have to keep moving on. Not everybody understands what propels a person through that search for contentment, for unity in themselves. Those that can't understand are usually the ones most bothered about why you just can't shut up and be content. They'll be relieved to know that I feel less anger towards them now that my journey is done.

Less anger, and more sympathy for their unhappiness.

Alpe

He's five kilometres from the top of the Col du Glandon but he's not sitting in his saddle; he's by the side of the road. Back down there just a minute ago he lost control of his breathing. It felt as if somebody had stolen all the air. Now his head is between his knees and he's wondering if he's even going to make it to Alpe d'Huez, let alone survive it.

At the Tour de France things can be going oh so well one day, then falling apart the next. His first stage win was at Bagnères-de-Luchon, just seven days ago, the only Pyrenean mountain stage that year. They climbed the famous cols – Aubisque, Tourmalet, Aspin and Peyresourde – and he beat this equally promising tour debutant called Pedro Delgado by a whisker after almost six and a half hours. What a day it was.

The Peyresourde introduces itself sourly with a rough jolter of ground at the bottom after the pleasant tarmac of the valley. He hit this strip with the Colombian José Patrocinio Jiménez by his side. Jiménez was from a town called Ramiriquí, almost 2,500 metres of air above sea level. Millar was from the 11th floor of Glasgow high rise and riding his first Tour.

When they hit the foot of the Peyresourde, Jiménez was still strong. Robert Millar had doubts about himself until about four kilometres in. Then, praise be, the sweat began sheeting from the Colombian's forehead.

Nearing the summit of the Peyresourde, the team car gave the warning that Pedro Delgado was in full pursuit. How many times in the next decade will one of them be in pursuit of the other? Millar allowed Jiménez to suffer some more, until about 500 metres from the top, and then he dropped him with a sprint. *Hasta luego!*

There were 15 curvy kilometres down the other side to the finish line in Luchon. Delgado was the crazy downhill guy. He stalked, he caught, he dispatched. A horror movie.

Gear ratios were limited back then. Millar had chosen a 13-tooth sprocket in order to prioritise the bigger ones he had for climbing. He knew that Delgado had a 12 and would be faster on the downhill, but without the advantage of his madness. Every second was vital.

The ride down was a hectic blur of pedalling and shouting. The tarmac was melting in the heat. The guys in the team car were screaming. Hairpins were negotiated by rider and car. Faster. Faster.

At the two-kilometres-to-go-board he still had a 15-second lead. He knew then. Finally. Pedro Delgado had run out of road.

Robert Millar of Pollokshaws swept into the main square. He donned the little cotton casquette. He did up the jersey. A last sprint from the final corner. Arms to the heavens like a man winning under that foreign sun on *World of Sport* with Dickie Davies.

For once the limelight felt soft on his face and some words flowed.

'I looked round at three kilometres to go, and I could see the guy [Delgado] coming. So I put myself on the rivet again. And then at 500 metres, I took the hat out for publicity, put the hat on nice. And put the arms up. Always have to remember that.'

Pascal Simon, his friend and roommate, finished third on the day and took the yellow jersey from the knotty shoulders of Sean Kelly. Perfect. Simon had a persuasive lead of 4 minutes 22 seconds on second-placed Laurent Fignon. What an evening that was. Two friends sharing the same room. The stage winner and the new maillot jaune. It felt like the beginning. Robert Millar had arrived. Simon was a good climber and no one would be able to drop him in the mountains. With that advantage, they quietly expected him to go on and win the Tour.

Leaving Bagnères-de-Luchon the next morning the future never looked better. That day's leg to Fleurance should have been uneventful. Alas, luck hides its tripwires in the best places. Simon crashed and landed awkwardly. In considerable pain, he got back on his bike. Helped along by his teammates, he finished in the bunch and held on to his 4:22 lead. He assumed it was just a broken collar bone. If only … he'd broken his shoulder blade.

The yellow jersey blurred Pascal Simon's vision. He should have headed back to his home village Mesnil-Saint-Loup that very evening, but the jersey imprisoned him. They bandaged up his shoulder, gave him a room to himself.

'What will you do, Pascal?'

'I will ride on.'

His team stayed with him. They pushed him along when no one was looking. There were a lot of tears – from the pain and from the emotion of having the yellow jersey but not being able to defend it properly. Meanwhile, Fignon stalked him with a patience that belied his years.

For five days Simon clung to his lead. He held on until his fingernails bled and came away from his flesh. On the sixth day the pain was no longer to be borne. Five minutes behind on the road and with Alpe d'Huez looming, he pulled in and stopped. His race was done and the formalities had no respect for his heroism. They stripped him of his race number and put him in the broom wagon with the quitters and drop-outs.

Now on the road to Alpe d'Huez, Robert Millar finds himself sitting on the side of the road, desperately trying to calm himself. He'd tried to stay in a group that contained his friend and teammate Stephen Roche. This had proved to be beyond him and now he was having a panic attack.

He sits for five minutes in the shade of a lone tree. Then he sets off again with barely enough composure left inside to stay on the bike. He has no idea how he might reach the finish line after the 21 corners up Alpe d'Huez. This life. Just days ago he was bulletproof. His friend Pascal was going to win the Tour while Robert rode shotgun. Now he's a wreck and all that glory is already a distant memory.

He still feels like 60 kilos of crap going into the valley to Bourg-d'Oisans, but he settles into a rhythm of sorts. Once he reaches the last climb, the zig-zag ascent up the sacred mountain, he just gets by, counting down the hairpin turns as he rides. One, two three ... 18 to go. Halfway up, lo and behold, he comes across Stephen Roche again. Roche is crawling up the mountain, in something of a state. Not for the last time in their careers he asks Roche if he might want help. A shake of the Dubliner's head. Nope. The team car comes alongside and offers to stay with Roche. Millar goes back to counting the hairpins.

There were many new young riders on that 1983 Tour. The race let each know their level. In the end, Fignon, just 22, became the youngest winner of the Tour since Felice Gimondi in 1965. For Millar, those final days, just riding towards Paris, were days of tiredness and elation. He was going to complete his first Tour.

And Paris! He knew the sights, the smells and the streets but he saw them afresh. He gawped and grinned like an American tourist as they rode down the boulevards and took the garlands. Finishers! The dourest ranks of Glasgow could scarce forbear to cheer.

That season his salary was £6,000. Annual, that is, not monthly.

the girl in the hotel

November is bloody cold in the Alps.

He was a Tour de France jersey winner and now Kellogg's wanted his face. The King of the Mountains eats this stuff. Maybe you should eat it too.

It was going to take five days to film a message endorsing the cereal, but down these treacherous roads skirted with ice a sporting celebrity must go. They stayed in a hotel in a small, lost village that wouldn't see strangers' faces again till spring. Travelling back and forth each day to the filming locations involved early departure and late returns, a busman's holiday for a racer. He consoled himself that at least he got to sleep in the same bed every night.

It was during the off-season for rider and hotel. Robert and the crew were the only guests, the hotel remaining open just for them. Outside, the village itself had already shut down for the season.

The hotel was a family-run place. The standard nuclear family, he noted on arrival. One mother, one father, one son, one daughter and one old dog that roamed listlessly about reception when it wasn't asleep by a radiator. It had been a long season. Robert envied that dog.

Robert rose the first morning and shambled down for breakfast. He noticed that the daughter of the family was taller than the son. She seemed a little withdrawn. He thought he saw something of himself there. A surly, grumpy teenager stuck at home? Been there, bought the unisex T-shirt.

The air stung his face as soon as he went outside in the mornings. By the time he returned to the hotel in the evenings it took him ten minutes under a hot shower to chase the ache of ice out of his bones. When he went down to dinner on the first evening, he noticed that the tall daughter from breakfast was actually a boy. A boy who was transitioning.

She was 17 years old, maybe 18, and just under six foot tall. Robert felt a pang for her there. He was small and slight. Perfect for climbing, perfect for passing himself off as a girl. This kid had light brown hair flowing halfway down her back. She'd been letting that hair grow for quite some time. The hair told Robert that the girl's family had accepted her choice. They had accepted what she needed to do to be happy. He felt a little pang for his younger self.

In the 1980s information was sparse. Every story Robert read about transitioning was sad and cautionary. Young people were thrown out of their homes. They wound up as prostitutes, hoping to scrape together enough money for medical care. They ended up in isolation, shunned and unloved when their medical history was revealed.

Here, in the remotest corner of the snowy Alps in brooding November, was a young girl in a supportive family in a public-facing business. She was transitioning. Right here was the proof of the possibility he had dreamed about.

None of the crew passed any comment about the girl. He wondered whether they whispered about her. He hoped not. They seemed respectful and accepting. Robert knew that had he been surrounded by riders, soigneurs and mechanics, the air would have been polluted with their horrible mockery. Anything not straight, white and male was grist to that mill.

He was the King of the Mountains and he was being visited by irony. He'd swap his kingdom for what this girl had. This girl quietly transitioning in her home with her family around her and nobody inflicting any pain. By contrast, Robert wore an earring as a modest signifier of individuality. To listen to the abuse he sometimes got at races, it was as if the earring was confronting people with some unimaginable deviance.

Robert wanted to speak to the girl and to her family. He felt inhibited by doubts, though. What could he say? He was seven or eight years older. He'd missed his chance. Deferred it? Suppressed it? Swerved it? He wasn't sure which. He'd certainly lacked the knowledge to see clearly what his own issues were. He'd kicked that can down the road.

How could this girl in this high village have known any more than a city boy like him?

Here he was, Robert Millar, this famous cyclist, this sample of the male species judged fine and wholesome enough to be an ambassador of breakfast cereal, fronting a TV commercial for Kellogg's Start to be shown to millions. Eat like the King of the Mountains! Be like the King of the Mountains!

Inside he felt nothing but failure. He was weak, trapped and ashamed, confined in the narrow corridor of the life he'd chosen. He was jealous that he hadn't done what this young girl was doing.

Every evening he watched her. He worried if words of empathy from him would imply that he'd judged the situation to be in need of empathy. It didn't. That was just the world that he lived in. Back in that world, people crapped on you if they thought you were different. An earring, for crying out loud. Here in this little village, otherness seemed less threatening.

He held his silence. For five days in the Alps he did what he had to do. He tried not to be affected by this young girl, but every atom of him wanted to scream, scream so loud that his voice echoed through the peaks and passes.

Me too.

Me too.

Me too.

When he left the mountains, winter was closing over the place like a white envelope. The valleys were silent, the snowstorms were gathering and the village was hunkered down. People wouldn't put one foot in front of another on the soil till spring, when the sun would assert itself once more like a larval dream hatching.

He buried his own feelings all over again. He tramped down the earth. He said a prayer that by the time he was finished with bikes the world would be as secure with itself as this family in a tiny hotel on the remotest alp.

He went back to the headlong rush of life as King of the Mountains – but he felt differently about it all for a while.

Vuelta skelter

11 May 1985. The day before the finish and the race is a two-horse deal: Robert Millar versus Spain.

Spain needs this. La Vuelta has been stolen for the last two years by Frenchmen. 1983 with Hinault was bad, but at least it was Hinault. If you're going to be plundered, let it be by Blackbeard. He leaves you a good story to tell.

But in 1984 Éric Caritoux won the Vuelta. He had just a six-second margin over the Spaniard Alberto Fernández. *Perdón?* Éric Caritwho? Six months later, Alberto 'El Galleta' Fernández (the town where he lived was famous for making biscuits), after losing the Vuelta by the smallest margin in the history of the race, died – with his wife – in a traffic accident.

This Vuelta, the 1985 edition, is about the honour and the sadness of Spain.

That's how Spain feels anyway. Also if foreign hands are going to steal their race again, Spain would ask that those hands not be attached to the scrawny arms of Robert Millar. Not the sour Scot who's more expressive with his hair than with his words. Not this cranky whippet who wears an earring. An earring? They say he doesn't even eat meat.

'*Españoles, valientes, que no gane el del pendiente*' reads a roadside banner that presumes to speak for all patriots. 'Spaniards, be brave, don't let the one with the earring win.'

This has been one crazy Vuelta. Miguel Induráin, 21 years old, was second in the prologue and in yellow two days later. Spain swooned. But chaos overtook Induráin. In Galicia the rain fell in jugfuls. Big crashes were the story of the days. A sheepdog bounded heedlessly into the peloton. Another crash turned into a fracas, Belgian riders swinging fists at each other.

And then it all subsided and everything was all about Perico. Mythical Covadonga. On stage 6, Pedro 'Perico' Delgado banished Millar among those sacred hills and finished the day in yellow. Spain slept well that night.

If Robert Millar is too salty for Spain's palate, Pedro Delgado is the perfect snack, a *tapas* to love. Dark, sturdy and talkative, he comes with a fat new contract from the Seat–Orbea team. He has a matador's bravado that runs to the edge of foolhardiness. Spain wants its daughter to marry Perico, regardless of her wishes or taste.

Alas! *Qué tristeza!* Perico cracked the next day on the road to Alto Campoo. He vomited on the descent from Palombera and lost four minutes at the Brañavieja station. Spain winced. No, not again.

So now, on this, the last day of genuine scuffling, Perico is six minutes and 13 seconds behind Millar, stuck in a thicket of gloomy also-rans. The new Spanish hope is his young team-mate, the third-placed Peio Ruíz Cabestany, a rider who possesses a modest amount of Spanish charisma and a lot of Basque grit.

For Spain, Peio will have to do.

He enjoyed three days in yellow before Millar gave a show of strength on the 10th stage over five big climbs. Now Peio's in third place, one minute and 15 seconds behind the wiry Colombian Pacho Rodríguez. And Pacho is ten seconds behind Millar. Neither Pacho nor Peio carry the weight of realistic hope today.

The race is Millar's to lose. He has the climbing genes of a sprightly goat, a grandmaster's appreciation of tactics and the serenity of a biking Buddha.

It's also cold and wet. Millar is of Glasgow. Billy Connolly once said that Glasgow has two seasons, June and winter. Tomorrow's stage is a formality, but for today the menu is all mountains, just mountains. Millar may not eat meat, but he devours mountains. He has the polka dot jersey from last year's Tour de France, his reward for having tucked in to so many mountains – and so heartily. And he has those ten seconds in his pocket. He need only stay on the wheels of Pacho and Peio today and it will be done. The first English-speaking winner of a Grand Tour will be Robert Millar.

Easy peasy!

Still, *Spain hopes*.

When Velázquez painted the majestic Sierra de Guadarrama, he reached for his pots of blues and greens and golds. Today a stick of charcoal could have drawn the dreary grey and the creepy mists. The 18th stage of the Vuelta a España. When these sullen hills have been tamed, La Vuelta will be all over bar the shouting. There will be lots of shouting.

Guadarrama is tough. Three ascents – Morcuera, Cotos and the long haul up the Puerto de los Leones – then a 43-kilometre gut buster to the finish outside the DYC whisky distillery in Palazuelos de Eresma.

They ride half blinded by fog, whipped by sleet, battered by unhelpful gusts. On the flanks of the mountains there's nothing to see but the bonnet of cloud, nothing to feel but the cold in your bones, nothing to hear but rubber on gravel and the chattering of your own teeth.

The first climb is the Morcuera. They're led over the crest by the Russian Alexandr Osipov. Now to business, the Cotos.

Near the bottom, Millar punctures. Sometimes there's a civility about such matters. Today, none. All hell breaks loose. In the chaos, José Recio of the Kelme team pushes on. The peloton gets stretched all over the mountain, but nobody really cares about Recio. While Millar's wheel is changed, Pacho Rodríguez and Peio Ruíz Cabestany try to get away. Too little, too soon. Pascal Simon, loyal teammate and friend, helps Millar track them down.

Yesterday was a time trial in Alcalá de Henares. Millar punctured yesterday too. He lost half a minute but kept the yellow jersey. Oddly, his team, Peugeot, asked all its riders to bust their guts in the time trial. Gilbert Duclos-Lassalle rode full pelt for fifth. Pascal Simon was tenth. For what?

Now Pascal Simon has no gas left and Robert Millar has no lieutenants. Half of them have been dropped on the first climb.

The Cotos tops out at 1,830 metres. Its neighbouring peak is Navacerrada, just 25 metres higher. Seven kilometres of scrabbly road separate the two climbs – a traverse through the clouds of the high Sierra. Somewhere on that ride you pass from the province of Madrid into Segovia, Perico Delgado's home turf.

Even blinded by clouds, fogs and sleet, Perico knows every rut, pothole, crevice and juniper bush. Descending Navacerrada, he plays every card his upbringing has dealt him. Gravity isn't enough. He attacks the descent with everything. Head down, feet a blur, Perico hurtling half-blind down slopes not made for men.

In the mist of confusion, nobody in the stretched peloton notices. The weather stays brutal. A gauze of mist and rain hangs. Communications along the road fail. It's a time before the race radios that will tout every move and break. This is old school, and the lessons are ruthless.

Perico's boss, his wily directeur sportif Txomin Perurena, drops behind Millar's group in his team car. Ostensibly he's there to babysit the third-placed Peio Ruíz Cabestany. Perurena's presence reassures Millar. Nothing amiss.

Millar hadn't given Perico Delgado a thought that morning. Too far back.

Before Navacerrada has bottomed out, Delgado has caught up with José Recio. Now the two Spaniards are in cahoots. Recio can have the stage win if he helps Delgado win the race. All of Spain via television or wireless radio knows what's happening. Very few people on the mountains know.

The last climb is Los Leones. Millar, oblivious, is still shepherding Pacho and Peio. If he gets to the top with both of them, La Vuelta will surely be his.

Ahead on the road, Perico and Recio's heist has everything going for it now. They ride just behind the lead caravan of press cars and camera motos, slipstreaming the circus shamelessly.

Back in the Millar group, Peio Ruíz Cabestany knows that a coup is afoot. He's the decoy. He knows his job now is just to allow Millar to think he has everything under control.

'What a bastard. What a great bastard,' he grins to himself, thinking of Perico. 'He will! He will win the Vuelta.'

Peio just has to keep his mouth shut while Delgado steals the race for Spain.

If you sit at a poker table and can't figure out who the sucker is, you'll spot him immediately if you go look in the bathroom mirror. Today, Robert Millar's hapless directeur sportif is Roland Berland. When Berland figures out that there's a Spanish heist in progress, the face in his mirror looks old and ruined. Like a surgeon admitting to his patient that he has removed the wrong organ, Berland delivers the bad news to his rider. Pacho Rodríguez and Peio Cabestany riding adjacent to Millar just shrug.

Millar's teammates Ronan Pensec and Pascal Simon are back down the road. Berland implores them. The game has changed. One last push for Millar. He needs you, guys. Pensec and Simon dutifully bend to their task but they arrive at a level crossing. The barriers are down. Three minutes pass. No train comes. The barrier lifts.

Berland frantically tries to broker deals with rival teams. There's less than 40 kilometres to go. People find it hard not to laugh.

Every Spaniard on the road is singing from the same sheet. Spain's pride is to be restored. The Spanish riders near Millar ride slowly and obstructively. Everybody else is just wasted.

Millar gives chase as best he can, but in the end he loses 6 minutes 49 seconds. He's 36 seconds down. Tomorrow he'll lose La Vuelta by 36 seconds.

Millar the lone wolf has never seemed more alone than when unclipping himself from his pedals and making his way to the team car at the Destilerías DYC on the outskirts of Segovia.

All of delirious Segovia are hanging off him just to get in his face. *Perico! Perico! Perico!*

Spain has its race back. How they did in the foggy mountains isn't important. What mattered was *la madre patria* – the motherland. What nation would do differently?

Millar clenches his teeth and swallows hard as Delgado takes the crown. 'My victory is Spain's,' pronounces Perico. Spain weeps. Pure joy.

'That's racing,' says Robert Millar. 'Your friends today aren't your friends tomorrow.'

Ha! He could have won the climber's prize but he'd let it go to a Spaniard, José Luis Laguia. He figured that he was going to need some friends in the endgame. The irony of it.

The gap between history and legend is soon filled. The media abhors a vacuum. To Millar – who never says anything – are attributed a strong of colourful quotes concerning the theft of the Vuelta, the enemies he has made and a vow never to return to the country again. In truth, he carries a small grudge for Recio, who doesn't show for the last stage into Salamanca, but otherwise he's stoic as ever

Beaten by Spain, by bad luck, by the weather and mostly by his own bumbling directeur sportif. A perfect storm of imperfection. Nothing for it but to briefly sob his sorrow, go home and get ready for the Tour de France. He knows, too, that it would have been different if he'd been strong enough to dominate them.

There were some who laughed in his face at the end. He'd always known pro cycling wasn't throbbing with nice people. Because in this game they can't be nice people.

At the end of the year he'll leave Peugeot.

Chapter 17

21 July 2022
Stage 18, Lourdes to Hautacam – 143.5 km

When the time comes to look back and pinpoint the moment Jonas Vingegaard killed off Tadej Pogačar in the 2022 Tour, it's Hautacam in the Pyrenees that we'll remember. This was the last day in the mountains, and as they neared the top of the climb, the main men were virtually side by side, following the pace of Vingegaard's teammate Wout van Aert.

Vingegaard stayed tight on Van Aert's wheel, by no means comfortable but well able to keep up. Alas for Pogačar, he had no more to give. The yellow jersey that he won at the last two Tours was now on the man in front of him. Soon that jersey started to move away into the distance, getting smaller and smaller until Pogačar could barely see it. Then it was gone.

Coming to the finish line, Vingegaard smiled and grimaced; his spirit and his body talking in turn. He twice raised a clenched right fist, not high because that's not him. Indeed, there was nothing that could be called a celebration. Mostly he was just pleased it was over. Not the end of the 18th stage, but the conclusion to his battle with Pogačar.

The Centre de Presse is a sports hall at Argelès-Gazost, 17 kilometres from the finish in the ski resort of Hautacam. From here back to the Hôtel Stella in Lourdes is just 16 kilometres, but it's going to be another slow one.

Lourdes is a slightly surprising town whether you believe in miracles or not. You expect the Catholic merchandise, a torrent of trinkets, medals and statuettes. But the pilgrim trade is slowly dying, and Lourdes is trying to reposition itself as a gateway to the Pyrenees for hikers and bikers. You can see how it might succeed.

Meanwhile Pippa and I are still talking.

DAVID: When you look back, is it a source of comfort and joy that, so far, you and Linda have survived?

PIPPA: Yes, both. I do appreciate this, because during the years where I was transitioning – from 2000 to 2003 – there were some dark times. They were quite painful.

DAVID: What caused them to be so painful?

PIPPA: I thought I was coming out of depression, but it just continued into the transition. And I'm dealing with all the physical and mental changes that happened. From probably 1995 to 2005, I don't have any really strong memories of enjoying life.

DAVID: Because you were at that crossroads?

PIPPA: No, the whole period of depression was so bad. And then the transition process wasn't any happier.

DAVID: Even though you were doing what you really wanted to do?

PIPPA: Even though I was doing what I needed to do to be happier. There was no real happiness in that situation. And it's not what I wanted to do. It's what I needed to do. I've rarely met any trans people who wanted to do it. That's because of the upset that it causes to everybody.

DAVID: So when you were transitioning, what was the cause of the unhappiness?

PIPPA: Oh, just the strife involved in the process, the difficulty of managing the relationships that were important, worrying about what my life was going to be in one year's time, in five years' time? The uncertainty of what was going to happen to everybody around me.

DAVID: You're thinking of Linda, of your daughter Lydia, of Edward?

PIPPA: You think about all the people that you've known. I'd be thinking about people that knew me as a rider, people that I'd shared a room with. I was worried about what they might think. The people that you have respect for, people whose judgement of you as a person you value. To deal with this, I've not disappeared, but I wasn't in contact with any of them. I needed space. You're not an island, you can't just put up a barrier and think, *I don't care what anybody thinks*, because, you know, you're still human. It's just that you can't function very well until you've fixed a few of your problems and issues.

Chapter 18

16 September 2020
Stage 17, Grenoble to Méribel (Col de la Loze) – 170 km

Eleven months before the race started, the route for the 2020 Tour de France had been announced. For directeurs sportifs and riders, that was the moment they discovered what awaited them. Back then they knew – Grenoble to Méribel, stage 17, would be the day. All outstanding issues would be resolved on the brutal Col de la Loze.

So it came to pass, stage 17. The drama began even before the race began. Egan Bernal, the previous year's winner, could no longer carry on. At the start in Nice he'd spoken of a lingering back injury, and though the Tour has been described as many things, no one's ever recommended it to the man with an aching back.

By the end of the previous day's stage, Bernal knew the score. The pain wasn't going away. 'It was increasing. On the last climb, it switched to my knee. I'm screwed up on all sides.' Occasionally these guys do listen to their bodies.

Even at his best, Bernal might not have been able to come between the two Slovenians who've dominated the battle for the yellow jersey. Primoz Roglič, 30, is a former international ski jumper who retired from that sport in 2012 to concentrate on bike racing. He came into this race with the backing of the best team, Jumbo–Visma. His compatriot, Tadej Pogačar, nine years younger, has been the revelation of the Tour.

Don't ask how Slovenia, a country of 2.1 million people, managed to produce two riders of such quality at the same time. A thousand times asked, but not once answered. At least, not consistently, because sometimes there's no plausible explanation for why things happen the way they do.

At the foot of the final climb, the 22.5-kilometre Col de la Loze, Roglič and Pogačar were in the same group. In the overall standings, Roglič had a 40-second advantage over his rival. The mountain stretched out in front of the challenger: if you've got anything else, this is the place to show it.

This 170-kilometre stage began in Grenoble. There, on Boulevard Clemenceau a little after midday, Tour officials moved among the riders with their open plastic bags collecting Covid-19 masks. The time had come for those with ambition to show what they had.

Mikel Landa, 30, did not see it as a shoot-out between Roglič and Pogačar. He got his Bahrain McLaren teammates to set a tempo that ensured a day of sustained suffering. Almost imperceptibly, the bunch thinned to a long, narrow train, each man's gaze fixed before him and each one unwilling to look up and take in what was coming.

The climax played out exactly where everyone knew it would. 'I couldn't find a similar place in the whole of the country,' said Thierry Gouvenou, the man responsible for designing the route. 'It's a unique road in France.'

He was referring to a murderously steep climb with gradients so uneven that they first break a climber's rhythm, then his heart.

Four kilometres from the finish, Richard Carapaz of Ineos Grenadiers led by 42 seconds. How quickly this would change.

One of Pogačar's teammates went to the front pursuers and increased the pace. Some were left behind, Carapaz's advantage dwindled.

Pogačar then attacked, and only Miguel Ángel López, Richie Porte and Roglič, with his ever-willing sherpa Sepp Kuss, could follow. After Pogačar eased, López counter-attacked and he'd not be caught. Carapaz was swept up by López, Roglič, Pogačar and Kuss. He hardly saw them fly past.

López, 26, was strong enough to stay clear, though the more important battle was happening behind. Roglič accelerated clear, Pogačar countered. For almost two kilometres, the two Slovenians had their *mano a mano* on the seventh-highest mountain pass in France.

Roglič got ten seconds ahead of his rival, Pogačar fought back to within five seconds, and just when it seemed he'd latch on to the man in yellow, Roglič went again. He was second to the finish line, 15 seconds behind López, 15 seconds ahead of Pogačar. It seemed appropriate. The rider in the yellow jersey had increased his lead from 40 to 57 seconds, reached the top and, metaphorically speaking, driven his flag into the ground.

'I was happy with the position as it was before the stage,' Roglič said. 'Now I'm even more happy.'

Pogačar gave it all that he had. 'In that hard finale I was happy to not lose more time. It's still reachable – tomorrow is another hard day.' Admirable though his defiance was, the race had swung Roglič's way. The tallest mountain in that year's Tour had decided.

* * *

The evening of the Col de la Loze stage, Pippa and I stayed at an Ibis hotel in Albertville. We found a nice restaurant in the town and at dinner we fell into conversation with Klaus and his partner, whose name we were never told. He did say they were on a holiday, one where he'd ride his bike and see the race. His partner didn't seem that interested in the Tour.

Klaus was from Germany and had been a high-level amateur bike rider in the former German Democratic Republic. After he stopped competing, he stayed in the sport and had just spent time coaching Turkey's U23 cycling team.

For an hour or so we shot the breeze with Klaus, and then … well, it's a long story. Pippa and I spoke about it as we walked back to the Ibis.

DAVID: From the beginning you had the sense that Klaus was halfway between being a cycling nut and a cycling bore. His partner knew him well enough to just stay out of the conversation.

PIPPA: He came across as one of those angry cyclists, never quite good enough to do what he wanted to do. And, of course, that was everyone else's fault. Everyone else was a cheat and the world was against him. As he talked, you could see him getting more and more red in the face. He'd said he'd ridden five hours in 30 degrees today and he was sunburned.

DAVID: I'm guessing those five hours were the best part of his partner's day.

PIPPA: Did you notice that when they finished eating and polishing off a bottle of wine and were about to leave, he just suddenly ordered another bottle of wine? The wife had a look on her face that said, 'Oh no, here we go.' You could see her thinking, *There's going to be no stopping him now*.

DAVID: He was talking to me a lot in the way that some men do. There's two women in the company and he's just ignoring them.

PIPPA: Yeah, because we're not relevant. That's one of the things I learned when I transitioned. Males expect females to be quiet. Just listen. You don't have an opinion, you don't have any experience. He latched on to you: 'Excuse me, are you David Walsh?' Then the next words were, 'I read your book about Lance Armstrong.'

DAVID: He then took us on his tour to Turkey.

PIPPA: Yawn. You could see his wife letting out a sigh, and she was sinking down into her chair. And I was watching you, your expression never changed and you were asking him why it turned out bad in Turkey. It triggered him to tell us his life story.

DAVID: Mea culpa. It was actually my fault, encouraging him.

PIPPA: Even you were getting bored. The only moments he stopped talking were to slurp his wine. That was your chance to jump in, and I could see you were thinking, *Let's throw a grenade in*.

DAVID: Well, I asked you first. I checked if it was OK to tell him who you were.

PIPPA: I was fine. It's not a secret.

DAVID: 'Do you recognise Pippa?!' He looked so confused.

PIPPA: He nodded but he hadn't a clue.

DAVID: So I bring up your Wikipedia page on my phone and pass it to him. And he looks at you, and he looks at the phone, and he looks at you again. The cat's got his tongue.

PIPPA: I had no idea what he was thinking.

DAVID: He was blushing beneath his sunburn. He was looking at you with this mixture of sympathy and incredulity. I knew something bad was coming.

PIPPA: It was coming! He actually said it! 'If only you hadn't taken drugs as a pro cyclist, this would never have happened.'

DAVID: He said he'd seen this in East Germany. Women athletes took male hormones and became men. He just needed to explain what had happened to you.

PIPPA: And you said, 'That's not how it works, Klaus.' You explained it all and he just looked lost. His wife was glaring at him.

DAVID: She totally got it.

PIPPA: She knew Klaus would keep digging and then pull the dirt down on top of him. You looked totally disgusted.

DAVID: I was. I thought you were going to freak.

PIPPA: Ah yeah, but I've seen it before, I've had this conversation before.

DAVID: Were you OK about it?

PIPPA: I wasn't really enjoying it, but I wasn't surprised. I find it quite funny; maybe not funny, but amusing. It's amusing, that level of, I don't know …

DAVID: Ignorance.

PIPPA: Maybe not ignorance. He just hadn't come across someone like me before. The opinions he has now are the opinions he had as a teenager. He's had no reason to change them. Then he's confronted with something different and he has to fix it or at least explain it.

DAVID: Maybe. But I was mad. It was such a stupid and insensitive thing to say.

PIPPA: That's one of the myths. It was the drugs you took as a cyclist. I've said to people, if that was the case, there would be a lot of us in the same boat. A very big boat! Honestly, I wasn't too bothered. I've heard worse.

DAVID: Really?

PIPPA: I read a similar thing in the Spanish press around the time that my transition became public. 'Took so much shit as a rider it turned him into a woman.' I laugh about it, because how can you think that?

DAVID: Still, it's a level of ignorance that I couldn't believe existed.

PIPPA: Every bad thing that happens to a bike rider, it's because of doping. It's no wonder they end up crazy. And look, that one's turned into a woman. Oh yeah, and anybody who dies early or gets cancer or their wife leaves them, it's because of the shit they took.

DAVID: Didn't Laurent Fignon say in his autobiography that he thought his doping might have contributed to the cancer that would end his life as a relatively young man?

PIPPA: Yeah, and when you think about what riders once did, obviously no one's immune to its effects. So if you get worn out earlier it kind of makes sense. I can't remember, did we shake hands with Klaus and his wife as we were leaving? I don't think we did. We'd had enough.

DAVID: Yeah, we just left. His explanation for what he saw as your problem was a dampener on the evening. It just pissed me off.

*   *   *

Robert Millar was somebody I admired but would probably have gone to great lengths to avoid being alone in a car with. He did, though, intrigue me. From a distance it seemed like he lived on an island, detached but self-sufficient. Pippa is very much at ease with Robert Millar and his achievements, and she indulges my thirst for recollecting him. I do, however, realise that we can't talk about Milar all day, every day. If Pippa has moved on, so can I.

Something else that astonishes me is the fact that Pippa is now a media colleague. As a rider, Millar regarded the press room as a nest of unwelcome and sometimes nasty distractions. Our questions, whether valid or trivial, ate into his rest time and his preparation time. He always wanted less of us, but some of my colleagues were gluttons for the punishment of his indifference. Mostly, I stayed far away.

Keith Bingham was an English journalist who didn't mind taking the ferry to Millar Island. I'd watch, from a distance, and silently root for Keith because it wasn't easy. There's a magical cameo in *The High Life*, ITV's documentary about Millar, that showed Bingham doing his best after a mountain stage of the 1985 Tour.

Millar is sitting in the open boot of a team car, his feet on the road, a towel on his lap. Bingham approaches and leans towards him with a tape recorder in his outstretched right hand.

BINGHAM: The race was going well until what point?
MILLAR: Until the Tourmalet.
BINGHAM: Until the Tourmalet. And what was that like for you?
MILLAR: It blew me in the middle.
BINGHAM: In the middle?

MILLAR: Yeah.

BINGHAM: Did you … er … recover at all?

MILLAR: [shakes his head, looks away] Nobody would ride at the front with Phil [Anderson, teammate].

BINGHAM: Why not?

MILLAR: I don't know.

BINGHAM: So, I mean, how do you sum up the ride?

MILLAR: Eh?

BINGHAM: How would you sum up your effort today?

MILLAR: Not so good.

BINGHAM: Not so good. On Saturday you gave the impression you might topple, or you might get Herrera [in the battle for the polka dot jersey]. Now, I don't think that's possible.

MILLAR: Nah, I don't think so.

BINGHAM: Is the stage win possible?

MILLAR: I doubt it.

BINGHAM: Doubt it?

MILLAR: Yeah.

BINGHAM: OK, Robert, cheers.

The interview lasts 50 seconds. Bingham wasn't expecting to get much and wasn't surprised by what he got. Throughout, Millar looks to his left, then towards the ground but never in the journalist's direction. Bingham did as well as he could.

Pippa York has more reasons than Robert Millar ever had to be allergic to the media. On the way to becoming Pippa York, she and her family had to endure unkind and unpleasant stories. At times the newspapers made her life hell.

After getting Klaus out of our systems on the walk back to the Ibis Budget, we talk about Robert, Pippa and the media.

DAVID: Robert Millar, you have to admit, had a jaundiced view of journalists, leading to strained relationships. Now that Pippa York has defected to the other side, how do you feel about journalists?

PIPPA: [long pause] I see it differently now. As a rider I had the impression that the journalists went to the start, had a cup of coffee, talked to a couple of people, drove along to the finish, probably stopped for lunch in a nice little restaurant, sitting in the sun as they ate.

DAVID: Only half watching the race?

PIPPA: If there was four of them, one of them would be watching the race, the other three are having a laugh.

DAVID: And if they came to you as you were getting ready to go to the start, they were likely to ask a stupid question?

PIPPA: Yes. They would.

DAVID: As I said, pretty jaundiced. Robert Millar gave the impression that he'd as soon tell a journalist to fuck off as say good morning. So I just didn't go there. Does that surprise you?

PIPPA: No, it doesn't. That would have been my strategy. Cycling was tiny. I'd go to races and sometimes I'd be the only English speaker there and there would be no English-speaking journalist. It could be an important race. The journalists that I got fed up with were the guys who'd just come to the Tour de France for a few days. I got tired of that pretty quickly. And I began to judge them as they judged me, based on their performance. I said this to them and it frightened some of them off. I didn't mind that.

DAVID: Because then they wouldn't bother you?

PIPPA: Yeah. I didn't want to give them half an hour of my time. I understand why I was like that, but now I see it very differently. Mostly because I realise that journalism isn't the cushy number I thought it was. As a rider you don't understand that the guys have been stuck in an hour's traffic jam to go five kilometres to the top of the mountain. A rider sees only his own feet going up and down. Now I'll be in the Centre de Presse and the journalists will be talking about some rider, saying he's really difficult. That's the rider I'll want to talk to.

DAVID: Because you understand where he might be coming from?

PIPPA: I didn't realise there's a camaraderie among journalists. I thought you were all slitting each other's throats.

DAVID: You think we're not?

PIPPA: No, there's a bit of an esprit de corps, you help each other out. I remember recording stuff at a press conference and my iPhone lost the recording. Disappeared. I had to go to the other people who were there and explain I've lost it, and they say, 'Don't worry, we'll send you the audio file.' I'm thinking it's not as cut-throat as I imagined and these guys actually hang out together.

DAVID: Seeing you in the press centre, I'm amazed at your patience. You finish most days long before me as I'm really slow. So often we're the last two people to leave the Centre de Presse. Always in the last five or six.

PIPPA: Oh yeah, always.

DAVID: You never say, 'Look, can you not hurry up?'

PIPPA: I'm thinking that I'm travelling with the chief sportswriter of the *Sunday Times*, who's also reporting for *The Times*, and I'm learning from you.

DAVID: Jesus!

PIPPA: So I can't say to you, 'Are you going to hurry up?' In terms of the hierarchy, I'm at the bottom.

DAVID: Remember that 40 years ago, I was the guy afraid to approach Robert Millar.

PIPPA: I'm never going to say to you, 'Look, we're in the last four again and the guys dismantling the press room have taken away every table but ours.' Since I've transitioned, I'm a very different person to the person I was before. I don't have that same level of angst and ego and ambition, all of the things you need to be at the top level in sport. I don't have that. When Google now says it's going to take three hours 55 minutes to get to our destination, I no longer say I can do that in 3:30. I now have patience with people, I say 'Please' and 'Thank you', which I never said before.

DAVID: Your calmness and politeness make you really easy to travel with.

PIPPA: One last thing about the journalists. When we get to the Centre de Presse, the first thing anyone says is, 'What's the buffet like?' Every single time.

DAVID: But that's a big moment at the Tour. Discovering the quality or otherwise of the day's buffet.

PIPPA: I find this hilarious.

the place of bones

In the year AD 721, a stop was put to the gallop of the Moors (or the Umayyad Caliphate, to use the proper term) when they lost the Battle of Toulouse. Retreating back across the Pyrenees, the Moors decided it would be a nice morale boost if they sorted out the pesky Asturians of northern Spain. The Asturians were refusing to pay their taxes for not being Muslims.

So in 722 there was another battle. The outnumbered Asturians led by Pelayo ambushed their Moorish foe. It was written that their bloody victory was aided by a performance-enhancing miracle from none other than the Virgin Mary, a convenient landslide finishing off the remnants of the Umayyad forces. The Virgin does landslides if needs must.

The battle is the founding tale of modern Spain, the beginning of the *Reconquista*. Like many things in Spain the *Reconquista* took a while. Until 1609, in fact. That defeat of the Umayyad took place in Covadonga, which, to Spaniards, is a sacred place.

In 1985 the rivalry between Pedro Delgado and Robert Millar was in its third year. In the Covadonga stage that year Delgado defeated Millar. His triumph gave the first glimmer of hope to Spain. Delgado eventually won that Vuelta, his first Grand Tour. Some call it the 'stolen Vuelta'. No Spaniards call it that.

In 1986 another battle loomed. Millar and Delgado riding into the pass of Covadonga again. The Virgin Mary was told to stay out of it. Both men rode with new teams.

The ride up to the Lakes of Covadonga suggests that the mountains are any rider's true enemy, but to the public this was personal, an account waiting to be settled. Millar, the man from whom the Vuelta had been stolen last year, had returned to Spain to win the Volta a Catalunya the previous September, but Covadonga just feels different.

If he's to restore his honour, it will be at Covadonga. It stands alone.

It's *l'etapa reina* – the queen stage – mythic and feared, often compared to Alpe d'Huez. The elevation and the average gradient are similar. The climb in the French Alps is unique with its hairpin bends, but the ride to the ski station is smooth. Covadonga is a climb to nowhere, almost straight up into the clouds. In the 1980s they rode a path as rough and wide as a goat track. Lightweight bikes and lightweight wheels wouldn't last five minutes on those rutted tracks.

It's a stark beauty, this long climb that finally winds around the two pristine lakes near the summit. It's another world up there, with the tips of the Picos de Europa looming everywhere. When the Vuelta used to take place in late spring, those peaks were capped with snow.

Spain was poorer back then, in the 80s. Decades of Franco still hobbled the place. Crowds gathered in the towns and cities when the race came through, but few people had the luxury of a motor to whisk them to the mountains, nor did the country have the money to service the stony goat paths and potholed drovers' ways that led to nowhere.

So the peloton climbed in relative peace, past the towering Santuario de Covadonga church, onwards past plunging waterfalls, cool caves and dense forests. Cows observed the race with suspicion, each the colour of a new penny and each with a clanging bell hanging from its neck. On and on went the riders to the plateau of the lakes.

In 1985 Robert Millar had botched his ending. He'd ridden too hard through Covadonga's cruellest section, La Huesera, the Place of Bones. He'd spent his gas recklessly. When Delgado had attacked on the last tough elevation, Millar was stuck in the quicksand for a few seconds.

Today he's older and wiser.

The going gets tough just after the 10-kilometre board. The Spaniard Mario Lejaretta takes over. He has form on Covadonga. He won the stage the first time it was ever held there. Now he turns the thumbscrews.

Millar saves himself for what lies ahead. He hangs in the group and dodges the wind. Even when you're being clever, though, this isn't an easy climb.

The yellow jersey rider, Pascal Jules, got drifted right at the start of the climb. The bespectacled Laurent Fignon now has the lead in the general classification. Millar takes a look at his rival. Fignon is struggling.

Lejaretta drives them on for a good four kilometres. The peloton bursts out from the cover of trees. There's stark rock face stubbled with ferns and gorse to the left, the vast valley below to the right. And to the Place of Bones Robert Millar comes again. La Huesera is a brutal slash cut straight up the side of the mountain. Average gradient 12 per cent, finishing at 15 per cent up where the road gives onto the platform of the Mirador de la Reina.

Lejaretta leads as they hit that 15 per cent segment. Delgado, ah the bold Perico, attacks. The group fragments. The gradient is so brutal, the surface so bad, for every rider rhythm is hard to find.

Millar had slugged it out with La Huesera a year ago. Today he picks his line, swerves the potholes and dodges the patches of gravel that just spin your wheels. And screw pride and appearances! He stands up out of his saddle for respite when he needs it.

He comes out of the steepest ramp, 100 metres down on Delgado. He has Perico on the hook, though. He just has to reel in the line. Only Reimund Dietzen and Álvaro Pino are left, chasing with Millar.

The gradient eases. Millar reels Delgado in and hits the front.

The wind is coming from the right now. The smoothest surface is on the right too. Quick calculation. To use Dietzen, Delgado and Pino as a shield from the wind hands them the best surface. The road is pummelling them now. Why change that?

He takes the right side, with the yawning valley below him. He plays the role of torturer. Speeding up, slowing down, then accelerating again. No rhythm and no recovery. Sorry, boys.

Four kilometres left. A tough climb after the Mirador de la Reina platform before the road sweeps down past Lake Enoi. He keeps his rivals in pain along the little flat section. Then the haymaker. The road gets wall steep and he throws in one last big acceleration.

This is just the spot from which Delgado attacked a year ago. Millar was hurting when Delgado rode away. Today the roles are reversed. He gives it everything. Soon he has two hundred metres of clear road between himself and the group.

The road winds down to the lakes now. Millar can't wind down, though. Seventy kilometres per hour, jouncing over cracks, bumps, craters and potholes. A fall or a puncture will do for him, but so too will fretting about a fall or a puncture. The finish line has been washed away. He just rides into where the people narrow the road, to where the race cars block the way entirely.

They say it's payback for the year before. They can respect vengeance. He won't play, though. He won't obligingly fit himself into the frame they make for him. It's another day, another dollar. It's racing. It's why he loves racing. Yep, another day. Something learned and applied.

But inside, he loves Spain and all this amiable chaos.

crème caramel

By the middle of 1985, Robert Millar had grown tired of Peugeot and their French ways. After the lost Vuelta of that year, he knew that he needed a change.

In a hotel on the Route de Grenoble on a rest day during the 1985 Tour de France, he bumped into Peter Post, the directeur sportif of the Dutch-based Panasonic team. For much of the previous decade, Post's team (previously TI Raleigh) had been the Manchester United of the peloton and Post was their Alex Ferguson, their guru. He was authoritative and feared.

Post was a tall and handsome man, some six foot three in his stockings. He needed a climber, though, and the breed tended, pre-EPO, to be small. He made Millar an offer. Slightly grudgingly, he explained he preferred taller men, but for Millar he'd make an exception.

So Millar started life with Panasonic in 1986. Early on they went to the GP Zurich. The race is just laps of a circuit and it started in 30 degrees of sunshine, with the riders hiding from the sun.

Post loved Switzerland, so he'd sent his A team, and they were expected to win. In the first half of the race they made hay while the sun shone. They got two men in the break and everything was under control.

Then a thunderstorm broke and the temperature dropped from 30 to 15. Suddenly it was freezing cold, there was water everywhere and Panasonic guys were getting dropped like mosquitoes. A new break goes and none of Post's guys are in it. Post orders his men to chase the break down. They can't. They're freezing. A few of them stop with one more circuit to go.

The inquest happened later in the evening. They were in the Hilton. 'Only the best for my riders,' Post would say. Having said that, he'd dine in the restaurant while his team ate in the cafeteria. Tonight, when his supper was over, he came down to chide his team. Everybody was aware that it was time for the inevitable bollocking.

Millar was indifferent. He was new. Post hadn't started picking on him yet. This evening it was Eric Vanderaerden and Eddy Planckaert who took the brunt of Post's rage. They absorbed it all in front of anyone who happened to be in the cafeteria.

'You two were useless. I'm paying you a lot of money and you've done nothing.'

Finally the bollocking, like a summer storm, wore itself out and Post began expounding upon other things. When the desserts began to appear from the kitchen, Post was joking with a rider about having a BMW when he, Post, was always telling people that a Mercedes was the only car for a man to drive.

Robert Millar had long been a careful eater, some would say fussy. He hadn't been going to have a dessert anyway, but he most definitely wasn't going to consume one of the crème caramels that were now being slung in front of the riders

He'd developed a list of things he was tired of having to eat. Spaghetti and thin apple tart were top of the list, crème caramel not far behind. He decided now was the time to quietly take his leave. Post had finished with his main tirade, so Millar rose and made his way towards the lift.

He'd just pressed the button when he heard Peter Post's roar. Post had spotted the uneaten dessert.

'Where are you going?' he boomed.

'I'm going up to my room.'

'You haven't eaten your crème caramel.'

'I've eaten enough. If there isn't anything else about the race to discuss then I'm going to rest.'

'But you've haven't eaten your crème caramel,' Post says again.

'I don't want it.'

And Post went red in the face. What sort of man spurns a crème caramel?

'But you have to eat your crème caramel. I've paid for it.'

With that the lift door opened, and Millar stepped in and pressed the button for his floor.

Post was now incandescent with rage. Insubordination on top of the hurt a man feels when his crème caramel is spurned.

'Come back and finish your crème caramel,' he roared. 'I've paid for it. You have to eat it.'

The doors slid shut and for Millar the shouting just faded away as the lift rose.

For three days Post refused to speak to his climber because of an uneaten crème caramel. Millar was twenty-seven years old and a married man.

And a very insolent boy.

pasta stroppetti

He was stroppy. OK? Now get over it.

The triumph of Covadonga isn't actually the first thing Robert Millar will recall about the Vuelta of 1986.

He'd returned to Spain as leader of his new Panasonic team. His directeur sportif, the famed crème caramel devotee Peter Post.

As with the year before, things went well until they didn't. As race leader, Millar had a poor time trial and fell back to second place on GC. He stayed there until the end of the race in Jerez. Second again, and to another Spaniard, Álvaro Pino.

What he remembers about that Vuelta though is Albacete. And his dinner.

The Spanish have a saying about Albacete. *Albacete? Caga y vete!* (Albacete. Take a shit and leave.) Millar wouldn't argue.

After the 15th stage the team were billeted in Albacete. In its heyday Albacete was a transportation hub, hence the 'shit and leave' tag. And the cheap hotels. The team hotel was shabby like a cheap motel in a bad horror movie. Panasonic were sharing the accommodation with three or four other teams. Millar had been in exactly the same charmless place the year before but this evening the hotel surpassed itself.

He was late for dinner. Delayed at the podium, which is a better excuse than most. This was his second year to the fore of the Vuelta story. He'd hoped that the hotel might be a little pleased and perhaps push the boat out.

He was further delayed by being last off the massage table, and in the end he came down quite late for dinner. The team was eating in a conference room that had no windows. The lighting was too strong. Yeah, déjà vu. The memory of exactly how bad the place was returned.

This year he'd restricted his diet still further. His dietary preferences he'd made perfectly clear. OK, pasta for dinner, but he patiently specified no oil of any kind, no sauces or buttery substances on that pasta. Just plain old undressed pasta, thanks.

A miserable plate of soggy pasta arrived. The stuff was swimming in olive oil. He asked, in Spanish again, if he could have pasta with no olive oil. Just pasta. Simple.

Another plate arrived. Just pasta. Simple. OK. First mouthful, it's cold. They've rinsed the olive oil off the pasta by running it under cold water.

So he asked again if he could have a plate of food that had no olive oil and was also hot. Perhaps he should have specified last time that hot was preference. Not feeling he was being unreasonable but sensing restaurant staff were getting cheesed off, Millar could feel some stroppiness coming on.

He sat seething and starving in this overlit room for another five minutes. He nibbled the half-stale bread. He regretted not just having had a box of breakfast cereal.

Another plate arrived. The cook had obviously declared war. The pasta looked as if it had fallen on the floor, been trampled on by flamenco dancers and then cooked again.

The fluency of a Glaswegian with swear words is never lost. Millar addressed his teammates.

How had they'd eaten this crap? Why had they eaten it?

They shrugged back at him. This was the crap we were served. It's the crap we ate.

He lost the plot now. He swore some more. He stood up. He took the plate in his two hands and launched it skywards. It hit the ceiling and the pasta stuck there, stuck up there as a gooey mess.

The riders at the table stared upwards, mouths agape.

The plate stayed on the ceiling for a second or two, but it seemed like an eternity. When the plate came back down it landed smack in the middle of the table. Riders jumped back out of the way, thumping the underside of the table with their legs. The table shook violently. It was the little plate of gloop that made an earthquake. Bottles of water flew everywhere, glasses smashed, fruits rolled to the floor, bits of bread and yoghurt pots flew as the table was almost upended.

The rest of the room watched in silence.

Millar walked out. He fetched his money and walked across the road to a restaurant where two other teams were dining.

'A table for one, please,' he said.

'No, señor,' they said, 'you have to go back to where you came from.'

He showed them his money. They sensed the nuclear intensity of his mood and they relented.

He ate alone while the other teams stole glances at him.

He smiled to himself later on.

A thought. 'I don't think it would be presumptuous to say that was one of the best strops that I have ever thrown.'

Eddy the knife

The day after the pasta strop, the word went around that Robert Millar hadn't eaten a thing. Some disputed that. No, they'd seen him eat alone. His glower had heated the whole room. Others said no, he was half-starved and hungry. He was there for the taking.

The race started as if it were on fire. They attacked each other with the table manners of jackals.

After an hour, things calmed down. Eddy Planckaert was greatly relieved. Eddy was a sprinter out of Flanders. A character. Along with the other Panasonic riders, he'd been following moves or shutting them down. Eddy was fed up and he needed to pee.

Eddy rode to the front and indicated he was stopping to do his business. Etiquette demanded that a nature break signal a truce, but Eddy had only pulled up for a minute before a rider from one of the smaller Spanish teams, Zahor, took a flyer off the front and the whole race reignited.

Other guys had stopped with Eddy for their comfort break. Now they were all back and pedalling like fury to catch the race. What was going on? And who was to blame?

What the culprit hadn't realised was that Eddy had been to the shops in Albacete. He'd bought himself a souvenir. Then, for reasons only known to Eddy, instead of putting his souvenir into his suitcase, he'd placed it in the team car. He remembered this as he furiously chased down those who'd broken the unwritten rules of pee breaks.

Albacete is well known for its manufacture of knives of all shapes and sizes. Eddy being Eddy (he has since made a reality show about himself and his family), he'd bought himself a knife that resembled the hunting knife Sylvester Stallone had used in *Rambo*. That morning before everybody mounted up, Eddy had gleefully demonstrated just how sharp his new knife was by slashing through sheets of paper.

Struggling to come back to the bunch after his pee stop and carrying a bee in his bonnet, Eddy now retrieved his knife from the team car and put it in his jersey pocket

It had taken a good 10 kilometres for Eddy to reappear at the front of the race. Red-faced and soaked in sweat, he began asking questions. Who exactly had been responsible for attacking while Eddy and others were stopped for business?

All fingers pointed to the little Spanish guy, a repeat offender for attacking at the most annoying times but never when the going was really hard.

Aha! That's when Eddy reached into his jersey.

Holy shit.

He's got a knife!

That's a knife in Eddy's hand.

He glared at the Zahor offender as the blade slid out of its protective sheath. Then with a manic growl he began waving the knife about.

The little Spaniard was shaking.

Nobody expects the Spanish Inquisition. Nor does anyone expect it to be conducted by a bug-eyed bicycling Belgian with a Rambo hunting knife.

He pleaded with Eddy to forgive his sins. It wasn't his idea. The team car had made him do it.

Just behind this scene, the peloton was in stitches. Then Eddy himself burst out laughing. He waved the knife above his head one last time and asked if there was anyone else who wanted to attack.

No, Eddy! Nobody wants to attack!

The rest of the day unfolded in an orderly fashion to the finish. That was the Vuelta and why Robert Millar always loved racing there.

*　　*　　*

The peloton always provided an odd sense of fraternity. Its unity was often cracked by egos, petty kingdoms, the uneven divide of talent and ambition. The peloton struggled with diversity as cycling became globalised, but some days on the road, suffering as a band of brothers, doing deals, swapping gossip and laughing, the peloton was its own world and Robert Millar had his place in it. He had the respect of a lot of those guys.

He could be of the peloton and yet separate from it. There were days when he recalls seeing a woman leaning over a railing in the sweaty chaos of a stage finish and instead of wanting to have her in the way so easily vocalised by his brothers, he just wanted to be her.

He'd never thought that bike riding would be a solution or a cure for his dysphoria. He loved the roads and the mountains for their own merits anyway. He just thought that being immersed in something he loved that much – something that asked so much of him – would allow him to bury that other need. At least for a certain time.

Maybe by doing something extraordinary I can be normal, he'd thought. *Whatever normal is. Maybe I won't feel like this. If I appear normal, is that not the same thing as being normal?*

But those days and those women, carefree and comfortable within their being, always shook him.

Chapter 19

29 June 2021

Stage 4, Redon to Fougères – 150.4 km

The story of Mark Cavendish's heroic return to the 2021 Tour de France can be told in many ways. In the brilliance of the sprint, mostly. At Fougères, where he won for the first time since 2016, he delivered again. For the 31st time in the race. Foolishly, we'd wondered if it could happen again. Thirty-six-year-old sprinters don't rediscover winning form at the Tour.

But that's to forget that Cavendish doesn't play to others' expectations and isn't bound by sport's standard mores. His birth certificate might say 36. What he says is that he wouldn't be still riding his bike if he didn't believe he could win. Cavendish was right. In Fougères, where he won in 2015, he somehow won again.

Only he could have done this. Other sprinters have had the same speed, a select few have been just as adept at weaving through the pack, but Cavendish has a character like no other. He was born to win, so he finds a way. Seeing him sprint has been one of the joys of the sport for the past 13 years.

Time may blur the sprint itself in Fougères but it will never erase the memory of the joy unleashed by this return to the top. It was his victory but the sport's as well. And then there were the reactions, Cavendish's and those of so many others.

Emotions swirled, euphoria washed over the peloton and the crowd knew they'd just seen the greatest finisher in the history of the sport.

The three-times world champion Peter Sagan stretched out his right arm as he passed Cavendish and patted him on the back. The old warrior André Greipel was next to slow and embrace him. After him the Dane Mads Pedersen and then Tim Merlier. They came to genuflect at the altar of greatness.

All wished to express their joy at his victory. Remarkable. As they did, his Deceuninck teammates formed a queue to hug him. There was Michael Morkov, who'd guided Cavendish back to the front of the peloton late in the stage, as well as Julian Alaphilippe, Tim Declercq and the others. They laughed, Cavendish cried. Memories to be cherished.

Afterwards he was asked if this was the most special of his 31 stage wins. You might as well have asked him to pick his favourite child. 'Every time I stood on the podium since winning the first in 2008, it's been the same. It's almost been forgotten how difficult it is to win a Tour de France stage, and now I've won 31 of them.

'This race has given me the life I've had, and I've given it the life I had. I'm just happy to be back, it sounds silly but it means so much to me. From the first time to now, I'm living a dream, an absolute dream.'

Before the 2021 Tour, Cavendish had already done enough. Then, somehow, he found a way to do more.

* * *

Something Cavendish once said to me during an interview stuck in the way that not much does. He was talking about the arc of his career, the first four wins coming in the 2008 Tour and from there he soared. No one could see the bad times coming, but they came and they knocked him low. From 2016 to 2021 he struggled with his physical and mental health.

His world changed. 'When I was winning, lots of people had attached themselves to me. No matter what I asked for, they said "Yes." A few people said "No," but they were overruled. When the tough times came, the number of people around me dwindled. What I noticed was that the people who'd always said "Yes" had gone. The few who said "No" were still around.'

Pippa and Mark are friends, I can see that when they're together. When he was down, she was one of the few who was there for him. That's the kind of thing he was always going to remember. Luckily, we were staying at Hôtel Le Flaubert in Fougères, where Cavendish got back on the winning trail. That meant we had time to find a decent restaurant. We spoke a lot about Cavendish, which is easy.

We also dug into the aftermath of the surgeries Pippa had undergone in Thailand.

DAVID: So how long after you got back home to Dorset did it take you to recover from the operation?

PIPPA: I think it was a year later before I'd say that I was properly recovered from the surgery.

DAVID: And when you say recover, did it take that long before you could get on a bike again. I imagine that was something you had to approach gingerly?

PIPPA: I'd done research before I went to Thailand. It might be that I wouldn't be able to ride a horse or a pushbike ever again. I'd accepted that. At best I knew I wouldn't be comfortable on a push bike for something like eight weeks. I gave it like three months before I got the bike out. No miracle. It was uncomfortable. There were times after San Francisco when it wasn't safe for me to ride; my bones needed to heal properly. I'd gone four or five months without riding, so I was familiar with withdrawal from the saddle. Going riding again was uncomfortable. That didn't settle down for a year. I had to change saddles and stuff; the previous ones I used weren't comfortable as my anatomy had changed. I needed support and relief in different areas, so I had to find something more comfortable. Women find it quite difficult to find a saddle that's comfortable. That part of your anatomy feels different sensations to having a penis. So that was a process – a soft saddle, a hard saddle. It's like shoes. Depends on the person.

DAVID: Let me tell you an absurd story from the 1984 Tour. What you've just said brought this back. At the time, five-time Tour winner Jacques Anquetil did an 'Ask the expert' column in *L'Équipe*. That was the year that the first women's Tour de France took place. A few of the riders were well known, but the race itself didn't get a huge amount of attention. The questions for Anquetil were invariably about the men's race, but one day somebody wrote to Anquetil asking about the women. The reader wondered why women rode a bike at all, because it's not natural for them and certainly not natural to ride a race as tough as the Tour de France Féminin. The only thing the reader could come up with was that women got some kind of sexual satisfaction from rubbing that part of their anatomy on the saddle. And Jacques Anquetil, the great legend of the Tour de France, replied that yes, he'd often thought the same thing himself. And there was no outrage.

PIPPA: That doesn't surprise me. But people don't realise how vulnerable all that stuff is. It's not being rubbed against the saddle. It's being crushed between you and the saddle. In male terms it would be like having your testicles pressed. Not comfortable. The saddle is definitely not a sex toy. Riding over cobbles does not bring a smile to your face.

DAVID: Do you remember that first women's Tour de France?

PIPPA: We read about it in *L'Équipe* but we never saw them. They were 'tidied away', so to speak, before the men arrived each day. We saw them at the end in Paris. Maria Canins, the Italian, was well known; Jeannie Longo was well known; Marianne Martin, an American, won, I think. I remember there was a woman on the podium and it was like, What's that about? Oh yeah, it's that thing that was in *L'Équipe*. But we saw none of it. We had our own selfish attitude and all the focus was on us. If there was a little piece in *L'Équipe* it was because it was their race and they were paying for it. They weren't exactly promoting it. It just wasn't a thing.

DAVID: You know when you told me about the final surgeries related to your transitions, you didn't say what happened to the male part that gets severed? Does it just get washed down the drain?

PIPPA: It's a question that people ask me, and I'm glad they do because it's an interesting thing and whenever I talk about this it's a chance to explain something a bit spiritual.

People want to know, what did you do with the bits, and I have to remind them that it was in Thailand that I had the operation. Dr Chettawut is a Buddhist, and in Buddhist tradition it's usual that they allow you – encourage you, I suppose – to retain all the things they remove from you. In their belief system it's part of your soul. You have to keep everything you were given. It's part of the unity of life. You have to keep them close to you. So they give them to you in a jar. It's a nice jar and you can take them home. Some people may bury them. But I still have them at home. I keep them in the living room above the fireplace.

DAVID: Wow. So, they did actually give them to you. Is that really where you keep them?

PIPPA: No, David, it isn't. But you're the most gullible journalist on this race. For the record, I've absolutely no idea what happened to the parts.

DAVID: I think I preferred you when you were surly.

Chapter 20

18 September 2020
Stage 19, Bourg-en-Bresse to Champagnole – 166.5 km

Emmanuel Macron had been at the summit of the Loze two days before and patted the day's winner Miguel Ángel López on the shoulder. The French president, however, didn't come simply to laud the riders and admire the scenery. Rather he was there to lend his support to the race and to thank the Tour director Christian Prudhomme for putting it on. Taking place at the very moment France was experiencing a ghastly rise in Covid-19 infections, many believed staging the Tour to be dangerously reckless.

The Tour, of course, is more than a race, something that Macron was eager to acknowledge. 'When we talk about this French way of life,' he said, 'we're talking about our culture, our gastronomy, our conviviality and our great sporting events. The Tour de France is an absolutely exceptional event.'

Just before the race set off in Nice three weeks earlier, the Côte d'Azur had become a red zone, denoting the highest attainable rate of new infections. Putting on a huge sporting event that travelled around the country, through villages, towns and cities, seemed like an invitation to Covid: do whatever you want.

'One third of French people want the Tour to go ahead,' said Alex Roos, the *L'Équipe* journalist, at the start in Nice, 'another third think it's crazy, and the final third will wait to see how the French riders are doing before making up their minds.'

By the time Macron appeared, it was clear the Tour de France was going to be a success. It had turned into a compelling spectacle, and infections within the race were remarkably low – only two positives among the teams' support staff and in the Centre de Presse.

It was safe, then, for the president to reiterate his message to the French people. 'We must learn to live with this virus,' he said. What he didn't say but did imply was that if you could safely stage the Tour de France, with all its variables and so many spectators at the roadside, then it was surely possible to live with this virus.

The race has been an affirmation of the French way of life.

Speaking of the affirmation of life, on the hour-long drive from Champagnole to our hotel in Besançon in eastern France that night, I asked Pippa what it was about this particular Tour that pleased her most.

'It's the fact that my friend Allan Peiper is directeur sportif of UAE Team Emirates and basically has guided Tadej Pogačar through an exceptional first appearance at the Tour. That's the highlight for me.'

When York was Robert Millar, the outstanding British rider of the 1980s and the first English-speaker to win the polka dot jersey at the Tour, Peiper was his teammate at Peugeot and then later at Panasonic. They were always good friends.

DAVID: You really do respect and like Allan?

PIPPA: He was two years younger than me but he was like my older brother. Allan looked out for me, and whenever I did something stupid, he'd be the first to tell me. I could take it from him because he cared about me, as he cared about a lot of people. 'Do that again,' he'd say, 'and I'll smack you.'

DAVID: You never resented his threats?

PIPPA: No, because he was quite right. I was a mixture of ambition and angst and not easy to deal with.

One day in Paris–Nice, when they were both in Peugeot colours, Peiper got in the break while Millar, not paying attention, missed out. From the team car, they told Peiper to slow down and wait for his Scottish teammate. 'He was there cursing me, all kinds of swear words, before he then put his head down and rode for me. He was that kind of bloke.'

Five years ago, Peiper was diagnosed and treated for prostate cancer. He has been dealing with it ever since. In April of last year it had spread to his lungs and bones. The bosses at the team Peiper managed, UAE Team Emirates, ensured he got the best possible medical help. There were six rounds of chemotherapy and much else. Peiper wasn't sure he'd survive, let alone would ever return to the team.

PIPPA: It was around October last year that I decided to go to Belgium because I believed it would be my last chance to see Allan. Then the word came that he'd survived the treatment better than his doctors thought possible and was officially deemed to be in remission. And so he returned to his job, though with the coronavirus infecting so many, he has had to be exceedingly careful.

The thing is, Allan Peiper wanted to live, not just survive. He wanted to come to the Tour and see if he could help young Pogačar. Pippa isn't joking when she says that Peiper has more wisdom than a whole peloton of directeurs sportifs.

Seeing her old friend play so central a role is the memory Pippa will cherish from this Tour. 'It would have been enough for me just to see Allan at the Tour. Seeing him working with one of the stars of the race has been something else.'

Halfway to Besançon, apropos nothing, Pippa says there are always things that remind her that her path wasn't a well-worn one.

PIPPA: Do you know what a GRC is?

DAVID: I've no idea.

PIPPA: It's a Gender Recognition Certificate. You have to apply for one. It's where your personal life collides with bureaucracy. A GRC allowed me to change my birth certificate and then for whatever reason be placed on a government list. So to get this GRC, a piece of paper that would officially confirm what I was, I had to fill in all the forms and supply all the paper evidence they asked for. I did that, and sat back and waited to receive the discreet brown envelope containing the letter that would then allow me to apply for an updated birth document. But when my application was processed, I failed because someone on the approval panel had decided that I might have detransitioned. I've no idea how that happens. They asked me to please send more information. This was baffling, as I'd sent more documentation than they required in the first instance. I gave in and sent off even more dull paperwork. The second time I was lucky. The whole episode was a reminder of how fortunate I'd been to be able to sidestep the needless scrutiny of the NHS gender system, not to mention the long waiting lists and appalling administration.

DAVID: Did you think at one time that you might work full-time in cycling, say some kind of role in a pro team?

PIPPA: Years after I stopped racing and had transitioned, I was approached about a working role that would have been suitable. A pro team needed somebody to coach, advise and integrate young riders who were coming into a professional structure. The riders of different nationalities and backgrounds would be experiencing a number of different challenges that they hadn't yet been exposed to. I'd adapted to all of those things as a young rider and I felt I was as well qualified for the job as it was possible to be. The team agreed. 'Yeah,' they said, 'this would be good. Very good. You certainly know what's needed. We're excited about this.' We all agreed that the times they are a-changin'.

After that initial gust of enthusiasm there was a long silence. I put that down to the team's pre-season prep. Everybody was busy. They'd get around to the mentoring of the younger riders soon enough. More time passed. Things had been quiet for just a bit too long, so I called and asked what was happening. The reply was that I wasn't going to be working with the team after all. 'Oh,' I said, 'and why is that?' The reason given was that a few of the staff didn't want a trans person there. When these staffers had been pressed for a reason why they might not like having a trans person, they apparently came back with the classic line, 'What are we going to tell the riders? How do we explain this person who is supposed to work with them?' The times hadn't changed very much after all.

DAVID: This stuff has hurt you?

PIPPA: To me it really didn't seem like such a complicated question. They could tell them that I was trans. Being trans has got nothing to do with my ability to help them improve as cyclists or people. Being trans didn't remove my 16 years as a pro rider. Being trans didn't erase the experience of 11 Tours de France. Or ... in the context of the times that are supposedly a-changin', you could say nothing at all because it's not actually relevant. The response I got, however, was yes, yes, but at this point the team didn't want to have deal with any of that stuff. So, all the big talk of how things had changed had been just rubbish. On the outside the PR was saying all the right things to look modern, inclusive and open to change. On the inside, it was another thing entirely. Same old story. It's much easier to talk about principles than it is to live by them.

It cost me a friendship and the rejection brought on another depressive period, another year on anti-depressants. I managed on a lower dose than before. I knew if I let myself fall into the endless grey days' existence that I had endured on higher doses, it would be hard to recover from that. Dealing with crap from people who are as thick as mince and know no better is bad enough. Going through that when a friend has told you that it will all be good made it ten times worse. So, to answer one of your other questions, there have been a lot of things much worse than being in the media room at the Tour de France.

post hoc planning

The 1986 Tour de France had begun in Boulogne-Billancourt, the home of ACBB. Robert walked the old avenues and boulevards of his former stomping grounds and saw some old friends. That was as good as that year's Tour de France got for him. He fell apart in the third week, most particularly on the trip up Alpe d'Huez. He stopped riding two days from the end. Peter Post was most unhappy. Again.

That he just about made it to the end of that season was because he didn't have to do any more stage races. He was dispatched to one-day events, usually in Belgium or northern France. There was less pressure and more travel. Usually, he rode in service of the team's sprinters or whoever was the protected rider in the race.

Winter duly came, and Post decided that Robert Millar needed to be coached by Phil Anderson's trainer, Ludwig van de Putte. It was an interesting suggestion. The rider had always set his own training levels. Very few cyclists were more acutely attuned to the needs of their own body than Millar.

The thing, the obvious thing, that Post didn't get was that Anderson was a lot stronger than Millar. The two friends were almost different species. When Ludwig van de Putte set out a virtually identical programme for both riders, it quickly became too much for Millar. He was willing, but his body cracked by the time he got to the end of March 1987. Granted, he did learn certain useful things that improved his time-trialling and better prepared him for the hilly classics, but overall he was unhappy.

If Millar was unhappy, Peter Post was stressed. His relationship with Millar was always full of friction. One day Millar's phone rang at 9.30 a.m. Millar was only vaguely and reluctantly familiar with the concept of 9.30 in the morning.

Peter Post was checking to see if his cyclist had left or was just about to leave to go training. Millar explained that he was going to train later. Post exploded into a rant about how much he was paying his riders. If Robert Millar wasn't at the front of the next few big races, he'd get someone else to replace him. Riders should be out riding early because the crack of dawn was what made them proper bike riders. Other teams were doing better because they got up earlier. Post reproached himself. He felt that his kindness was being abused. He looked after riders too well; they ended up soft and overpaid, and the worst of the ingrates were still in bed at 9.30. Things weren't like that in his day, Post said before he hung up.

Millar was glad that the call had been brief. He could get back to sleep. He didn't get the chance to interrupt or to explain that he went training later so that his ride finished round about the same time that most races did. That way his body was used to performing according to its circadian rhythms.

'Circadian who?' Peter Post would have asked. 'What's he even won?'

Liège-Bastogne-Liège, *La Doyenne*, first held in 1892, is the oldest of the five Monuments of the European professional road cycling calendar and usually comes as the last of the spring classics. In late April 1987 there was the infamous incident when Stephen Roche and Claude Criquielion had the Liège–Bastogne–Liège race stitched up between them. Neither Roche nor Criquielion were great sprinters, so having left the field behind, they tried to outfox each other playing a game of 'After you …', 'Why no, sir, after you …' They both figured that whoever led off into the sprint would lose the race.

There were no radio earpieces then, so when the two leaders glanced behind them in the last kilometre they saw only the team cars. They had no idea that a group containing Moreno Argentin, Yvon Madiot and Robert Millar was closing on them.

Millar was as unlikely to win a sprint as either of the front pair, but he and Madiot seemed content to pull Argentin along. The Italian claimed to be bushed after the Ardennes, and he assured Millar and Madiot that he wasn't planning any sprint finish. Millar didn't really want to tow Argentin along to the finish but, from his car, Peter Post decreed that Millar should ride for a third or fourth place.

Fine.

The next race on the calendar was scheduled for a week later in Limburg – the Amstel Gold Race, one of the three Ardennes classics and basically Post's home event. The number of World Cup points that Post's team accrued before the race would dictate where the Panasonic car was placed in the convoy in the Netherlands. So even though Argentin was perhaps going to do Millar and Madiot over at the finish, Post was more worried about where his Mercedes would be located within the race convoy at the Amstel in Limburg. It would not do for the homecoming hero to be seen bringing up the rear.

Millar duly helped tow Argentin into position so that when the race turned the final hairpin bend at the top of the Boulevard de la Sauvenière, Argentin burst into life and sprinted to win his third LBL in a row.

No one was happy.

In the debrief with the whole team present, Post now attacked Millar for not striking up some kind of deal with Argentin.

'You rode like an amateur just to get a placing.'

In his frothing fury he lapsed, as usual, in and out of his native Dutch.

When he subsided, Millar pointed out coldly that it had been Post's decision that he ride along with Yvon Madiot, with Argentin hooked on the back. They'd towed Argentin along in order to secure Post a better place in the convoy the following weekend. Millar repeated that he'd wanted to wait for the others but he, Millar, didn't call the shots.

The room sat in stunned silence. Right or wrong, nobody had ever argued with Post.

There were repercussions. The Giro d'Italia hadn't been on Millar's race programme for 1987. He'd fallen apart from trying to do two Grand Tours one after another in previous years. In 1987, however, he got packed off to the Giro at the last minute. Revenge is a dish best served antipasto.

red, red wine

The 1987 Giro d'Italia has long been remembered in Italy not so much as a race but as a Shakespearian drama in lycra. Stephen Roche 'betrayed' his Carrera team mate Roberto

Visentini. Or did Visentini betray Roche? In Italy there's only one answer. In 1987 there was only one winner.

Robert Millar had a ringside view. He'd been friends with Roche since the ACCB days in Paris. In 1979 Millar and Phil Anderson were the two pros to emerge from the ACBB hothouse. As was the custom, each was asked to nominate an English-speaking successor to the amateur team they were moving on from. They both recalled racing the Tour of Ireland that year. Ron Hayman of Canada had won, but the dark-haired Dubliner Stephen Roche had been better than either Anderson or Millar. They'd had to put their heads together and beat him tactically, just to get Anderson in to second place, with Roche finishing third and Millar behind him.

So they nominated this Stephen Roche, and, years later, Millar naturally gravitated to Roche's side during the Visentini dispute. When Roche and Visentini began cutting each other's throats on the Giro, Carrera – being an Italian team – backed the home favourite and Roche became isolated pretty quickly. His domestique Eddy Schepers stuck with him, but from everybody else came the cold shoulder.

One particular day lodges in the memory due to its drama – the monster mountain stage crossing the Gardena, Sella and Pordoi passes and finishing over the Marmolada in the ski resort of Canazei.

The Italian media was by now seething with hostility, their fury reflected in the *tifosi* on the roadside and even within Roche's own team. It had even been rumoured that Roche wouldn't start the day, but Roche and Schepers showed up at the start. On a long day, Visentini attacked twice on the clos-ing climb, but Schepers, along with Millar, twice helped

Roche to close the Italian down. The fans hissed and whistled at the Irishman, with some of them filling their mouths with red wine and spitting fountains at him, the arc iridescent in the sunshine. Others leaned in towards the rider with sticks and rolled-up newspapers. Nobody was trying to tickle him.

Roche rode on defiantly, however, with Millar and Schepers serving as his Praetorian Guard on the climbs. Schepers was paid to ride with Roche his teammate, but Millar took it upon himself out of friendship.

kermesse whispers

After weeks of listening to Peter Post's grumbles and quibbles about the way he, Millar, was riding a race he'd never wanted to take part in, Millar won the final mountain stage of the 1987 Giro. He'd secured the green jersey and had wound up in second place on the general classification.

His almost accidental podium finish didn't fill him with joy. Peter Post's cup didn't run over either. Post was still annoyed that Millar had bumped Erik Breukink, his (tall) new (Dutch) star, down to third place. Post had told Breukink not to worry because he'd take the position back from Millar in the final day's time trial. Having overheard Post's comments, Millar rode flat out, fuelled with spite. Breukink posted a better time but it wasn't enough for him to get second place back.

That was it. Millar was done with Peter Post. He decided that evening that he wouldn't be going through another year of the Dutchman's tantrums. The riders and most of the staff were fine – he'd had really good fun and learned more in his first six months there than in the previous six years at Peugeot – but Post was just too much.

After the Giro, Millar was granted the following weekend off but then received a countermanding fax telling him that he had to turn up for a midweek kermesse race in southern Belgium.

On the morning of this unscheduled outing, the actual green jersey winner from the previous weeks' Giro arrived to sign on for the race in a bar just off the main square of a small town somewhere in Wallonia.

Fully kitted out in his Team Panasonic kit, he made his way to the room where the pros were being handed their numbers. A hammy hand placed itself softly on his chest and barred his way.

'No, son, the juniors are in the other room over there.'

'I'm a pro.'

'What?'

'Here's my race licence.'

'Hmmm. But my son is bigger than you!'

With his number secured, Millar went back to the car and removed his bike from the boot for a mechanic to put some race wheels on. That was the deal. You brought your frame, clean and ready. The team checked it and put the wheels on.

Except today. At these street races, every rider gets an appearance fee and is obliged to bring their own bike wheels. So Millar's mood was soured still further by the half a bollocking he received for turning up with no wheels.

Oddly, practically the whole Panasonic team was present for the race. Nobody knew why there had been a full muster. Perhaps there had been some sort of 'you scratch my back and

I'll scratch yours' deal, but they'd been at the Giro not ten days earlier. No back needed that much scratching.

The race set off and after the first corner a break of about 25 riders went up the road. Panasonic had no one in it, nobody from the team chased it down, some even quit, and by the time the riders had done a big 100-kilometre loop and come back to the town for the finishing circuits, Team Panasonic were chittering along, ten minutes behind.

Which was when they heard the all-too-familiar honking of the team car horn. The car hadn't insisted on anybody chasing the break, but now they were asking everybody to ride hard. Odd.

The reason became clearer when they spotted Peter Post looming on the side of the road ahead and screaming abuse at them. Millar was exhausted and contemplating how many more laps he was going to do before packing it in. There was nothing to be gained by riding on, and the thought of going past Peter Post on each lap made the prospect even more depressing.

A minute after they'd passed Post, the insistent honking of the team car started up again. What now?

Peter Post had installed himself in the passenger seat and was furiously shouting orders out the window. Millar was sitting at the back with Eddy Planckaert and they both pretended to be deaf.

Finally, Post screamed at Planckaert that he must move up. The sprints were coming soon.

'EDDY! EDDY! Eddy, you have to move up. Move up.'

Eddy smirked, slid forward on the saddle a couple of inches and said innocently, 'Like this, Peter?'

A few weeks later the Tour de France started in Berlin. Old Berlin. They flew in and out above the motorway. The Wall was covered in graffiti, machine guns poked out of the watchtowers above and nobody was free from the vague feeling of being watched. It was fascinating and slightly worrying at the same time.

Day later in the Strasbourg Sofitel there was another Panasonic moment. Peter Post got in the hotel lift only to discover that there was a hotel room door standing there in the lift, just resting against the mirror. He checked his room list with a sinking heart. Fear confirmed. The number on the door was the room number of Eric Vanderaerden, the team's other sprinter. While he'd been having his after-race massage, one Eddy Planckaert had unscrewed the door from its hinges and placed it in the lift.

Millar fell apart in the third week of the Tour but wasn't permitted to abandon. Physically he ended the season as a mess and it took till mid-November for his recovery to be complete. Tests revealed that his thyroid had packed up.

braced

On the 1991 Tour de France, Robert Millar noticed that things had changed. An entire team just vanished, claiming to have eaten bad chicken. He'd figure that out later. First he had to get through the Tour himself.

It didn't start well, and then it got worse. On top of that he'd had a busy and disappointing early season. The low point had been riding the Amstel Gold Race while suffering from smallpox.

As the Tour de France gathered for *le grand départ*, Millar was already riding at his minimum weight. He liked to start races at 56.8 kg and meticulously monitor that down to 56.2 kg after ten days. Anything less than that, and what power he ever had on the flat just deserted him. But now in 1991 he started the race at his minimum weight, and he felt tired right from the off.

Greg LeMond, the Z team leader, was jumpy as always, but in good form on the flat. He'd had a day in yellow before Rolf Sorensen took over the race lead. In the mountains, Millar and the Norwegian Atle Kvålsvol would be doing the grunt work for LeMond.

Stage 6 was a well-remembered day when the French rider Thierry Marie made a break on his own, riding on all alone for six hours and 234 kilometres to finish at Le Havre in Normandy and win the stage. France rejoiced.

It was also the day that Robert Millar crashed.

He was the first to fall in what quickly became a massive pile-up. Miraculously, nothing was broken, but when it came time to stand up again, he noticed that his neck didn't work properly anymore. He could neither turn his head nor hold his neck up straight. These were two things that he liked to do as much as the next man. Furthermore, he had holes all over his body and his right arm had taken a bad hit too.

The ambulances came and filled up quickly with riders with broken collarbones and fractured arms. Millar didn't feel too good and an ambulance looked like a nice way to spend the next few hours, but the team just gave him a fresh bike and a slap on the back. Off you go.

The replacement bike was one of the really early carbon rides that was meant for back-up. He hated it. It was too stiff and the saddle kept slipping. He finished just inside the time limit that day, having ridden ten miles on carbon before his original bike was repaired and handed back to him

That evening he was too inflamed and too sore for any physio work. The team summoned Bruno, an osteopath, who drove up from Paris to treat the rider. Alas, the inflammation was so bad, Bruno announced that couldn't do a thing for the patient either.

Bruno decided that the only way for Millar to continue in the race was for him to wear a neck brace. They scoured Le Havre the following morning and came back with several different varieties of neck wear. Millar chose the softest, most spongy model and rode the Tour de France for four of the next five days in a neck brace.

Roger Legeay, the Z team boss, told Millar to take it easy so he'd be ready for the mountains, when the holiday would be over! Millar would be earning his corn helping team leader Greg LeMond on the slopes.

At night the only way Millar could sleep at all was face down. He woke every few hours in pain. More worryingly, his right hand didn't work. That meant no rear braking and no getting food from his jersey pockets. They got around this by putting race food in a bidon that had been cut open. Meanwhile he had to change gear with his left hand. His steering was off so he had to ride well away from the other wheels so that he had a bit of space for manoeuvre. He knew that he ought to have stopped but it was the Tour de France and you just don't do that sort of thing.

The time trial from Argentan to Alençon a couple of days after his injury was a fiasco. He rode without the brace, thinking he'd make the 73 kilometres without too much pain. He was dead wrong. But LeMond took back the yellow jersey that day, and Roger Legeay in good cheer instructed Kvålsvol (who'd also taken a fall) and Millar to relax, recuperate and recover for the mountains. That luxury was beyond them, though. The team were riding flat out just to survive.

On the first day in the Pyrenees, on the road to Jaca in Spain, LeMond got thirsty. Millar and Kvålsvol, his wingmen for the mountains, were too dilapidated for domestique duties, indeed they were labouring well behind with the rest of their Z teammates. There was nobody to drop back and fetch water, so LeMond just ploughed on, getting weaker as he went. By the end of the stage, he'd surrendered the yellow jersey and, still parched, his confidence was gone.

The next day brought a handful of climbs back over the French border to Val-Louron. On the first climb of the day, a Gatorade support car clipped LeMond and he went down. He got back up and rode on. Three hours later he tried a bluff on the imposing Col du Tourmalet and went for a solo break-away. Miguel Induráin and Claudio Chiappucci hunted him down like two lions stalking a wounded wildebeest. Things were bad. Kvålsvol then dropped out, looking like an old man. Millar hoped to do the same, but to abandon LeMond completely was unthinkable.

By the time Alpe d'Huez arrived the following week, Millar was still suffering and was dropped on a Category 3 climb before they reached the Alpe. He finished 75th, nearly nine minutes behind the stage winner Gianni Bugno. Left alone, LeMond did not go well on Alpe d'Huez either.

When Millar got dropped, Roger Legeay spoke to him from the team car.

'I was relying on you today,' he hissed at his wounded rider.

Some years the Tour just flashed by as a blitz of experiences and disappointments.

rare air

Isn't it rich? Are we a pair? Two twilight riders together again, up here where the air's so fine and rare.

Ten years earlier, on the high road to Bagnères-de-Luchon, Robert Millar was about to win his first Tour de France stage on his first ever Tour. It was Pedro Delgado who came after Millar towards the end of an epic day at altitude. Millar held the Spaniard off, but since that day they've toiled against each other up and down countless mountains.

Today is 15 July 1993, the 11th stage of the Tour de France. They were in the mountains yesterday but worse lies ahead today. In Tour terms, Millar and Delgado are old men and this should be no country for them. Their best days are behind them, smeared on countless thousands of tarred miles. The culture has changed, and the peloton is now awash with EPO and men doing things they shouldn't rightly be able to do. But today's stage, from Serre Chevalier to Isola 2000, has something that seduces both the old rivals. The masochism of mountain climbers has no known cure.

Some 263.5 kilometres of riding lie ahead, generously spiced with 180 kilometres spent in the mountains. It's a day that dangles the prize of ascending the Col de la Bonette, 25 kilometres long and ascending to over 2,800 metres in the clouds. The col holds Europe's highest through road and has been visited by the Tour only twice before, in 1962 and 1964.

On each occasion the first man to cross the col was the remarkable Federico Bahamontes, the greatest climber the sport has seen. Bahamontes was the one who on his very first Tour de France in 1954 raced to the top of the Col de Romeyère and stopped for an ice cream while he waited for the team car to catch up with him.

To follow Bahamontes into the history books was a worthy objective of two men whose time had come to think of legacy. The martyrdom of the born climber beckoned them again.

This was a day and a place for making memories. In 1861 Emperor Napoleon III had cut a track through here for his mules. He needed to connect the Ubaye valley in the Alpes-de-Haute-Provence to the Tinée valley in the Alpes Maritimes, thereby making a pathway to the pebbly shores at Nice. The path was used in desperation again during the First World War. It took many decades for asphalt to pave that track used by soldiers, mules and goats.

People talk of the silence up there, the awe-inspiring purity of that silence. They talk of the air – the thin, elusive, oxygen-stingy air. And they whisper of the bare grey slopes of the lunar landscape on either side of that slow, interminable climb. Nothing but sky and stone above.

The riders begin with the Col d'Izoard, Claudio Chiappucci reaching the top first with his customary bravado, followed by Davide Cassani and Toni Rominger. Cassani wears the polka dot jersey but Rominger covets it. The descent is a killer, and some of them ride down as carefully as pensioners on frosty footpaths. Charly Mottet, though, descends like a lunatic to catch Miguel Induráin's group. This is a serious day for the big players.

Tony Rominger was a stage winner yesterday, and when he's within sniffing distance of that jersey on Cassani's back he suffers a puncture. This allows Cassani to press his advantage. On they go to the Col de Vars, another colossus. Cassani goes over first, just a minute ahead of Chiappucci and Rominger. By the time they reach the flat road before the Col de la Bonette, Cassani has been caught and the subplots of the day are soon forgotten.

The real attacks and jostlings begin among the emperors of the air when they reach the first foothills of La Bonette. Millar attacks, along with Delgado, Johan Bruyneel, Iñaki Gastón, Yvon Ledanois, Jim Van De Laer and Rolf Aldag. It's the two old stagers, Scot and Spaniard, who emerge from the scuffling.

They're 18 kilometres from the summit when Millar and Delgado set off alone, establishing a 30-second lead. They pull away, helping each other like two desperadoes making a break for the border. They can settle their differences later, when the posse are out of sight somewhere far behind.

So it goes until 14 kilometres from the top, when Perico Delgado can no longer match Millar's strident rhythm. On this day of all days, his legs desert him. Delgado falls away. Millar reaches the top of the granite col alone. The mountain makes him look like a flea on the back of a great bear, but he has conquered the beast.

All hopes of winning a grand tour have been swallowed by now, but these are the days that nourish him. This is a triumph only knowable to true climbers. Today's twist, though, is that the Col de la Bonette isn't the final act. There are fifty kilometres left to ride before the finish high up at the ski resort of Isola 2000.

Pippa York & David Walsh

On the descent of the col, Millar keeps a lead of 1 minute 20 seconds over the yellow jersey group of eight riders. Down in the flatlands, a group of 13 riders pedal hard now in pursuit of Millar. Across the plain they chase on, towards the foot of Isola.

By the time Millar is heading up the last climb of the day his lead is back down to 35 seconds. The peloton is now strung out all over the Alps. The damage is widespread. Cassani knows that the polka dot jersey is lost and he'll do well to finish within time. At the foot of Isola, Laurent Fignon gives up and just abandons his tenth and final Tour de France.

Millar climbs the initial slopes, but he knows enough to understand that his lead won't hold. Chiappucci and Bjarne Riis break free from the chasing posse and reel him in at the fourth hairpin. Six kilometres from the top, and now they're all here feasting while Millar succumbs. There go Rominger, Induráin, Riis, Álvaro Mejía and Chiappucci, with Zenon Jaskuła hanging off the back.

The stage settles into its own grim momentum. Those six are going to fight it out between them. Induráin says later that this day asked more of him than any other day ever had.

The TV commentators have paid their respects to Millar and honoured his heroics over La Bonette, but now they have forgotten him, along with all the other broken casualties of the epic day. The limelight belongs to Rominger and Induráin, the heavyweights of the general classification. Rominger is already certain that he will be in polka dot this evening when he steps from the podium. Induráin is content to mark him and make sure he steals no seconds. The camera car cruises alongside the pair until, suddenly, a small figure with a ponytail overtakes them on the inside.

Induráin, obsessed with Rominger, looks briefly startled. The commentaries turned apoplectic. Robert Millar is risen. He's back from the dead. He sails past them with four kilometres to go. He has scraped together the last of his strength and flung it on the table to back himself on this final climb.

For two gruelling kilometres he manages to stay in front. All his Tour wins have been in the Pyrenees; to win in the Alps in this manner, on this day of all days, seems impossible. But on he pedals, as defiant and hungry in his 11th tour as he was on the first. Finally, Induráin, who has been left to do all the work leading the chase, catches Millar and the group of six devours him again.

Rominger takes the stage, a wheel's length ahead of Induráin, but the day is Millar's, his name engraved forever across the granite brim of La Bonette.

Delgado finished the Tour in ninth position. Millar finishes in 24th place, but covered in so much glory. It was the last Tour de France for the two of them, Millar and Delgado, with Col de la Bonette their last and greatest duel.

car parking

On 17 July 1988 the Tour de France rolled on from Blagnac in Haute-Garonne to Guzet-Neige in Ariège, a stage of 163 kilometres with three climbs to cross, including the finish.

What a nightmare. Robert Millar isn't in great form. He knows that the stage is one of the few chances to put in a decent ride at this Tour. Usually he likes the Pyrenees, but this year he's dog tired by the time the mountains loom.

They've gone 70 kilometres or so when a group of 15 pulls away. Millar goes with them, but he can only drag himself into the group with pure grit and willpower. He's as cussed a rider as ever put bony ass on skinny saddle.

Everybody's feeling it today. From that escape group they start tumbling out the back, until at the foot of the final ascent there are only four left: two Italians – Ennio Vanotti and Massimo Ghirotto – the Frenchman Philippe Bouvatier and, to his own surprise, Millar. Millar is confident that he can drop the other three for what will be his second stage win at the ski station of Guzet-Neige in four years.

Bouvatier is from Normandy. For a while he's been the next big thing. This is his third Tour, though, and it's high time for him to add something memorable to his palmarès. Today he's riding like fury, taking the lead on the ascent and setting the rhythm. Vanotti is the first to crack. Bouvatier knows his enemies by now. Massimo Ghirotto is a scrappy, combative rider. Millar is Millar. He has the legs, the experience and the cunning. Bouvatier makes a private calculation. If Millar is still on his wheel approaching the line, Millar will win.

Bouvatier is feeling lucky today, and sensing that he's stronger than his two companions, he attacks 250 metres from the finish line. Ghirotto responds. Millar loses a few bike lengths before he can find a response. But a response comes.

One moment, the stage has got to be Bouvatier's. The next moment, it looks as if Millar has timed things perfectly and is going to take him down. Millar has raced this climb just a month ago at the Route de Sud. He knows the road and the finish well. Bouvatier rides to the left, while Millar takes the line behind him, closing all the time. Ghirotto is some way back now. The road is narrow, the race convoy is crowding the riders.

Ahead a burly police officer in a sky-blue shirt is sorting the cars from the bicycles. One vehicle must go straight. The other must go left. Bouvatier flies straight past the policeman, who's all swirling arms and tooting whistle. Millar is closing on Bouvatier. As he passes the policeman he glimpses to his left.

Oh!

The policeman throws his arms in the air.

Oh fuck, thinks Millar. *Oh fuck. Oh fuck. Oh fuck.*

He has just followed Bouvatier straight into the car park. The damn car park, not the finish line. *Fuuuuuck*. They've both sailed past the policeman and the sharp-angled turn to the finish line.

Now manna from heaven is dropping on Massimo Ghirotto's hapless shoulders. He takes the left turn at the policeman's suggestion – Thank you, sir! – and he rides serenely to the finish line. Millar is the first of the Car Park Two to recover his composure. He reappears on the course just in time to take second place.

The media want to know what that feels like. Two guys who miss the turn to the finish line are always going to be more interesting than a winner. There's a winner every day, but a comedy double act stealing glory from themselves is a real novelty.

Unfortunately for the media, one half of the double act is the straightest of straight men. No funny lines fall from his lips today. Millar leans over his handlebars and stares at the ground. The monosyllables drip from him slow and black, like the tar.

Fagor

He reached a point where he'd had his fill of riding Grand Tours as a general classification contender. The pressures didn't sit well. Robert Millar was a loyal but generally solitary fellow. He didn't ooze the charisma that inspired fealty in everybody around him. So he signed for Fagor, to ride with Stephen Roche. It seemed like a good idea at the time.

Roche had won the Giro for Carrera in a way that made his future with the team untenable. Millar joined Fagor for the same reason that a heap of other guys did. They liked Stephen Roche and the way that the team was being built around him. Having won the Giro, the Tour and the Worlds in 1987, Roche was being given a hand in choosing his own team. It was sort of an *Ocean's Eleven* ensemble but without the neat ending and the big payoff.

From Millar's perspective, he could race the Vuelta and he'd have less stress at the Tour. It really ought to have been OK. It ought to have been better than OK. But ...

If cycling is a team sport undertaken by individuals, Fagor ended up being a waste of time for a team and those in it. There was no team spirit between the collection of odd bods and swollen egos who happened to be wearing the same jersey. The only race where Fagor functioned as a unit was at the Tour of Britain, which Malcolm Elliott won. After this, nobody could figure out how to replicate that cohesion.

The 1988 season was one disappointment after another. Stephen Roche was hobbled by knee problems and never raced properly. At management level, order vied with chaos – and chaos generally won.

Power seemed to reside in a grumpy old head mechanic who decided which riders rode in which race. Nobody trusted anybody. If you grumbled privately, your grumble was magnified to the level of a pending coup by the time it got back to the paranoid management junta. And it always got back.

And then, as night follows even the crappiest of days, the 'who said what about whom' business would be served up with a dollop of spicy spin in some Spanish newspaper.

Guys from the Fagor factory would arrive junketeering heroically on a day off. They'd get loudly drunk with their friends or with journalists, while taking the mickey out the team. Being able to deliver that sort of fun seemed to satisfy the sponsors. Fagor never showed much interest in being associated with a team that might actually win something.

Millar left at the end of the year. He needed to return to his roots and just be a climber again. He went back to Peugeot. Not with his (pony) tail between his legs, but because it seemed the pragmatic thing to do.

Zed LeMond

With Panasonic and then with Fagor, Robert Millar had spent three years unmoored from a Peugeot-themed structure. He returned to Peugeot in 1989. The team was by then known as Z–Peugeot, Z being a French brand of children's clothes. To many observers, the move seemed like a step backwards for Millar – and in some ways it was.

But Velo Moto Club de Paris, who were still the organisation behind the team, were a competent operation. They had ambition aplenty but a realistic take on what they could achieve. In the years of Millar's absence there had been a refresh of the management and the team was now run, in part, by men whom Millar had raced with. For the first time in three years, mutual respect again existed between Millar and his own team management. Or perhaps he was just mellowing with age.

The pecking order was clear. Greg LeMond had returned from the hunting accident that almost killed him to win the Tour de France in 1989. He'd won despite riding for ADR, a team that offered him flimsy protection on the road. For the 1990 season he signed with Z–Peugeot, putting his name to a $5.5 million contract over three years, a landmark haul in the sport.

Meanwhile Millar's own take on what might be achieved in personal terms had become more realistic. He'd learned that being competitive in Grand Tours was his limit. Beating his head against that realisation was futile. As a rider he still had a real chance of winning stages or stealing races just below the Grand Tour level. Being one of the top climbers in the world and winning mountain classifications offered more satisfaction than finishing in the top ten of a Grand Tour.

The Tour is usually won by the strongest rider and Millar knew that he wasn't the strongest. He was among the best climbers, though, so he accepted that gift and chose to just enjoy racing again. Z provided the freedom for everyone to have a chance of succeeding at what they were good at.

The arrival of Greg LeMond took away any individual pressure Millar might have felt at the Tour. The quid pro quo was an expectation that the team all had to step up when needed. Millar had watched the 1989 battle between LeMond and Laurent Fignon from the saddle of a rival team. In 1990 he was there to witness the pressure that a Tour winner experiences when defending his title.

Millar was fascinated by LeMond. They'd been friends for a long time, an odd pairing. If Millar was at one end of the intensity spectrum (call it 'Glasgow') LeMond was at other end (we'll call it 'California'). Instead of hurling soggy pasta at the ceilings of Spanish cafés, LeMond might bring a book to read in the interminably long gaps between courses of dinner being served. If his room was too warm for his liking, he'd simply send Otto, his Mexican soigneur, out to buy a portable air conditioning unit. No fuss.

That he fiddled with his race shoes was a constant source of bemusement for Millar. LeMond cut holes in the front so that his toes stuck out inelegantly. He constantly adjusted the Velcro straps in search of the marginal gain of more comfort, the reps from Time who supplied the shoes being sucked into a never-ending vortex of modifications. LeMond was a dude who'd arrive at big races jangling with nerves but then ride his way into relaxation.

Halfway through the 1990 Tour it was obvious that he was in good shape, and as defending champion he looked likely to be wearing the yellow jersey when the big show rolled into Paris.

Early one morning, the mechanics, up before the larks as usual, went to their workspace to discover that LeMond's bikes were missing. All hell broke loose among the staff, the air thick with Gallic oaths. Somebody was dispatched to Paris immediately to fetch replacements. It was decided not to immediately distress LeMond with the news of the theft. That revelation could wait until he came down for breakfast. By then, fingers crossed, the situation would be somewhat in hand. LeMond was duly informed of the larceny. He was assured that the youngest of the mechanics had left two hours ago for Paris and that he was heading *à toute vitesse* to the team HQ.

Greg looked oddly sheepish. The previous evening after the stage was won, he'd happened upon the room where the Z–Peugeot mechanics were working. So he took his own bikes, hid them in his bathroom and went to sleep chuckling to himself. Now he had to confess his prank. The unfortunate guy facing the 1,000-kilometre round trip was contacted before he got much further and he turned back. Amiable race leading superstar or not, LeMond wasn't forgiven for several days, but the Z–Peugeot got LeMond to Paris in the yellow jersey – and also won the team classification.

ta da! it's TVM

By the time Robert Millar joined TVM, cycling was changing from the old ways and catching up with how elite sports organisations were running themselves. All the top teams had by now acquired a team bus. TVM was no exception, although its budget didn't permit a custom-built bus. So TVM just hired a bus. It was owned by Sauna Diana, a sex club near the Belgian–Holland border. The bus didn't have the sex club advertising splashed all over the outside, but it did have rather dubious wipe-down seats. There was no shower, no massage area, no washing machine or fridge. Nothing other than the dodgy leather seats. And there were no maps. TVM seemed to be allergic to maps. The team spent a lot of time getting lost.

There was one thing TVM were excellent at, though. Team presentations. These always had an element of surprise, sometimes merging into shock and horror. Their first presentation was staged on a canal boat, all very quaint and nicely Dutch, until the low roof and the thick smoke from the barbecue combined to make a meaty fog from which the assembled herd of suits had to be evacuated. Next year the proud Dutch theme continued regardless. TVM staged an extravaganza in a posh hotel that was connected to a windmill. And they had fireworks. The twist being that the fireworks were held indoors, just for that war-zone atmosphere that sponsors love.

Chastened, the following year TVM opted for a normal hotel with a normal conference room. The riders disgraced themselves by going for a bike ride on their nice new machines and coming back with their drivetrains covered in sand, having ridden on the Den Haag beach. Still the show had to go on. For once, the team presentation seemed suitably banal and unambitious. A dollop of team promotion, a side course of rider interviews, a sugary dessert of short sponsor films.

The only curiosity was that in the middle of the room sat a giant cake on a raised platform. Speculation about the cake and what might lurk within ran from the fearful to the bawdy. Maybe this was a mafia-style deal, and a guy with a fedora and a machine gun would emerge and tat-tat away at the riders who'd had messed up their bikes. Perhaps the team had gone back to the Sauna Diana sex-club theme and the cake contained a tasselled stripper. Worst case, it was a clown, a magician or a rider. Or a rider dressed as a clown who'd do magic. Finally, the presentation music struck up, the lights dimmed and the spotlight hovered on the cake. What next? Who? Why?

Then there was a soft explosion, and confetti and streamers hung in the air while out of the cake popped the team boss's teenage daughter dressed, well semi-dressed, in a scanty outfit. She was 17 or 18 years old. Mouths opened in silent horror. Please, please don't let her do an exotic dance routine or sing a song or do magic tricks. What happened next was arguably worse. The girl just stood there frozen in mortification.

Her father glared around in anger. He'd been expecting applause and wild cheering, and all he got was a shocked silence from his assembled troops and guests. Finally the tension and the silence gave way in the only style possible. Waves of laughter rolled around the room.

The next day it was drizzling and freezing cold. The team got sent out on their now-squeaky-clean bikes for a biblically long ride. They knew they were being punished for not enjoying the exploding cake spectacle. But they relived it all for hours and hours, their laughter making the miserable day shorter and warmer.

goodbye

Back near the beginning, way back in 1978, Robert Millar was beaten by Steve Lawrence in the Isle of Man International Road Race for the Manx Trophy. One week later, Millar beat Lawrence to win his first British National Amateur Road Race Championships and the course of his career looked set.

In June 1995 Millar returned to the Isle of Man and won the British Professional Road Race Championships for the only time in his career, the race that day doubling up for the Manx Trophy. Millar won in a style that underscored his best qualities as a rider, hauling his way back to a leading group of six riders whose break he'd missed. He'd fallen three minutes and 40 seconds behind, having taken his eye off the race situation for a few seconds. When he finally caught the group on the climb of Creg Willey's, he left each rider behind in turn and rode the last miles alone in the sunshine, knocking nearly ten minutes off the course record.

His win was the first national championships won by a member of Le Groupement team, which had been founded some months earlier. Le Groupement was a French door-to-door sales organisation. Afterwards, as much of a hubris-free zone as ever, Millar described the ride as 'nothing special', and said he was looking forward to getting back to France on Monday. Commenting on the imminent *grand départ* of the Tour de France, he added, 'You have to go to the Tour feeling 100 per cent, I don't believe you can ride yourself fit as the Tour goes on.'

Two days later, on the eve of the Tour, Le Groupement folded. Millar and 19 other riders had, it appeared, been riding for a sponsor that ran a pyramid scheme linked to a sect controlled by an American evangelist. Sales had fallen by 35 per cent in the first half of 1995.

While the other riders scrambled to get themselves on to other teams, Millar, fast approaching his 37th birthday, just stepped away. Having won his final race, it seemed a good time to dismount. He'd become Scottish junior champion in 1976, worked for 16 years as a pro (the average career duration is four years) and had come to the conclusion that he'd have swapped it all just to have transitioned at 16 and lived a happy and anonymous life since then.

Chapter 21

The penultimate day, and this was the cruellest scene. We're in a sports hall that's been converted into a press centre at Ronchamp in eastern France. Sitting at the top table is Tadej Pogačar, vibrant in his yellow jersey. Around him 200 journalists hang on his every word, almost wanting to bow before asking a question.

Thirty metres to the right, unknown to Pogačar, his Slovenian compatriot and great rival Primoz Roglič waits his turn.

Pogačar has just blown Slovenia and the Tour de France apart. The 36.2-kilometre time trial has seen him gain almost three minutes on his compatriot. He has taken the yellow jersey from his hero's shoulders and tomorrow he'll wear that jersey riding into Paris.

Roglič can hear every word as Pogačar recalls how he woke that morning thinking only of holding on to second place. 'For myself, I was never thinking of the yellow jersey. I don't really know what happened. After Col de la Loze [on Wednesday], that I was solid in second and I just wanted to secure that. Today, incredible.'

Even if no one else did, maybe the rider himself in all his youthful innocence believed in his chance of turning the race upside down, as Greg LeMond had against Laurent Fignon in 1989? No, the kid never saw it. Now he was the champion. He was asked if he'd spoken to the president of Slovenia, Borut Pahor, a keen cyclist who'd been following the Tour. Alas, the telephone signal was bad.

He joked that if he'd spoken to his mum and dad, he'd have thanked them 'for the genes'. Twenty-one years earlier, those genes sprinted from one body to another to create a new being. Let alone get tired, those sprinting genes wouldn't even have taken a shallow breath.

So fresh on this second-to-last day, Pogačar looked like he'd just joined the Tour rather than being the neophyte with 3,340 kilometres in his legs. He was asked about Roglič, the one standing unseen by the door who had victory in his pocket but then had his pocket picked. Slovenians, or at least most of them, had willed Roglič to do it.

'Roglič was the best rider in the race, with a really good team [Jumbo–Visma],' Pogačar said by way of an apology. 'They did a fantastic job. I have so much respect for him, he's a good friend of mine. I feel for him. I feel his loss. To lose the yellow jersey on the last day, it's really difficult. That's racing. We all try to win.'

Though he'd ridden a brilliant time trial, Pogačar's press conference was for some part a request for forgiveness. He was applauded as he walked towards the exit. He then realised Roglič had been there all the time. They shook hands and instinctively knew that wasn't enough. They embraced. Roglič walked to the table as a Tour official asked Pogačar if he could sign a replica yellow jersey.

Roglič spoke of his pain while Pogačar was writing his name on the sacred jersey.

*   *   *

We left the press centre sometime after 9 o'clock that night. Our work was done and we had a 410-kilometre journey ahead of us to Paris.

Small, twisting roads made the first part of the journey torturous, but as always we talked. We'd talked a lot about the media on numerous days.

Being a sportswriter had been the plan since I was a child. I've never done anything else or wanted to do anything else. People think it weird and absolutely unbelievable when I tell them that I knew what I wanted to be at age six. They're thinking, *No one knows at six*. Except I did.

One of my earliest sporting memories was Nicolaus Silver, a beautiful bright grey, winning the Grand National. For years my assumption was that I must have been 11 or 12 when this happened. It was March 1961. I was five. As a very young kid, I liked writing stories and watching sports, so it wouldn't have taken Einstein to put those two together.

It came as a surprise to me when I arrived in the newspaper world and more cerebral journalists from other sections of the newspaper referred to the sports section as the 'toy department', but I could see where they were coming from. Every story Pippa tells me about her experiences with my colleagues from the more serious sections of the newspaper helps me to appreciate the toy department.

We're getting to the end of our first Tour together. I'm not sure she sees it that way, but it seems that being in France for the last few weeks has enabled Pippa to return to the continental European cycling world entirely on her own terms. I want to ask her to sum up how she got to this stage where she's working and writing as Pippa York on the Tour de France. This evening, like every other for the last three weeks, she's driving away from a media centre with her press accreditation around her neck. Considering what she's been through, being thought of as part of 'the press' must have seemed unimaginable at one point.

DAVID: How did that happen?

PIPPA: It's a long story, so we've got to go back a bit. By the time I'd finished with the medical part of my transition in 2003 I wasn't following cycling closely. In fact, I wasn't following it all. During the Lance Armstrong years I never really noticed who was winning or losing. I still went out cycling when I felt like it, doing more riding in the summer than the winter. With the anatomical and mental changes brought about by transition I had no desire to go fast or far. Even if I'd wanted to, I couldn't. I didn't have the stamina or strength. That was OK. I was more than happy with being Philippa, and establishing some depth and history to the new identity. It also takes time for everything to settle down after major surgeries. Moving from the Midlands – and being in the centre of the country – to south-west England, away from major roads, cities and millions of people, was a relief too. There was space and the opportunity to just enjoy life. That was until summer 2007.

Then a book came out about my life – *In Search of Robert Millar*. The author is deceased now, so the less said the better. I knew that books, TV programmes or films that have *In Search of ...* as a title usually have an ending where whatever's being looked for is found. And so it was. I was found. Six days after publication, the *Daily Mail* came into our quiet lives.

DAVID: Yes. I remember a horrible newspaper story with a photograph of you dressed as a woman?

PIPPA: I'd been cleaning things in the garage and noticed this car driving past slowly, somebody peering in. I thought little of it. We lived in a cul-de-sac, and it was common for people to take a wrong turn and end up on that road. Then I saw that the car was parked up at the top of the street, which seemed a little strange. I became suspicious when they drove down and back a couple more times, but then they left. I'd finished in the garage and was in the house. I had a vague concern about how the two men in the car had behaved. The doorbell rang.

My daughter Lydia opened the door. And our lives just became really shit for the next two or three years. I heard a man's voice say, 'Is Philippa there?' Lydia shouted for me to come.

I knew immediately it was the same people who'd been sitting outside in the street. It was me that the men from the *Daily Mail* were stalking. Linda went to the door and told the man who was standing there to basically go and do one. She said there was no one at the house of that name. He said he didn't believe her. Linda closed the door and she burst into tears. Poor Lydia was nowhere to be seen. Later we found her hiding behind the sofa. I was hiding in the kitchen so the *Daily Mail* man wouldn't see me. Think about that. I was hiding in my own home as if I was some sort of criminal.

I knew if the media had found where I lived then there would be some crap story with all the usual rubbish spouted about our concerned neighbours or friends worrying about my situation. That's what the *Daily Mail* and co. specialise in, moral outrage in the entertainment and lifestyle pages. The man came back half an hour later, and he told Linda that we'd better speak to him as there was a story being prepared for the weekend. What did we have to say? Again, she told him to go away, but we knew for sure then that our lives were about to become a whole lot worse. Basically, they spied outside my house and took pictures of me without my consent. Which is against the law, but you're arguing with somebody who's got lawyers already.

DAVID: Was it in 2007 that they talked about the Queen of the Mountains?

PIPPA: Yeah. That appeared in the *Daily Mail* in the entertainment pages, with the photograph, taken without consent. We were living just outside Dorchester in Dorset. The *Daily Mail* printed our names and roughly described where we lived. All it took was two clicks on the internet to access the electoral register and obtain our home address. So they'll find a picture of you from before and after. They love that shit. Because it makes who you've become less valid. It makes it almost a performance, that you're now performing as a female. And that's how it was presented in the *Daily Mail*. And then in the *Scotsman*. When the newspapers come, it feels like they've decided to make an example of you. It's almost as if they're teaching you a lesson: you should just crawl back under that stone again.

DAVID: You'd been through this before, though, Pippa? You have some experience and you probably had an idea that somebody was going to turn up at some stage. Did you have a lawyer in place or anything like that?

PIPPA: No. Our peace of mind was just gone. We were just in emotional shock. So I phoned my sister to ask her for advice on what to do. She recommended getting a lawyer, fast. The first company she recommended were called Carter-Ruck. I've no idea if they were the first hit on Google or if she knew who they were, but they turned out to be excellent. I phoned them and explained my situation, and thankfully they took the case.

DAVID: What can they do at that stage? Were there grounds for an injunction, a warning letter?

PIPPA: Apparently, papers like the *Daily Mail* have their own lawyers, whose job it is to decide if what they print is legal or isn't legal – they advise on what it will potentially cost them in damages if they publish. From what Carter-Ruck said, the other side had decided that my story was worth the damages. It was worth the risk because they knew we weren't rich people. The *Mail* didn't care about the fallout for us, they weren't worried about the hurt or my medical history being discussed in the entertainment pages. It was all a formula. We print this. It costs this. We'll go with that. As far as the *Daily Mail* were concerned, they were going to say that it was all in the public interest. A translation of that would be that they wanted to present the whole thing as a scandal, a freak show, and something to laugh about. They'd been doing that for years to trans people and they still do. Anyway, Carter-Ruck couldn't stop the story being published on the first day of the 2007 Tour de France.

I don't really remember how we got through that weekend. It was all just a mess of stress. People were ringing our door bell asking for a comment or offering to write 'sympathetic' pieces in the pages of their magazine or paper. They just take your privacy and destroy it. The most deeply personal feelings that you and your loved ones have struggled with for so long just become crass headlines and photos for entertainment. And any peace of mind that I had living at home was totally gone, even to this day.

DAVID: I'm assuming that once the story appeared it drew more attention.

PIPPA: It changed everything. Now we were exposed to all manner of gawkers and idiots.

We told Lydia she could stay off school on the Monday, but she insisted on going. We phoned the school on the morning and alerted them that there might be media or someone outside the gates. Our concerns were noted and her teachers informed. That was reassuring, so off she went to school. Next, Linda went to work and everything seemed normal outside. Around midday, though, Linda phoned me in tears to say she was coming home early. Some journalists had turned up at her place of work and they were hanging around outside. They were asking other people for comments and quotes. The reporters had been removed but the damage was done. Linda was traumatised. I waited for her to come home. I checked through my emails to see if there was any news from Carter-Ruck. I got a message from the author of *In Search of Robert Millar*. Book sales were going well, apparently.

Just when Linda and I had composed ourselves enough to act normally for Lydia coming back from school, we heard the worst thing you can ever hear from a child. She'd been approached inappropriately at school. Not by a dumb pupil but by a teacher. She wasn't taught by this person and yet they'd said something to her that suggested they might want to exploit any vulnerability that she now had. This teacher had come up to her, mentioned the *Daily Mail* story, asked her inappropriate questions and been, as she put it, 'weird'.

That opened up another can of shit. The school defended the teacher. We phoned the police and it just got worse. They asked, 'Where's the evidence?' They said it's not a matter for them, contact the school governors. In the end, the teacher left at the end of term, which was just two weeks later, never to return or be mentioned again.

The mental abuse from people staring and sniggering in the street was bad enough, but then one day Linda was threatened by a young lad. I won't repeat the words used, but they were awful. I believe the term is 'corrective rape'. We'd already decided that we needed to move house – that incident meant speeding things up. It was hard to find a place that gave us privacy, but two days before Christmas we started our lives again somewhere else.

Those months looking for somewhere else to live were tough ones.

DAVID: So you had to set up a new home in a different place?

PIPPA: People have no idea. One day a policeman presented himself on our doorstep and demanded to be let in. I wouldn't let him in. He said if I didn't let him enter, he'd arrest me for breach of the peace. So I let him in. He proceeded to tell us that he was sick and tired of hearing complaints about us! He said that if he came back again it would be because he was used to dealing with rapists, paedophiles and weirdos, so he'd make sure we were convicted. We phoned the police complaints number when he finally left. We were given the contact details of a LGBT liaison officer, who found out that our visitor hadn't been dispatched to our address. He had no official reason to be knocking on our door.

So now the PCC was involved in our lives. Goodbye, quiet life.

Eventually the *Daily Mail* settled out of court. They'd factored that in from the start. Did it repair the damage? The money we received wasn't relevant. The whole process just makes you feel dirty. You're insulted from start to finish and then you're left to get on with it. Pick up the pieces while they look for the next victim. At least the *Daily Mail* half admitted that they thought my medical history was entertainment for their readers. You know, I never thought I'd begin a sentence with the words, 'At least the *Daily Mail* …', but dealing with the *Scotsman* was much, much worse.

Carter-Ruck don't operate up north, so we had to hire a local set of lawyers instead. I don't know what's so different about Scottish privacy law but the *Scotsman*'s defenders were dreadful and the case dragged on and on. Every exchange was more hurtful than the previous one. It became clear that they were willing to spend years just prolonging the insults. I was worn out from the *Daily Mail*, the PCC thing was under way and I got tired of being compared to every type of criminal they could think of. When someone says that the public needs to know about people like you for their protection, it's really bad. When you're being compared to a child murderer, how do you deal with that? You can't laugh in the way you laughed when some guy suggests it was doping that made you trans. I was back on antidepressants just to cope with the anxieties. In the end the *Scotsman* case was settled. The lawyers got paid and again there was no apology.

In comparison, the PCC was relatively civilised. There were a few visits from police officers, some were professional and some were less considerate, but maybe that's how the process works. In the end a letter of apology was delivered. The good was taken out of that when the messenger who arrived to deliver the letter advised us to just keep our heads down.

We'd been keeping our heads down before other people decided to stick our heads under a newspaper headline.

DAVID: In the end things settle down. But the damage has been done and people were hurt. You try to get back to your quiet life in a new house and start again. How do you go from there to press centres on the Tour de France?

PIPPA: Well, first of all you asked! I blame you. But that whole period when I didn't have a public profile was great. I could be out and about and nobody recognised me or cared other than the few people I worked with or was still in close contact with. I was just another woman. That was the whole point of changing sides – to feel more at ease, in a more natural existence. So I had that time and it helped me. I'd definitely lost touch with cycling. I just had a lot of other things on my plate. But after a while you say to yourself, *How do I make a living?* I was asked to do some pieces. Nobody was making any other offers that paid. So I wrote. It's not normal work. I found it hard judging people because I didn't like being judged when I was doing it. But getting back into that world helped me process my career and Robert Millar. So, in a way it was also therapeutic. Therapy that paid me money.

DAVID: Had you known beforehand that you could write?

PIPPQ: Well, you probably remember that I never really looked at journalists all wide-eyed with wonder at how many years they'd spent mastering their craft. It's not brain surgery.

Oh, and I did get a re-education! That sounds a bit North Korean, doesn't it? I was told I needed to go to a team HQ to observe how modern cycling works. It sounded like they thought that in my day we'd been going around on penny-farthings. So I went along to that. And yes, they had some new tech and some training improvements, but no bionic cyclists.

DAVID: So the next transition, how did that come about, because for a while you were writing as Robert Millar but living as Pippa York?

PIPPA: Yes, my pieces were appearing under Robert Millar's name and at the start I was happy with that. I thought it gave me back some privacy. It was a form of protection.

We need time to recover. But in the end I decided that I wanted to publish things as Philippa York. That started the process, I suppose, of returning to a more public profile. It would go well for a while, but then something would happen and I'd go sliding back down to the bottom of the confidence ladder again.

DAVID: What sort of things happened? Were these things related to the media or your work?

PIPPA: Put it this way, I'd been subjected to all the basic levels of hostility during my transition, but nothing gets you ready for the shock of being threatened and sexually assaulted when you're walking to the car after a night out in central London. Not one but two separate incidents. It was awful, and I've no doubt that both things happened because they suspected I was trans.

DAVID: Really?

PIPPA: There's such a dirtiness to it. You wonder afterwards, *Was it misogyny? Was it transphobia, or drink- or drug-induced opportunism? Is this just the shitty part of being a woman?* And then there was the question of who do I tell. *Do I report it to the police and then have to deal with all that?* I was exhausted from confrontations over privacy and dealing with bureaucracy, so I did what most women do and I said nothing, just because I didn't want more upset. I couldn't handle more intrusion or more abusive comments. That's a terrible thing to say, isn't it, but there's always some idiot who'll suggest that whatever happened was in some way your own fault.

I fell back on things. I went back to doing Taekwondo and I made it to black belt and then 2nd Dan. That was a good experience. And a real education. I liked the way males and females were treated equally. It's a martial art, but there was no macho boasting or showing off. It was quite respectful, which may be related to its military origins. And there had been no shock or horror or scandalised looks when I changed my details. That would never have been the case with cycling. Can you imagine?!

DAVID: Well, you don't have to imagine. You had the thing with the pro team that offered you a job and took it back again because they couldn't 'explain' you?

PIPPA: The pro team thing?

339

DAVID: Yes. The ones who gave you the job and then changed their minds because they didn't know how to 'explain' you?

PIPPA: That definitely hurt, although it's turned out to be a blessing. It took a while, but I calmed down and recovered from the disappointment. I'm sad that it cost me a friendship, but it was a wake-up call. The whole episode reminded me of the 'First they came for … and I said nothing' quote by Martin Niemöller. Minorities have to stick up for each other.

*   *   *

We've been travelling for almost three hours. I wonder whether Tadej Pogačar will sleep in his brand-new yellow jersey tonight. It will be after midnight by the time we get to the hotel I've just phoned. No answer. I'm afraid to mention this to Pippa, but there's a chance we're not going to be able to get into this hotel when we eventually get there.

Time to brighten things up.

DAVID: OK, tell us some good news. Who are the good guys? I've been around you a lot on this Tour and so many people are happy to see you and have great affection for you.

PIPPA: That's the point, there are also good people out there too. There are people who give you confidence, support and make you feel appreciated. Without them, that whole ten years from 2007 and the *Daily Mail* crap, right through to taking on a public profile again in 2017, would never have happened. We went through so much crap while I was

just trying to live my life peacefully that I wasn't exactly
enamoured by the idea of emerging as Philippa to the
whole wide world. If trying to be private had turned into
such a nightmare, what would stepping into the light be
like?

DAVID: Name some names. The Pippa York Honours
List …

PIPPA: If I'm giving out honours, should I say, 'One is
eternally grateful'? So, all my decisions I make, I ask my
family for their opinion on whether I ought to do it or not.
My children were really supportive, especially Lydia. So
eternally grateful to my family. I'm eternally grateful to
David Millar and his mother Avril for shepherding me
through the first steps of the re-emergence process. Guy
Andrews and the crew at *Rouleur* magazine were brilliant.
They kept my privacy intact until the moment came when
it seemed right to step back into the limelight and take the
chance of being burned by the public gaze. That came
about in a strange way. I was at my friend Holly's wedding.
She married a certain cyclist called Matt, and Ned Boulting
– off the telly, as they say – was there. I didn't speak to Ned
when I was at the reception. I'm shy like that and I'd very
rarely invade other people's space if it's not work-related,
but afterwards I got an email from him asking if I'd
consider doing some commentary for ITV4's Tour
coverage. That was an opportunity with a level of gravitas.
It was television, though. Pros and cons. ITV4? It was
basically mainstream television but the amount of negative
press and comment was hopefully going to be pretty
limited. I asked my family for their opinion. My children
were really supportive, especially Lydia. She said that

things had really changed and it would be a good thing to do, not just for me but for the LGBTQ+ community as well. She said I had the chance to use the platform of being on TV and in the media not as an example of someone there for being transsexual but rather for having been a top-level cyclist who just happened to have transitioned. That was such a wise thing to say. For those people worrying about their gender or sexuality, the world keeps turning and they should be part of it and not ever feel excluded.

I asked Dan Benson of Cyclingnews and Will Fotheringham of the *Guardian* about what they thought might be the best way forward. They agreed that we needed to control what was put out there. Don't just pop up on ITV4 and be Philippa York. I needed to tell that story in the way I wanted it told and not have it construed as a freak show. What I sent the guys first was too emotional and too personal. They sifted through it until there was nothing to add on or to speculate about or criticise. We included a few well-chosen photos. No one had to turn up and hide behind our hedge to take sneaky shots.

So, I love this bit. Ten years to the day after the *Daily Mail* and co. trampled all over my privacy and caused carnage in our lives, the article appeared that I'd worked on with Dan and Will. I look at those ten years between the *Daily Mail* intrusion into our privacy and the official re-emergence as Philippa as a lost decade. But it was a decade we got through. I was often reminded of what my friend Leanne said to me early on. She was one of the first trans people that I was lucky enough to meet, and she said something to me about having an unconventional path.

'Different. It's not good or bad, right or wrong, it's just means different.'

*   *   *

We'd booked a hotel about a third of the way to Paris in a village called Saints-Geosmes, about five kilometres off the A5. After stopping for something to eat, it was well after midnight when we got there. Pippa's telling of her trials by media shortened the journey.

Near our destination, we fell back into chatting about cycling.

DAVID: Pogačar felt genuinely sorry for Roglič. Back home in Slovenia, it was Roglič they were hoping would win.

PIPPA: Yep. Roglič was their man.

DAVID: Crazy, isn't it? You're 21, you win the Tour de France and you disappoint 80 per cent of the people back home.

PIPPA: That moment where he embraced Roglič. I just thought they were friends up until then, even though they were racing, but that friendship was based on Roglič's assumption that he was still above him. That changed from the moment Pogačar took the yellow jersey. Roglič has to deal with his friend taking his jersey, a friend who's nine years younger.

DAVID: That isn't just a bad defeat, that's potentially a grim future for the older rider.

PIPPA: That's what made it worse for Roglič. It was his moment, his chance.

DAVID: Anyway, we're getting close to our shelter for the night, the Logis Jum Hôtel. The good news for you is that

343

the hotel ain't much. The rooms cost £52 each, breakfast included.

PIPPA: I never expect much!

DAVID: The bad news is that I couldn't get through to tell them we'd be late.

PIPPA: This place isn't going to have an all-night reception, is it?

DAVID: No. Maybe a night porter.

PIPPA: Doubt it.

DAVID: So, we're probably fucked.

PIPPA: Probably.

We get to the entrance of the hotel. It's 40 minutes after midnight. A steel gate bars entry. Everything is pitch black, not a light on anywhere. Fuck. Then the car headlights catch a keypad to the right of the gate. It's got a handwritten note attached – the code for the gate and another code to get into the hotel. Inside, we use the torch on a mobile phone to find our room keys, which have been left sitting on the reception desk.

After three weeks and one very long day, this may be the happiest moment of our time together.